Celebrations of *Connecting across Differences*

"*Connecting across Differences* describes how to communicate in a way that leads to greater understanding and more positive relationships. Ultimately, it provides not just practical methods; it espouses a philosophy of personal responsibility and respect for others and ourselves. The wisdom of this book is a great guide in living with full awareness and compassion."

—Daniel Pharr, Ph.D., Chief Psychologist,
Bronx Psychiatric Center

"A captivating book where we are shown tools to increase our understanding of one another and ourselves…and the compassion we so desperately want."

—Michelle Russo, Binghamton University student

"In my 26 years as a Professor of Communication, I have found that students rarely like textbooks. *Connecting across Differences* marks a major exception. Students love how this book is written —in a compelling and clear way—and how the examples deal with their everyday lives. Connor and Killian teach how we can communicate and connect, live and love in empathic and compassionate ways that meet our needs and the needs of others. In this time of war, both students and I feel thrilled to learn that alternatives exist to our traditional patterns of linear thinking, judging, criticizing, comparing and contrasting."

—Lois Einhorn, Professor of Rhetoric and Composition

"Empathy isn't limited to certain subjects—it works for situations being gay, straight, with school problems, roommate issues and even comes in handy when dealing with teachers. I think you should have great results with this book because the examples are all real life problems—and solutions."

—Jonathan Crimes, A Multicultural Psychology student

"NVC has been an invaluable tool for connecting with those around me—my clients, family, and friends. NVC has helped me to move beyond doing what is expected and customary to formulating goals and making choices that enrich me and truly meet my needs."
—Roxanne Manning, Ph.D., clinical psychologist, Raleigh-Durham

"As both a mother and a mature student, my communication skills have improved with *Connecting across Differences.* I find that my relationships, especially with my children, are dramatically changing for the better. Most of all, I have gained insight into how I communicate with myself. I am now learning self-empathy and how to heal some deep-rooted wounds."
—Maggie Clements, Binghamton University

"I taught Nonviolent Communication to a class of peace and social activists using Jane and Dian's book. The students found it inspiring and invaluable in their learning experience. I love the clarity, organization, and universality of their approach to NVC."
—Christine King, NVC Certified Trainer, Santa Cruz, CA

"*Connecting across Differences,* through numerous illustrations and examples, raises awareness about the covert, passive violence that M. K. Gandhi described as being more insidious than physical violence. Nonviolent Communication and this book offer an antidote."
—Cynthia Moe, Atlanta, NVC Organizer

"This book gives a step-by-step guide for getting closer to our inner world and achieving a better understanding of oneself and others. I especially like the exercises, the sequence of chapters, and how easy to read and understand the language is."
—Merike Kahju, empathy trainer, Talinn, Estonia

"Fabulous book for developing better relationships! If you want to build awareness, find peace, and make a difference, this practical book helps you communicate with love and compassion and shift from old ways of judging self and others toward connecting more deeply."
—Martha Lasley, author of *Courageous Visions: How to Unleash Passionate Energy in Your Life and Organization*

Connecting across Differences:
A Guide to Compassionate, Nonviolent Communication^{sm}

Jane Marantz Connor, Ph.D. and Dian Killian, Ph.D.

Hungry Duck Press
New York

ISBN 0-9770617-0-1

This book is based on the work of Marshall B. Rosenberg, Ph.D., founder of the Center for Nonviolent Communication (www.cnvc.org) but reflects the understanding and opinions of the authors and not necessarily that of Dr. Rosenberg or the Center for Nonviolent Communication.

Published by Hungry Duck Press, 120 4th Avenue, #2, Brooklyn, NY 11217. For information on ordering, contact info@BrooklynNVC.org or call 718.797.9525.

Cover design by Jill Connor
Book design by Charlotte Morse

For M.G., who is so determined to seeing the needs of the world met and who so contributes to meeting mine each day.

For my family, students, and the larger community who have nurtured and inspired me.

To those everywhere with passion and vision who are willing to take the leap of imagining and creating change.

An enemy is one whose story we have not heard.

—*Gene Knudsen-Hoffman*

Contents

PART ONE

INTRODUCTION:
Living with Awareness and Choice

"You just don't understand me. You never listen, do you?"

"How could I make such a stupid mistake again? It seems like I never learn."

"I just don't know what to do. There are too many choices."

"He's just a jerk. All he cares about is himself."

Reading the above statements, how do you feel? What do you notice in your body? Do you feel tense or tight? Do you feel anxious, sad, angry, or confused? If so, I'm not surprised. While addressing different issues, each of these statements involves some kind of judgment. Each indicates a level of miscommunication, disconnection, or blame. No one enjoys being judged—even by themselves. And none of these statements address the root cause of what's contributing to the tension and misunderstanding taking place.

Now read the following statements, fully expressing what each speaker was thinking and feeling:

"I'm so frustrated. That's not what I recall saying and I really value accuracy."

"This is the second time this year I've forgotten to pay my VISA bill. I hate getting those late charges and I really want to attend to my personal matters with care."

"Seeing that there are twenty-two different courses that meet the writing requirement I feel totally overwhelmed. I need to know which to take."

"I'm furious. There's no hot water left and my housemate just spent twenty-five minutes in the shower. That's not the kind of consideration I want."

Reading the second set, you may feel a very different kind of response. Do you feel more relaxed, connected, and at ease? Do you notice greater appreciation and understanding—especially when you read what each speaker is wanting (accuracy, care, clarity and consideration)? Do you find yourself more open to what the speaker desires, and more willing to engage with them?

If so, I'm also not surprised. In each of these sentences, the speaker takes responsibility for their own experience. Rather than engaging in judgment (which often provides little information), the speaker clearly describes what is bothering them, what they are feeling, and what they're wanting.

These two sets of sentences illustrate the practice we'll be exploring in this book: how to move past judgment and name our own experiences in a way that enhances people's ability to listen and care about what is important for each other and ourselves. In doing so, we explore a view of the world and human relations which we believe can vitally contribute to interpersonal and inter-group harmony. The communication tool and the world view support and enhance each other.

Different—Together

In taking this approach, we examine both the differences and commonalities among people. Of course, in many ways, we are different from each other. But we also have much in common. As living organisms, we all have numerous physical needs, including for food, air, water, and rest. We need clothing and shelter for comfort and protection from the elements. We need confidence that we can be safe, from illness and other physical harm. And we have needs for warmth, touch and intimacy, as well as tenderness, care and sexual expression.

Beyond physical needs, there are numerous other qualities that, as humans, we like to experience and express. These values include honesty, authenticity, and integrity; community and connection as well as spaciousness, autonomy and choice. Most of us value, at least in some situations, efficiency, effectiveness, movement, and ease, and many other needs for our well being, such as order, beauty, and meaning. There are dozens of other qualities, such as mutuality, companionship, and consideration, that could be considered primal and basic human needs.

In your life, what do you value and try to live by, especially in relating to others? Perhaps you value kindness, care, consideration, and autonomy, and the freedom to decide how you want to live. Perhaps you also value self-expression, empowerment and responsibility. You may also care about dignity, understanding, honesty, and trust. There are probably dozens of other values that you care about.

Now stop and think for a moment. Think about your family, friends, and colleagues and those you simply pass on the street. Is there anyone who would not enjoy experiencing the qualities we've mentioned? Is there anyone in the world who would not enjoy food and drink, warmth and shelter, consideration, care, support, ease and respect? All of these would seem qualities that humans everywhere could appreciate and desire. While humans address these needs in diverse ways and experience them at different times and in different circumstances, there is little doubt that, as humans, we share basic, universal needs.

Needs—Understanding and Acting on Them

We all have needs. That's the simple part. But how do we meet these needs in ways that we enjoy, in ways that are consistent with our values and also our desire for choosing how we want to live?

And if we all have the same needs, how can we be confident that everyone's needs—including our own—can be addressed? And if we have so much in common, how is it that we so often experience difference, misunderstanding and conflict?

These are the questions we take up in this book.

In doing so, we will explore two basic principles. The first is that when we disagree or experience disconnection with others, it is because we are disagreeing over strategies (what we want to do in a particular situation). If we focus first on connecting with others— hearing and understanding, and holding everyone's needs with care—strategies can be discovered that are far more satisfying, enriching, and unifying. In doing so, we are acting on what *we want* (not what we *don't* want) and actively moving towards our goal and what's satisfying in life and in relating to others.

The second principle is that connecting with and contributing to the well being of others are instinctive human behaviors and deeply rewarding. If we believe this second principle—that contributing to others is intrinsically satisfying—finding ways to meet everyone's needs becomes much easier to do. "Win-win" solutions become the ultimate prize.

The Contribution Test

Do you doubt these principles? If so, you can try them out in the laboratory of your own life. Just take a moment now and think about when you last contributed to another's well being. Perhaps you gave someone directions, helped a child with a task, did something kind for your pet, or ran an errand for a friend. Perhaps you listened with caring to a person who wanted your companionship. Or perhaps you told a joke, and added some humor, fun, and creativity to the day, or expressed gratitude, love, or appreciation to another person.

Pause for a moment and think about your action and the way you contributed. How do you feel? What sensations do you notice in your body? You may notice that you feel warm and openhearted, with an expansiveness in your throat, chest, or limbs. You may feel happy, calm, satisfied, or at ease. There may be a sense of fullness, peace, and completion. These are the feelings we typically experience when our needs are being met. And contributing to others is one of the most basic and compelling of human needs. We all have a desire to contribute to life, to enrich and enhance it.

Now imagine all the people you know enjoying the sensations you just experienced. What would the world look like, and our lives everyday, if people increased their experience of meeting human needs? What if there was confidence that everyone's needs mattered? How would we communicate and make decisions differently? How would we respond to difference and misunderstanding? How would our jobs be structured differently, our neighborhoods, our communities, our schools?

Given the number of people whose needs are not being met in the world today and who believe their needs don't matter, how do we imagine such a world, what it would look like, and how it would function? How do we go about seeing that everyone's needs be held with consideration and care?

Creating Abundance

These questions may at first seem overwhelming. But the model we offer in this book, known as Compassionate or Nonviolent Communication[sm1], offers what we think is the best blueprint for creating such abundance, in our own lives and the world around us. The more we know what our needs are—how to recognize and name them—the more resources we have to see that they're heard, understood, and acted upon. The more we experience how satisfying

---

[1] Nonviolent Communication is a registered service mark of the Center for Nonviolent Communication and we are using it here with their permission. Website: www.cnvc.org Email: cnvc@cnvc.org Phone: +1.818.957.9393

it is to respond to human needs, the more motivated we become to see how human needs can be addressed.

The communication skills and the perspective on human relations described here can also help you understand yourself. What do you truly value? What do you find unsettling or satisfying? How do you stand by what you believe in, even when others disagree? Increasing self-awareness and having the choice of saying "no" means you can say "yes" with power and integrity. And this honesty—honoring your convictions while not dismissing others—can in fact bring you closer. This is what we explore in this book.

Internationally Tried and Tested

The approach taken in this book is based on the model of Nonviolent Communication (NVC) developed by Marshall Rosenberg, Ph.D. In developing NVC, Marshall was fascinated by a basic question: What is it that contributes to human beings enjoying moments of profound connection and compassion for each other and, at other times, lack of compassion and even antipathy and contempt? At a young age, Marshall observed both first hand— acts of violence, such as the race riots in Detroit in the 1940s, and acts of immense compassion, as in the care his uncle joyfully gave his elderly mother. Wanting to understand compassion and how to foster it, he studied psychology, including with the humanist psychologist, Carl Rogers. After completing his studies, he worked for many years with youth and their families.

From years of experience, including working with gangs, those in prisons and detention centers, corporations, and other organizations, Marshall developed what's become known as Nonviolent Communication. The NVC model is now being used around the world, increasing understanding, cooperation, and the resolution of conflict between diverse groups and people. NVC has broad application; as well as fostering self-awareness and connection with others, NVC skills can contribute to decision making, mediation, and needs assessment and facilitating meetings so that everyone feels included and involved. The approach you learn in this book will help you live in your own skin and find mutuality with others—at home, school, work, and in your most intimate relationships.

Sounds Great. But How Hard Is It to Learn?

The principles of NVC are not hard to understand. As you will see, the model involves four basic steps: making clear observations, identifying feelings in relation to what you're observing, identifying needs in relation to what you're feeling, and making a request that might contribute to meeting your needs. Learning this new way of communicating, however, requires a willingness to step outside your comfort zone and to be a beginner at something. At first, it involves a certain amount of risk-taking, learning about yourself, and trusting that the "real you" (with all your feelings and needs) has something worthwhile to contribute and communicate to others.

To learn NVC, it is also essential that you practice. Learning a communication skill is not like learning history or math. It's not just principles or theory; it needs to be lived—and practiced— everyday. By applying NVC to your life, you will see how it works and you will gain confidence. To support this practice, the book includes exercises that can be done more than once. Each time, just think of a different situation that you would like to improve or understand better.

You may also wish to keep a journal while reading this book and learning to practice Nonviolent Communication. In this journal, you can respond to exercises that ask you to observe and comment on interactions during the week. You can work on choices you're making, or behavior you're interested in understanding and perhaps changing. You can also re-write and re-work situations you've engaged in where you didn't communicate compassionately or not as fully as you'd like.

Even knowing a few words of a language is better than knowing none at all. Similarly, even though learning NVC takes time, you will benefit as soon as you start. Just identifying feelings and needs is helpful in itself. Over time, you will develop confidence and be able to respond to the most challenging people and situations.

Representing Compassion

In many parts of the world, including North America, Nonviolent Communication is symbolized by a giraffe and referred to as "giraffe language" or speaking "in giraffe." There's a reason for this. Of all land animals, the giraffe has the biggest heart, weighing as much as twenty-six pounds. (It takes a big heart to pump blood through such a big body.) The giraffe also has a long neck so as to reach the foliage at tree-top. Nonviolent Communication is about connecting on a heart, not just a head level, so an animal with a heart this size can remind us about the intention of NVC. And like the long neck of the giraffe, communicating with compassion also means "sticking your neck out," reaching out to others and taking the long view.

Communication inconsistent with NVC or "giraffe talk" is sometimes represented by another animal, the jackal, which is small and energetic. The jackal means well, and has the same basic needs as the giraffe, but the way he expresses it often stimulates pain or discomfort in others.

These symbols are not used in every country where NVC is applied and are not necessary to understand NVC concepts. In this book, the authors have chosen not to use them. You may want to know about them, however, especially if you read other NVC materials or attend an NVC workshop or event.

Language, Choice, and Inclusion

Wanting inclusion of different genders and also ease and simplicity, in this book we do not use "he" to refer to all human beings. Consistent with trends in English towards gender neutrality, we use the third person plural, "they."

Also, while there are two authors of this book, when speaking about each of our own experiences, we use the first person singular pronoun, "I." If you are curious about which author is speaking when, Jane Marantz Connor lives in upstate New York with her husband. Dian Killian lives in New York City where she rides her bike and is very much in love with her partner, Martha, and her cat, Digit.

No Needs Met, No Peace

While what we describe here is a powerful tool for becoming aware of human needs and responding to them, this is not the same as ensuring that those needs are met. As Inbal Kashtan, coordinator of the Parenting Project for the Center for Nonviolent Communication, observes:

> As powerful and effective as it can be for addressing problems in the social and political arenas, the language of NVC by itself does not remedy the enormous challenges humans face when they don't have the financial or social resources to meet their own or their children's needs. NVC does not eliminate social inequalities that relate to race, gender, class, sexual orientation, physical ability, and the like.[2]

---

[2] Inbal Kashtan, *Parenting from Your Heart: Sharing the Gifts of Compassion, Connection, and Choice* (Encinitas, CA: Puddle Dancer Press, 2003), pp. 36-7

NVC can facilitate communication between those who may not otherwise understand each other, giving us the tools to see how everyone's needs can be addressed. It can help us express our concerns, including to those in power, who otherwise may not be attentive to our needs. But the work of creating change, and the harmony that results, comes from seeing that human needs are, in fact, met. This involves not only intention and communication but commitment, creativity, and vision.

Fostering Abundance and Connection

As human beings, we have learned to focus on isolation and difference. Some people are short, others tall; some fat, some thin; some smart, others stupid; some fast, others slow. Some people are my friends, others not; some people good, others untrustworthy and perhaps even mean or evil. Attached to these distinctions are numerous other attributes, also distinctions. The dichotomies are endless—like night and day, everything can be seen as having its opposite, and, from this perspective, everything is distinct and separate.

In addition to isolation and difference, we have all learned to view the world as involving scarcity. We're told that "you can't have your cake and eat it too" and that we need to "watch out for number one." We need to have a job and make more money, we need life insurance, health insurance, and a pension. We need to get there first, and do it better. Tied up with scarcity, there is urgency and, inherently, difference. If we are different, and some things good and some bad, we are determined to get the good—and get it before others can.

Given what we have learned about scarcity and difference, it can be challenging at times to imagine fullness of abundance and connection. Yet in each moment of understanding another human being and contributing to life by serving needs, there is a moment of connection and abundance. For a moment, scarcity and difference fall away. This book takes a radical view that each of those moments can be multiplied indefinitely. In doing so, you can enjoy more harmony, connection, and meaning in your life. You can also directly contribute to the well being of others. We hope you will take that step and consider where connection and plenty can lead—how it can enrich your life, those around you and, eventually, the larger world.

Integration: Questions to Further Explore the Introduction

A. Think about your personal and intimate relationships. What conflicts and differences arise? How would greater connection and communication contribute to the quality of your life, and those you care about?

B. Think about different situations that you see in the world today. How do these situations have their root cause in needs being met, or not?

C. Think about judgments you may have of others or yourself. How are these judgments rooted in concepts of isolation and scarcity?

CHAPTER ONE:
Another Way To See the World

"Feeling and longing are the motive forces behind all human endeavor and human creations."
—*Albert Einstein, 20ᵗʰ century American physicist and Nobel Prize winner*

"Sticks and stones can break my bones, but names could never hurt me."
—*Children's rhyme*

When people first hear the term "Nonviolent Communication," they can be surprised or confused. We are accustomed to thinking about violence as physical force and it can be puzzling to think of communication—mere words—as aggressive. In fact, communication is usually seen as an *alternative* to violence. Negotiations are attempted before acts of war and used to stop physical conflict. If a parent sees her child hitting a playmate or grabbing a toy away—an act of physical force—the child might be reminded to "use your words." The parent may be assuming, as the children's rhyme goes, "…names could never hurt me."

So what do words have to do with violence? If you think about it, there often is a connection. The language we use and the thoughts we have inform the kinds of actions we take. If we have critical thoughts or images of another group or person, it becomes far more likely that physical force will be used. If you reflect on physical violence and trace back what leads to it, you may at first blame a physical act or stimulus—"He hit me first!" or "He cut me off on the road!" But if you reflect further, you will find that before a strike is taken, even in perceived retaliation, that words or thoughts preceded it: "How dare you!" "What a jerk!" "I'll teach you a lesson." Violent actions follow from talking to ourselves in this kind of way. Violence most broadly defined can be seen as a breakdown of human connection and understanding. Certainly, when such fissures occur, opportunities for physical violence become more likely. In contrast, if we love and care for someone, the last thing we want is that they suffer or experience harm. While we may not be able to love and care for everyone in our lives with the same level of energy and attention, learning *how* to connect compassionately with others can contribute to resolving conflicts when they arise and to fostering even greater understanding where connection already exists. It is this kind of Compassionate Communication that we address in this book.

Beyond Boxed-Up Thinking

"Beyond right and wrong, there is a field. I will meet you there."
— *Rumi*

Communicating compassionately involves changing our thinking. It involves challenging a primary assumption that has informed our culture for hundreds and thousands of years. This assumption tells us that it is useful to classify people and things as "right" or "wrong." According to this kind of thinking, some people are good, some bad; some smart, others stupid; some heroes and others villains. This right-wrong thinking can be found at every level of our society. Comic book heroes fight arch villains; the current President of the United States talks about an "axis of evil." A popular bumper sticker reads, "Mean People Suck!" This assumes that some people are mean, others nice, and that mean people are mean all the time. Meanness is the very definition of who they are.

Who's right? Who's wrong? Who deserves our sympathy, understanding, and support? And who should be excluded, judged, or punished? When I was in college, I spent hours discussing questions like this with my friends. We considered relationships, family, and politics. We wanted to understand the world, and the choices being made. Even today, I find questions like this compelling. I want to understand the cause of a situation and who is responsible. I want to be informed and aware, prepared to face something similar and to have clarity about what

> "Reality is much more complex than any judgment of right and wrong encourages you to believe. When you really understand the ethical, spiritual, social, economic, and psychological forces that shape individuals, you will see that people's choices are not based on a desire to hurt. Instead, they are in accord with what they know and what world views are available to them. Most are doing the best they can, given what information they've received and what problems they are facing."
> —Michael Lerner

to do. I know I'm not the only one. The popularity of "confessional" talk shows and courtroom programs such as Judge Judy attests to a continuing interest in this kind of right-wrong thinking for solving problems and understanding the world.

So if right-wrong thinking has been used for thousands of years and is still so popular today, why change it? Clearly, this way of thinking meets some needs. It can offer us a sense of safety, meaning, fairness, and order. It can seem effective in making choices and distinguishing values. And it's familiar, so it can feel comfortable and easy—even intrinsic to human nature.

Yet right-wrong thinking doesn't foster connection. It separates us from each other and ourselves. It draws a line in the sand: You are either with us, or against us. Innocent or guilty. Right or wrong. Deserving of punishment—or reward. As such, it can be seen as lacking the complexity of life and full human experience. It implies a static view of human beings and their behavior. According to such thinking, "bad" people will always do "bad" things and "good" or "just" people must stop or control them. This world view focuses not on behavior—the particular acts we choose to take—but on who the person supposedly *is*. And if someone is intrinsically evil, what hope is there for learning, connection, compassion, or change?

> "I hate having to choose sides. Last year a guy I was friends with was going with a girl friend of mine. When they broke up I felt like I had to decide whose fault the break-up was, which one was the "bad guy." I chose my girl friend because we are very close and I didn't want to lose that friendship. But I really would like to do things differently."
> —Paula

Empirical research paints a very different picture of human behavior. It shows that behavior is not static but primarily determined by what we *think* about the situation we find ourselves in. Given the circumstances and our cultural conditioning, we are all capable of doing "bad" things. The proportion of college students, for example, who admit to behavior that could be classified as a felony is consistently over 90%. When asked if they would commit various illegal acts if they were "100% guaranteed that they wouldn't get caught," the proportion of students who said they would steal, cheat, or physically hurt someone who has hurt them in some way is very high. In effect, if you want to get someone to cheat, make the stakes high enough and the chances of getting caught low enough.

As the writer Jorge Luis Borges has observed, human beings live by justification alone—even if to bring a glass of water to our lips. What Borges means is that we all have reasons for doing what we do. The given circumstances and the needs we have—not who we are intrinsically—determine the course of action we take. It's safe to say, for example, that most human beings would abhor eating human flesh. Yet when stranded from an accident and given the choice of starving or eating the bodies of dead companions, you might perhaps choose to eat. There are well-documented cases, from climbing and airplane accidents, where this choice was made. If you reflect on an action you took that you're not proud of, you probably can find some need or important value that motivated that action—even if you're not fully happy with the choice or results.

The limitation of right-wrong thinking is that it doesn't promote compassion for ourselves or others. It doesn't help us make choices that can fully meet all our needs, or take actions fully aligned with our values. In this book we explore how a different kind of analysis, focused on feelings and needs, can enrich our understanding of human behavior and foster greater compassion and connection.

Exercise 1, Chapter 1: Force and Feeling

Take a moment and reflect on an act of physical force or violence that you have taken, considered, or fantasized about. This act of physical force could include simply slamming your books on the floor, breaking an object, or having the urge to physically hurt someone. What was the stimulus for the action you took or wanted to take? What were you feeling and thinking at the time of wanting to take this action? What is the link between the action and your thoughts?

Stimulis	Thoughts/Judgments About Stimulis	Feelings

The "F" Word

How many times a day does someone ask you, "How are you?" When you see a neighbor, coworker, or friend, this question most likely comes up. If you're like most people, you probably answer in passing. "Fine." "Ok." "Great." "Not bad." Yet like Morse code or short hand for what's really happening, none of these responses give us much information. Perhaps the only time we answer this question fully and frankly is when asked by a doctor, counselor, or loved one. But even when talking to those we are most intimate with, we may not fully express what we're experiencing and feeling.

In our culture, we're taught to be "polite" and not assume others are interested in us or our concerns. Wanting safety, we learn to be guarded and not too revealing. And we're certainly not accustomed to talking about our feelings. In the West, at least since the Age of Reason and the development of empirical science, feelings have been cast as subjective and untrustworthy. We are told instead to "use our heads" and not get emotional. The philosopher Descartes summed up our very existence in our ability to think— "I think therefore I am." And we're told that if we believe something, to "prove it." Logical thought, like a mathematics equation, can be written out and tested step by step. But how do we "test" human emotion and feeling?

For many men, feelings are especially a largely unknown and dangerous territory. Growing up, boys are told to "Take it like a man" and that "Only sissies cry." Men are not supposed to have feelings, especially feelings of sadness, fear, or loneliness. Perhaps the only feeling that men are allowed and even expected to express is anger. One NVC trainer from Texas, Ike Lasater, said that for years the only feelings he was ever aware of experiencing were *good, bad,* and *angry.* Whenever someone asked him how he was feeling about something, his response was either "good" or "bad."

While it is more socially acceptable for women to show their feelings, this expression is not valued. Historically, women have been discriminated against for the very qualities they are expected to exhibit. Hysteria, "wild, uncontrolled excitement or feeling," comes from the Greek for uterus, *hystera*, stemming from the notion that "women are more often hysterical than men."[3] Cast as overly emotional, irrational, and unstable— "the weaker sex"—women were told for centuries that they were unfit for many occupations, including driving, voting, and working as a doctor, soldier, or scientist. Women of course have now proven themselves in these areas. Statistically, they have lower accident rates than men. Yet as epitomized by the "Iron Lady," the first female Prime Minister of Britain, Margaret Thatcher, women who want to be successful are expected to exhibit toughness, "clear-headedness," and indifference.

This way of thinking about feelings is especially true in Anglo-American culture. In French, the word for feeling, *sentiment*, is not pejorative. Expressing feeling is socially acceptable and even desired. In English, the same root of *sentiment* turns up in "sentimental"—fake, over wrought, superficial, and cliché. We hear "don't be too sensitive" and so-and-so is "*over* sensitive." Rather than being "sensitive" (aware of our feelings), we're supposed to be thick skinned, with a stiff upper lip. The

> "If I am feeling bad I just try to talk myself out of it, to not let it show."
> —Holly
>
> "The last time I cried was when I was six years old."   —Samuel
>
> "If things go badly for you, my dad taught me you just gotta 'suck it up.'"
> —Jessica
>
> "I always figured it was a good idea to ignore my emotions. I thought they might lead me to do irrational things, things I would regret."
> —Patrick

[3] David B. Guralnik (Ed.), *New World Dictionary of the American Language*, 2nd College Edition (Cleveland, OH: Williams Collins, 1980), p. 693.

historical heroes we emulate are the pilgrims, pioneers, and cowboys—all "strong, silent" types who were resilient and tough. Our modern pop heroes are equally strong and unfeeling. Athletic stars and those on "survivor" programs are admired for their endurance and putting "mind over matter." Urban, "gangsta" culture is about "coolness" and disaffection.

In our fast-food culture, we're also proactive and product-orientated. We want effectiveness and immediate results. If something is "wrong," especially if it's unpleasant, stressful, or painful, we want a solution—*now*. Like changing a TV channel or popping a pain-killer, we also try to "fix" feelings—telling others and ourselves what to feel—or not. "Just get over it." "Just suck it up." "Get a grip." In doing so, we may not fully understand what we're feeling and why.

True to Life

> *"Trust your feelings, Luke…"* —*Obi Wan Kenobi*

We dismiss our feelings, thinking they're irrational and unreal. Yet our feelings in fact are very much linked to our physical bodies. When our bodies need something, our bodies tell us. If we're hungry, tired, hot or cold, we experience a physical sensation. Our bodies might tighten, our hairs may stand on end, or our stomachs grumble or churn. Similar to physical needs, when we're feeling an emotion such as anger, happiness, sadness or contentment, our bodies let us know. If we're angry, our bodies may feel tension or heat. If we're sad, we may feel tightness or heaviness. If happy or content, we might feel lightness, openness, and expansiveness. Each of us experience our emotions in different ways, with different sensations. But there's no doubt that our emotions have a physical impact on our bodies. When we experience an emotion, there is in fact a chemical response in every cell of our organism. That we use the same verb in English ("feel") for physical sensations and emotional states illustrates the close relationship between these two types of experience.

We are so accustomed to using our heads and not depending on feeling or intuition that, in some ways, we are cut off from the rest of our bodies. We may not be fully aware of what our physical needs are, never mind our emotions. Yet our feelings serve as an important indicator of what's going on for us. Because we can feel heat, we are able to pull back from a hot stove before getting burned. Because we feel thirst and hunger, we can nourish and hydrate our bodies. Emotional states, such as happiness and fear, equally provide us with crucial information. Our feelings tell us something about what we're experiencing in our environment and what we're enjoying or needing. In the next chapter, we will look more closely at how our feelings relate to our needs.

For the moment, I'd like you to consider the value of feelings. So related to our senses, feelings are part of being fully alive. Part of aliveness is being fully aware of our experience in the world. As seen in the etymology of "emotion," our feelings move us. They can lead us to action; they can foster self-awareness. When we pay attention only to our thoughts and dismiss our feelings, we're playing with only half a deck. And why play with half a deck, especially when the other half has some of the most valuable cards with which to play the game of life?

Exercise 2, Chapter 1: Emoto-Meters

Our bodies are like "Emoto-Meters," highly tuned and sophisticated gauges that can help us ground ourselves in the present moment and be aware of what we're feeling and needing. By tracking how our feelings physically manifest, we can gain greater awareness and fluency in naming them.

A. Observe your bodily sensations at this moment. What sensations do you feel? What feelings (emotions) do you associate with these sensations?

Feelings: _____

Sensations related to these feelings: _____

_____

B. How many different feelings are you aware of experiencing on any given day? Where do you experience these feelings in your body? How would you describe how the following feelings occur in your chest, your head, or your limbs?

An example from one student:

Feeling	Where Experienced	How Experienced
Fear	arms, hands	a feeling of tingling, contracting, tense medium intensity

What is your experience?

Feeling	Where Experienced	How Experienced
Fear		
Sadness		
Joy		
Relief		
Excitement		
Anger		
Annoyance		

Table A - Universal Feelings

Fulfilled Feelings			
AFFECTIONATE	INSPIRED	REFRESHED	EXCITED
Compassionate	Amazed	Enlivened	Amazed
Friendly	Awed	Rejuvenated	Animated
Fond loving	Wonder	Renewed	Ardent
Openhearted		Rested	Aroused
Sympathetic	ENGAGED	Restored	Dazzled
Tender	Absorbed	Revived	Eager
Warm	Alert		Energetic
	Curious	GRATEFUL	Enthusiastic
CONFIDENT	Engrossed	Appreciative	Giddy
Empowered	Enchanted	Moved	Invigorated
Open	Fascinated	Thankful	Lively
Proud	Interested	Touched	Passionate
Safe	Intrigued		Surprised
Secure	Involved		Vibrant
	Spellbound		
	Stimulated		

Unfulfilled Feelings			
AFRAID	ANGER	AVERSION	TENSE
Apprehensive	Angry	Appalled	Anxious
Panicked	Enraged	Disgusted	Cranky
Petrified	Furious	Dislike	Edgy
Scared	Livid	Hate	Irritable
Suspicious	Outraged	Loathe	Nervous
Terrified	Resentful	Repulsed	Overwhelmed
Wary			Stressed out
Worried	EMBARRASSED	SAD	
	Ashamed	Depressed	DISCONNECTED
DISQUIET	Humiliated	Despair	Alienated
Agitated	Mortified	Discouraged	Apathetic
Disturbed	Self-conscious	Down	Bored
Restless		Heavy Hearted	Detached
Startled	FATIGUE	Unhappy	Distant
Uneasy	Beat		Indifferent
Uncomfortable	Burnt out	VULNERABLE	Numb
Unsettled	Depleted	Fragile	
	Exhausted	Insecure	PAIN
CONFUSED	Tired	Needy	Anguished
Ambivalent	Worn out	Open	Devastated
Baffled		Sensitive	Heartbroken
Hesitant	ANNOYED		Hurt
Lost	Aggravated	YEARNING	Lonely
Out of it	Frustrated	Aching	Miserable
Torn	Impatient	Envious	Regretful
	Irritated	Longing	
	Ticked off	Nostalgic	
		Wishing	

Exercise 3, Chapter 1: The Rush of Feeling

Why do people like to see particular types of films? Clearly, seeing a film is a form of entertainment and can meet various needs, including stimulation, fun, and companionship. But each film genre can also be seen as eliciting particular feelings—such as apprehension, anxiety and fear (horror flicks) or tenderness, warmth, and hope (romances). Amusement park rides can also be seen as eliciting certain physical and emotional responses—roller coasters and other daredevil rides advertised as "thrilling;" the "tunnel of love" similar to that invoked by a romantic film. Sports also elicit strong emotions. Part of the appeal in watching a game is the apprehension, excitement, disappointment, joy and/or relief that we experience as "our" team misses, scores, wins or loses.

Why do we enjoy activities that elicit emotional responses? Why do we like feeling anxious, thrilled, or terrified? Feelings are our life-blood. When our feelings are "up"—our hearts beating, blood pressure increasing—we are aware of being fully alive.

Make a list of some of your favorite activities. This can include hobbies, sports, entertainment, or other pastimes you enjoy, even taking a walk or meeting with friends. What feelings come up for you thinking about the last time you engaged in this activity?

Activity	Feeling(s)
Sport:	
Film genre:	
Games:	
Hobby:	
Other activity:	

Playing With a Full Deck

There are hundreds of words in the English language for different feelings. Most of us, it's safe to say, are using only about ten percent of the vocabulary available. Like colors in a paint box, there is a huge array, with a range of intensity and shades. And out of all these colors, the majority of us are painting in only white and gray.

Happiness, for example, can range from pleased and content to jubilant and ecstatic. Sadness can descend to broken-heartedness and grief or lighten to blueness or simply "feeling down." "Good" and "bad," the words most commonly used to describe feelings, are so general, they could refer to many different experiences. "Good" and "bad" in fact are not even feelings—they're adjectives marking approval or disapproval.

At first you may find it challenging to identify what you're feeling and to distinguish between different shades. With practice, we can all develop this ability. Reading over the list of feelings in Table A (page 35), do you see any that are familiar to you? What feelings belong in a similar group or "family"? After identifying a group, you may wish to organize them in intensity and degree. You may also want to jot down feelings that come up for you on a regular basis or keep a list of feeling words with you, to refer to. The next time you answer "good" or "bad" in response to "How are you?" you may wish to stop and ask yourself: "What am I *really* feeling at this moment?"

Exercise 4, Chapter 1: The Movement of Emotions

Have you noticed how quickly feelings can change for young children? At one moment, a child may be smiling and laughing, and the next moment in tears. There's no evidence that children experience more feelings than adults; regardless of age, we probably all have similar ranges. The difference may be that children tend to be more in touch with what they're feeling and more inclined to express it. As adults, our feelings can also shift in intensity and degree—from apprehension to fear or terror, from satisfaction to happiness or elation. Our feelings change in response to what we're experiencing in the moment, and how we interpret that experience. We may be feeling perfectly excited, happy, and satisfied as we head off on a sunny day to enjoy a day at the beach. But after being stuck in traffic for an hour and being cut off on the road by a big SUV, we may be feeling completely different—frustrated, hot, and annoyed! Feelings are not frivolous or irrational—they are indicators of how we are responding to stimuli in the moment. That feelings change easily and quickly is simply a sign of how quickly circumstances can change in our lives and our thoughts about circumstances; being aware of our feelings can help us respond effectively to what is happening in the here and now.

Think back over the day or even the last three hours. What feelings have come and gone during the day? See if you can link those feelings to your thoughts about a specific stimulus in your environment.

Time	Feeling	Possible stimulus – Thoughts about stimulus

Exercise 5, Chapter 1: Stimulation and Response

What we see, hear, touch, taste, or think about can all stimulate feelings in us. Often these responses are conditioned by associations (prior experiences), even if these experiences are not fully conscious or currently present in our minds.

Part One: Examine each of the photographs on the following pages. For each one consider:

A. What aspects of the photo do you find stimulate thoughts or feelings in you (subject, lighting, location, interactions of people and animals, etc.)?

B. What thoughts, associations or interpretations do you have with respect to that stimulus? What experiences in your own life does it remind you of?

C. What feelings are stimulated in you by the thoughts you have as you look at this photo?

EXAMPLE: Person making "X" marks on electronic Lotto form

Stimulation:	Thoughts, Interpretations, Associations:	Feelings:
Pencil marks on scan form	Thinking about all the multiple choice tests I've taken; school tests, SAT tests	Frustrated, anxious, hopeless
Last part of the word "Lotto" on top of paper	Gambling, thinking about losing lots of money, family problems, paying bills, compulsive gambling	Tense, frustrated, worried, scared

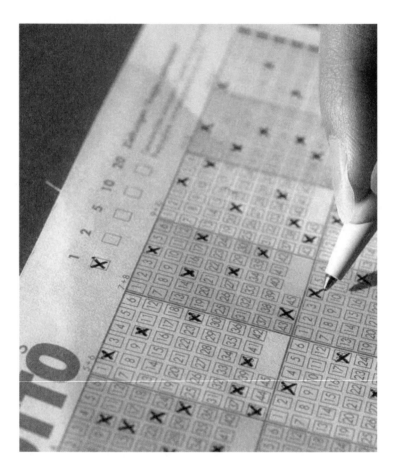

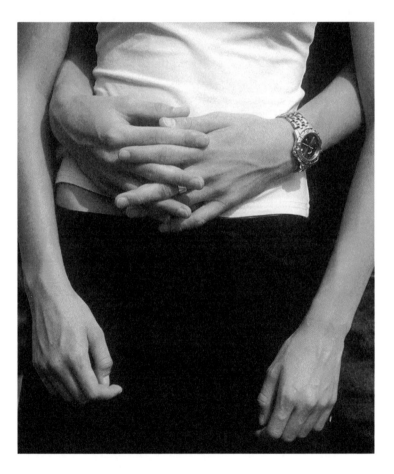

Part Two: Look in a daily newspaper and choose several photos that you find stimulating. Again, identify what you're seeing in the photo, how you're feeling seeing this image, and any thoughts and associations.

Part Three: Go to an art museum and/or look at some art work in a book. Choose a work of art that you find moving. How do you feel looking at this piece? What do you specifically see that's stimulating your feelings? What associations do you have with what you see?

Disentangling Thoughts and Feelings

It's hard enough to identify what we're feeling. But it's even easier to confuse feelings for thoughts. As we've already explored, the verb "feel" in English has different uses. We can talk about how we feel in relation to physical sensations and also emotions. We can also use "feel" to talk about thoughts, opinions, and judgments. When we say, for example, "I feel that capital punishment is wrong," what we're really expressing is what we *think* or *believe* about capital punishment—not how we *feel* about it. If we unpacked the feelings in this statement, we might find that the speaker is feeling angry, sad, or scared.

Often there can be passionate feelings behind our opinions. We're simply not naming them. Using the verb "feel" with an opinion can be an effort to express that passion. Sometimes we can say, "I feel that…" when wanting to give an opinion with a somewhat softer or gentler edge. In this context, we could easily say, "I personally believe" instead of " I feel." Regardless, when using the word "feel" in this context, as followed by "that," we are talking about thoughts and opinions—not feelings.

Looking for the word "that" can help us identify when we're giving an opinion or thought. But sometimes in English we can also give opinions where "that" is understood but not stated. For example, we can say, "She feels (that) because he left her, he has no heart." Or "Tom feels (that) it should be done by noon." "I feel (that) if it's packed this way, it will be safer." To know when we're using thoughts with "feeling," we need to look for where "that" can occur, not just where it in fact turns up. We can also look for subjects, such as "I," "you," "he," "she," "they," "it," or other words that follow a predicate in English, such as "because" or "as if." We also can check of course to see that the word following the verb "feeling" is, in fact, referring to the experience of a feeling or sensation— "hot," "aggravated," "joyful," "excited," etc. The following Table gives other examples of how the word "feel'" is used to express thoughts.

Sentences in which the word "feel" is used to express thoughts

I feel you look better in blue = I personally believe you look better in blue
(Pronouns—e.g., *I, you, it*— after "feel" indicate a thought)

I feel I am worthless = I'm convinced that I'm worthless
(Pronouns—e.g., *I, you, it*— after "feel" indicate a thought)

I feel John is sad = I believe that John is sad
(Nouns—e.g. *John*—after "feel" indicate a thought)

I feel *like* I'm a loser = I think I'm a loser
(Like indicates a thought)

I feel *as if* you hate me = I'm sure you hate me!
(As if indicates a thought)

I feel fat = I think I'm fat
(Fat is an evaluation, not an emotion)

Exercise 6, Chapter 1: Real Feeling

Complete the following sentences with a judgment or opinion. Then go back and "unpack" what feelings you are experiencing when thinking about this issue.

EXAMPLE: "I feel because he didn't call that I'm not important to him." Feelings: sad, disappointed, lonely

Opinion: _____

Feeling(s): _____

A. I feel as if… _____

_____

B. I feel if… _____

_____

C. I feel when… _____

_____

D. I feel that… _____

_____

E. I feel because… _____

_____

Wolves in Sheep's Clothing

Speaking English, we also confuse feelings in another way. Just as the word "feel" can be used with a thought, we frequently use words in English that appear to be feelings but in fact are feelings mixed with judgments. When communicating, these words occur in the same place where feeling words occur. We commonly understand them as feelings. But, upon closer examination, we can see that there is a thought or judgment mixed in with them.

How can we distinguish? Feelings concern what is going on *inside* ourselves (What am *I* feeling?) or what is going on for another person *inside* that person (What are *you* feeling?). Feelings are internal experiences. While there may be cues (such as tears, frowning, or laughter) we may not always be able to identify feelings from what we can observe from the outside. Thoughts and opinions in contrast, while they can seem very personal, concern what we see in the world.

Let's look at an example. When we say, "I feel abandoned," there is, in part, a feeling at play. We probably are feeling sad and lonely. But "abandoned" includes much more than a feeling. The thought wrapped up with it is a judgment of what someone (or circumstances) has done *to* us. Thus "I feel abandoned" could be translated as, "I'm so lonely and it's your fault because you left me." Or it could mean, "I feel scared and uncertain that no one is ever going to care for me." In effect, the word "abandoned" is a shorthand way of blaming a person or situation for what we are feeling inside us. It is a mixture of an internal experience (a feeling) with something we are imagining, thinking, or seeing (perception of the world).

There are many judgment-feeling words in English that mix feeling information with judgments or interpretations. Some of them include:

Judgment Mixed with Feeling		
Abused	Interrupted	Pressured
Attacked	Intimidated	Provoked
Betrayed	Left out	Put down
Cheated	Loved	Rejected
Cherished	Manipulated	Screwed
Defeated	Misunderstood	Threatened
Devalued	Neglected	Unappreciated
Discriminated against	Nurtured	Unheard
Forced	Overworked	Unwanted
Harassed	Patronized	Used

With each of these words, you can uncover both a feeling and a judgment. "Unappreciated," for example, could mean sad and disappointed combined with, "You did this by not expressing your gratitude." "Overworked" could mean disgruntled and annoyed combined with, "You asked that I work late every night this week." An easy way to identify these "judgment-feeling" words is to ask yourself, "Did someone do something *to* me in this situation?" "Have they *made* me feel this way?" "Whose fault is it?" If you're placing responsibility for your feelings (and circumstances) outside of yourself, you may very likely be using a feeling mixed with judgment.

Since judgment-feelings involve blame, they easily lead to breakdowns in communication. At the very moment we want to be understood, by using judgment-feelings, our words can trigger defensiveness and denial. This response is not surprising: No one likes to be judged. If we want mutual understanding, we will succeed more frequently if our statements of feelings reflect only our feelings and not our judgments.

Using judgment-based words can also obscure that we have autonomy, personal power and choice. No one can make us feel anything. By clearly stating a feeling without criticism or blame, we are taking full responsibility for our responses. In doing so, we can experience greater awareness and choice.

Exercise 7, Chapter 1: Like Oil and Water

Go back to the list of words that mix feelings with judgment. Choose five of these words and translate what the feeling and judgment might be. Harassed, for example, could be translated as "angry and stressed" with "you're pressuring me."

Judgment-Feeling word	Feeling	Judgment
1.		
2.		
3.		
4.		
5.		

Exercise 8, Chapter 1: Claiming Our Feelings

To gain more awareness of judgments you may have and what can stimulate feelings (and how these feelings are experienced in your body), you may wish to keep a log. Try keeping a "feeling log" one or two days this week. Check in with yourself ten-fifteen times during the day or every hour or two. At the moment you check in, what are you feeling? What sensations are connected to this feeling in your body? Does a "judgment-feeling" word come to mind for you? And what stimulus (thought, judgment, or evaluation) is connected to your current experience?

Sensation in body	Judgment-Feeling	Stimulus	Feeling
Tightness in my throat, heat and tension in my face	Disrespected, unappreciated	Told that I'm not good enough; dropped from the team	Sad, hurt, disappointed, scared

Moving On

In this chapter we considered how moving beyond right-wrong thinking can contribute to greater connection with ourselves and others. To move beyond this kind of thinking, it can be helpful to connect with what we're feeling and what our bodies are telling us. In the next chapter, we will examine how feelings can connect us to our needs and that in focusing on needs, rather than judgments or evaluations, we can find solutions that are more effective, satisfying, and consistent with our broader beliefs.

Integration: Questions and Exercises to Further Explore Chapter 1

Decide for each of the following whether you think it is a feeling (mark F) or not a feeling (mark N). If you mark N, write a statement that you think might express what the speaker is feeling. My opinion about each statement follows the exercise.

A. _____ "I feel he doesn't care about me."

B. _____ "I'm happy you're coming with me."

C. _____ "I feel very nervous when you do that."

D. _____ "When he leaves without me, I feel forgotten."

E. _____ "You're ridiculous."

F. _____ "I'm satisfied with my grades."

G. _____ "I feel like kissing you."

H. _____ "I feel manipulated."

I. _____ "I feel good about how I played at the game."

J. _____ "I feel fat."

My responses for this exercise:

A. If you marked "F," I do not agree. I don't believe that "he doesn't care about me" is a feeling. To me, it expresses what the speaker thinks the other person is feeling, rather than how the speaker is feeling. Examples of expressing a feeling might be, "I'm lonely" or "I'm feeling sad and want your company."

B. If you marked "F," I agree a feeling was verbally expressed.

C. I agree if you marked "F."

D. If you marked "F," I do not agree. I don't consider "forgotten" a feeling. To me, it is a judgment-feeling, expressing what the speaker thinks the other person is doing *to* him or her. An expression of a feeling might be, "I feel sad."

E. If you marked "F," I do not agree. I don't believe that "ridiculous" is a feeling. I believe it expresses what the speaker is thinking about the other person, rather than how the speaker is feeling. An expression of a feeling might be, "I'm annoyed with you."

F. If you marked "F," I agree that a feeling was verbally expressed.

G. If you marked "F," I do not agree. I don't believe "like kissing you" is a feeling. I believe it expresses what the speaker imagines doing, rather than how the speaker is feeling. An expression of a feeling might be, "I'm attracted to you."

H. If you marked "F," I do not agree. I don't believe that "manipulated" is a feeling. To me, it expresses what the speaker thinks the other person has done and a judgment of the other person's intention. An expression of a feeling might be, "I feel suspicious."

I. If you marked "F," I don't agree. The word "good" is often used to talk about feelings but in fact simply expresses approval—that you're happy with how you're feeling. A feeling might be in this case "satisfied, content, excited."

J. If you marked "F," I don't agree. I don't believe "fat" is a feeling. It expresses how the speaker thinks about him or herself, rather than how the speaker is feeling. Examples of an expression of a feeling might be, "I feel insecure about my weight" or "Thinking about my weight, I feel anxious."

CHAPTER TWO:
Getting to the Root of Life

Needs: The Primal Force of Life

As we explored in Chapter One, we can start being fully present to ourselves and others by attending to our feelings—our physical sensations and our emotions. In doing so, we give attention to what we're experiencing around us in our environment, to what is happening in the "here and now." Yet awareness of our feelings (and what might be stimulating them) is only the first step. Like a red flag, our feelings are a way of alerting us to the primal experience of life, our needs. Being aware of what we're feeling, we can know if our needs are being met or not. It is by focusing on needs—others' and our own—and seeing how everyone's needs can be met—that we can most enrich life.

If you think about it, all human beings share the same basic needs. We have needs for physical well being, such as air, food, touch, and water. We also have what could be considered non-material or "psycho-spiritual" needs, such as needs for honesty, connection, autonomy, and meaning. Our physical bodies need air and shelter to survive. But it could be argued that without dignity, equality, purpose and creativity—to name just a few "non-material" needs—that we also would not survive or thrive, both as individuals and as a species.

Human beings can certainly differ in our wants and preferences. There are innumerable strategies we can employ to meet our needs. But among different people and cultures we can observe the same needs underlying different behavior. Consider the need for food, for example. While many

> "Food, sex and sleep—and not necessarily in that order!"
> —Anonymous student

Americans may enjoy eating seafood, many South Africans view it as inedible and disgusting. Many Americans of European descent may have no interest in eating chicken feet and find them repulsive. But in Chinese and other cultures, chicken feet are considered a delicacy. Similarly, people in all cultures value respect. Yet how respect is experienced and communicated varies tremendously. In some cultures, respect is indicated by making eye contact, leaving space between people, or being silent. In other cultures, respect is expressed by lowering or averting ones eyes, allowing less space, or speaking up. Regardless of how expressed, each of these needs, along with many others, can be considered "universal"—valued all over the world.

As universal, needs are general, not specific. As such, they can be fulfilled in a number of different ways, by a number of different strategies. When you're feeling thirsty, for example, you can meet your need for hydration by drinking water, milk, or some other beverage, or eating a piece of juicy fruit. If you choose to drink water, you could choose to buy a bottle of water, pour some from a tap, or find a water fountain. How we choose to meet our needs can depend on a large number of variables—what other needs are "up" at the moment, and the ease or "do-ability" of how to meet them.

Regardless of how we choose to meet our needs, all needs are vital and important. One is not inherently more crucial or valuable than another. Nourishment and sleep are vital to physical survival. Yet it would be hard to privilege sleep over food. We need both, and won't survive without either. It could seem that physical needs are more vital than non-material needs. But human behavior suggests otherwise. We all have been willing at times to forgo sleep to study for a test or attend a party. In doing so, we are seeking to meet needs for effectiveness and confidence in how we will perform or, in the case of the party, wanting play, connection, community, and celebration. The physical need for food is compelling. Yet at times, humans choose not to eat out of wanting to meet non-material needs. In many cultures, for example, people voluntarily fast as part of a rite or ritual, contributing to needs for meaning, community, purpose, and belonging to the larger group. In some cases, people have chosen to go on hunger strikes when their needs for autonomy, dignity, choice, and fairness were not being met. In the 1980s, for example, Bobby Sands, an Irish Republican, wanted the British government to recognize him as a political prisoner. This recognition was so important to him that he was willing to fast until his death. He was not the only one who made this choice.

Sometimes it can be hard to see the universality of needs because our strategies to meet them can be so different and even seem at odds. The universality of needs can also be hard to see because different needs can be more "up" at different times. We all have needs for movement, rest, food, and water. But at one moment, we may be thirsty and, at another moment, hungry or tired. In a particular situation, we might be wanting care and consideration; the other person we're interacting with may be wanting spaciousness, play, and ease. Yet while each person may have different needs stimulated, we can all appreciate and understand the basic, universal needs that humans have. "Play" or "spaciousness" might not be needs up for us in the moment, but we can understand and appreciate them as valuable and life-enriching.

As life-enriching, all needs can be seen as "positive" and desirable. The need for food, for example, is a "positive" energy; it motivates us to find and consume food to sustain us. Similarly, all cultures value celebrations to mark events of importance to the individual and the community. These events, such as birth, death, and marriage, relate to primal human needs for life, hope, community, and connection (among others). If you look at the list in Table B (page 58), there probably is not one need that you wouldn't enjoy experiencing or seeing met for others. All people all over the world, for example, want a sense of purpose in life, and to enjoy integrity, love, peace, safety, and fun. Needs motivate and energize behavior; they sustain and enrich the quality of our lives.

Table B - Universal Needs

CONNECTION	PLAY
Acceptance	Joy
Affection	Humor
Appreciation	Adventure
Belonging	
Closeness	PHYSICAL WELL-BEING
Communication	Air
Community	Food
Companionship	Movement/exercise
Compassion	Rest/sleep
Consideration	Sexual expression
Consistency	Safety (protection from life threatening
Cooperation	situations)
Empathy	Shelter
Inclusion	Touch
Intimacy	Water
Love	
Mutuality	MEANING
Nurturing	Awareness
Reciprocity	Celebration
Respect/Self-respect	Challenge
Safety	Clarity
Security	Competence
Shared reality	Consciousness
Stability	Contribution
Support	Creativity
To know and be known	Discovery
To see and be seen	Effectiveness
To understand and be understood	Efficiency
Trust	Growth
Warmth	Integration
	Learning
HONESTY	Mourning
Authenticity	Movement
Integrity	Participation
Presence	Purpose
	Self-expression
PEACE	Stimulation
Beauty	Understanding
Communion	
Ease	AUTONOMY
Equality	Choice
Harmony	Dignity
Inspiration	Freedom
Order	Independence
	Space
	Spontaneity

Part of the life force, all organisms, not just human life, respond to needs. Plants and trees soak up water and grow in the direction of the sun. With sufficient water and light, a plant will survive. But with spaciousness and care—weeding, fertilizing, trimming, a plant will thrive. Humans are the same. If our physical and non-material

All organisms make use of diverse strategies to meet their needs. This fica, for example, has extended a branch five feet above a screen to benefit from direct sun light.

needs are met, like stretching towards the sun, we will experience "fulfilled" feelings such as happiness, satisfaction, and peace. When our needs aren't being met, we may experience "unfulfilled" feelings, such as anxiety, fear, impatience, or anger.

> "My friends and I don't talk about feelings and needs. We just talk. But when I listen and try to figure out what needs they might be having, whew! It really looks different!"
>
> —Gary

Seeing all needs as positive, life-enriching, and holding equal value and weight is crucial in seeing how all our needs—and the needs of others—can be met. By focusing first on what our needs are rather than moving immediately to strategies, we can create connection and shared understanding. We also can often resolve or avoid misunderstandings and conflicts and discover strategies that work for everyone. You may not understand why I like classical music and I may not appreciate the rock music that you like, but we can both relate to the fact that for each of us music satisfies a need for aesthetic pleasure and expression. This kind of awareness of shared needs can lead to very different outcomes. In one high school, for example, where the white students, the black students and the Latino students had different preferences in dance music, the organizing group decided to have music from the three different preferred styles at the school prom. The organizers recognized that all of the students wanted respect for their musical preferences and wanted to know that their needs mattered. At other schools, in contrast, where there is not such an understanding, the songs played were determined by majority vote. The students whose preferences were in the minority didn't get to hear any of the music they like best. Their voices were not heard.

"I wanted to have sex and she didn't. I sure was frustrated!"

—Matthew

"My best friend has been going with this guy who I think is a loser and a very manipulative person. I have been telling her to break it off and it's gotten to the point where we are barely talking because I think it's such a bad relationship for her and I have been pushing her really hard to leave him. After thinking about it, I realized that I was doing the same thing to her that he is—trying to get her to do what I want her to do. We sat down and talked and she told me how much she wanted me to be there for her even if I don't agree with her choices in boyfriends. And how much she wants me to respect that she has to make the choices because it's her life—even if I disagree with her and even if she does make some mistakes and get hurt along the way. And the great thing is that now that I have stopped pushing about what to do and become more accepting of her right to choose, she is opening up more, telling me more about her own uncertainties and confusion about the relationship."

—Sheila

Exercise 1, Chapter 2: Connecting the Energy of Feelings to Life-Enriching Needs

A. Think of a specific time that you recently experienced one of the fulfilled feelings shown at the top of Table A (page 374).

1. What were you feeling?

2. What was the specific thing that happened that stimulated that feeling?

3. What need(s) shown in Table B (page 375) did you experience as fulfilled in relation to that feeling?

B. Think of a specific time recently that you experienced one of the unfulfilled feelings shown at the bottom of Table A (page 374).

1. What were you feeling?

2. What was the specific thing that happened that stimulated that feeling?

3. What need(s) shown in Table B (page 375) did you experience as unfulfilled?

Form and Essence: Strategies and Needs

As discussed above, all needs are life-serving and "positive." We may not all agree, however, about which strategies are life-serving. A particular strategy might meet some needs and not others. A strategy might meet some needs for us, and not meet needs for another person, or group. For some people, eating at a fast food restaurant might meet needs for pleasure, ease, fun, and choice, as well as nourishment. For others, choosing *not* to eat fast food might meet needs for health, self-care, integrity, and choice. We could disagree and argue for hours about which strategy to take—do we eat at McDonalds or at a health food bar? Do we eat at McDonalds some days, but not every day? Yet regardless of where they like to eat and when, both parties can probably understand and appreciate the needs at play—for pleasure, choice, ease, and health.

Exercise 2, Chapter 2: Connecting the Dots: Strategies and Needs

For the following exercise, think about five choices or actions (strategies) that you have taken in the last week. Then consider the needs you were wanting to meet, and other strategies possible to address the same needs.

Action (Strategy:)	Needs at Play:	Other Strategies Possible:
Reviewing notes as part of studying for test	Effectiveness, competency, confidence, ease, efficiency, learning	Re-reading chapters in text book; meeting with classmate to review concepts; going to professor's office hours for additional help; listening to tapes of class lectures

Getting Clear about What We're Needing

In our culture, it is common to confuse strategies for needs. This confusion is easy to understand. Without strategies to meet our needs, we can be left feeling unsatisfied and incomplete. If we don't find ways to meet our needs, life will not continue or thrive.

And because we associate how we meet the need with the need itself, it can be difficult to distinguish between the two. Yet it is the needs we have, not the strategies, that are the primal energy and force of life. Strategies are simply the diverse ways we attempt to experience and address our needs. Clearly distinguishing between the two can help us in understanding our needs, having more choice and being more effective in the choices that we make.

In English, it's easy to mix strategies and needs

> "When I first started thinking about needs, I felt stumped. I just wasn't used to thinking of myself as having needs. I had no problem using the verb "need" in statements like "I need a coffee," "I need to sleep," "I need to study." I thought I "needed" those things. But then I realized that the universal needs underlying "I need coffee" could be a number of different things, depending on the situation. Sometimes when I want a coffee, what I'm really wanting is to take a break and get outside for a few minutes. I was mixing up needs with strategies. In doing so, I was not always attending to what the real needs are themselves."
> —Sarah

because we commonly use the word "need" when talking about specific choices or desires. We might say, for example, "I need a new bike... a bigger apartment...a faster car...a better job...a nice vacation!" You can substitute countless objects in this equation— such as a new jacket, a book you want, or CD! You can also substitute outcomes and behaviors. "I need to eat less." "I need to study more." "I need better grades." But none of these items are needs. They are particular ways of attempting to meet needs. Beneath each objective, you can find the true, universal needs at play—such as wanting pleasure, connection, fun, and learning (a new book) or warmth and beauty (a jacket).

Your desire may be so intense for a particular strategy that it can feel like an urgent necessity. How often have we heard, " I *have* to get X!" or "If I don't get X, I'll die!" Yet the intensity we feel for a particular outcome in fact comes from the energy of the needs we are experiencing, not the strategy.

We Live What We Learn

Another reason it can be challenging to distinguish strategies from needs is that most of us are not accustomed to thinking about universal needs. It's not something we learn about at home, from our friends, or at school. In our culture, we're most accustomed to talking about strategies, not the needs at play motivating them. At one point, the study of needs was included in psychology courses, primarily through the work of Abraham Maslow who wrote during the 1950s about human needs. Yet in contemporary American psychology, the concept of human needs and how needs motivate human behavior is not well represented. In six popular introductory psychology textbooks averaging over 600 pages each, the number of pages on the topic of needs ranged from zero to one. The number of pages, in contrast, devoted to cognition and thinking averaged twenty-five pages. At Binghamton University, the course Motivational Psychology, which included the study of needs, was removed from the graduate and undergraduate curricula in 1990. Given how little focus has been given to human needs, it's no wonder that we have little awareness or fluency in discussing them.

The Business of Mixing Needs with Strategies

This lack of focus on needs is not true of all disciplines, however. Roaming through a local bookstore recently, I found one discipline where the number of books devoted to the study of human needs occupied a full bookshelf seven feet tall! Can you guess which discipline took up so much needs-based shelf space? Business! The label for the set of shelves was "Business Motivation" and included books on how to appeal to human needs in how you market, hire, fire, advertise, manage, or seek to influence people.

All these needs, however, were clearly linked to strategies—to manage workers and sell products.

How does business mix strategies and needs? Think about it: The primary job of advertising agencies is to convince us that buying a particular product will meet a whole array of needs. In effect, what they're selling is a strategy. Is there really a connection between the product (the particular strategy advertised) and the needs it claims to meet? You might think, for example, that the most important thing to know in choosing what soft drink to buy is how it tastes and how likely you are to enjoy it. But many companies advertise soft drinks featuring words and images that have nothing to do with taste. They depict people in the company of others, talking, laughing, playing sports, kissing, and/or relaxing on the beach. These images suggest an association between the product and primal, universal needs, such as fun, rest, ease, intimacy, connection, spaciousness, and belonging. With these needs, we associate positive feelings—happiness, contentment, ease, and satisfaction. We associate these positive feelings with the product being advertised.

By implication, many ads suggest that only if you buy their product will you see your needs met. If you drink product X, or wash your hair with product Z, you will be popular, respected, "cool," sexually appealing, and part of the "in" crowd. All by drinking the "right" brand of soda! Of course we know rationally this is impossible. How can a soda meet needs for community, belonging, respect, sexual expression, and appreciation—not to mention fun, stimulation, play, and excitement? There are plenty of people who don't drink soda who enjoy these needs being met. And there are plenty of people sitting alone drinking Coke in front of a TV each night.

Many of the needs being "sold" to us can be met in other ways and are not specific to a particular product, or any product for that matter. A Mercedes-Benz, for example, as a mode of transportation, could be seen as a strategy to meet needs for ease of movement. But if these were the only needs a Mercedes-Benz were meeting, what would motivate a person to spend $100,000 on a Mercedes-Benz when a Honda for $25, 000 could also meet the same needs? If you want to sell a Mercedes-Benz, you need to convince people that transportation is not the only need it will meet. A Mercedes-Benz could be a strategy for comfort and beauty (aesthetic pleasure), or for connection or belonging (to a particular group that can afford such a car, or with those who value styling and speed in transportation). This car could also be used to experience and express energy, power, and self-expression.

There are other ways than buying a Mercedes to meet these needs, of course. And a Mercedes in the end may not be effective in meeting all the needs you'd like. I once read a joke about a man who responded to his mid-life crises by mortgaging his house to buy a sports car. He wanted to feel the excitement, spontaneity, and vitality again of his youth. But he ended up working so much overtime to pay for the car that he felt more tired and stressed—more "middle-aged"—than ever. Clearly, the sports car was a strategy, not a need. And in this case, the strategy was not effective.

Similar to the cartoon about mid-life crisis, do you think the Mercedes-Benz might be bought as a way of fulfilling a need for prestige or status? Or a need to impress others? These notions are certainly suggested by the advertisements for these cars. But all needs are positive, universal and general. By this definition, I don't consider impressing others a universal need. Do all people need status to have a quality life? Is the need for status found everywhere—among all people? Can a person have a high quality life and not have a significant amount of social status? I think so. So, if social status is not a need, what is it? In NVC terms, we would say that a desire for social status is a strategy, a way of meeting other needs. What needs might it be a strategy for fulfilling? Well, that depends on the person. For some people social status might be a strategy for acceptance. For others it might be a strategy for attaining self-respect, safety, belonging, or choice.

We wholeheartedly support your love affair.

Exercise 3, Chapter 2: Trying to Buy Love

Look at the ads on the following pages. For each ad:

A. Identify how you feel looking at it.

B. Identify the need or needs that the ad is attempting to "sell" you.

C. What in particular about the images and/or words stimulate your feelings and/or suggest that particular needs will be met?

D. How do you feel thinking about these needs going unmet?

EXAMPLE:

A. Feelings that I identify looking at the ad for Bud Light are sad, envious, nervous, self-conscious, suspicious and insecure.

B. The needs that I see the ad trying to sell are self-acceptance, fun, sexual expression, connection, stimulation, belonging and beauty.

C. Everyone appears very confident and open in their poses. The guy in the rear is incredibly open. All of the bodies are slim, muscular and shapely. The group is mixed in gender and race, suggesting that I will feel comfortable in a group of diverse people if I drink Bud Light. The implication is that not only will I be sexually attractive, but I will meet sexually attractive people who will be available and that I will feel comfortable with that. The openness of the poses of the two guys in front implies that they might be willing to welcome me into their group, but I am not so sure about that.

D. I would be extremely sad, maybe even despondent, not to have my needs for self-acceptance, fun, sexual expression, connection, stimulation, belonging and beauty met. They are fundamental needs that I value highly. However, I am also suspicious and not trusting that buying Bud Light will meet all those needs. I wish it were so easy!

A Need for Power?

Similar to how social status can be confused as a need, I have heard it said of people, "Bob is a very controlling person. He's bossy. A control freak—and power hungry!" But is power-over others a need? Do all people have a need for this kind of power? I don't think so. Like social status, power-over can be profitably viewed as a strategy. For some people, it might be a strategy for meeting needs for respect or acceptance. For others it might be a way of trying to enjoy peace, order, confidence, self-acceptance, or safety. We all have a need for power and empowerment—needs for autonomy, choice, movement, and independence. Having power can be seen as having the capacity to meet our needs. But power *over* others can be seen as a strategy. It is something we do to try to get something else—such as acceptance or respect.

Those who practice Nonviolent Communication distinguish between power-over and power-with. Power-over involves a belief in scarcity—that there's not enough to go around. And, according to this thinking, if there's not enough, we want to make sure that our needs get met first. Power-over structures are typically hierarchical and assume that the needs or concerns of some people are more important than those of others. So, teachers decide what happens to students, bosses decide outcomes for employees, bishops have authority over priests, etc.

In the power-with paradigm the needs of all parties are considered vital and interdependent. The assumption is that strategies for meeting needs may conflict but there is no inherent

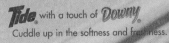

Works Wonders.

LOCTITE

Power Grab™

CONSTRUCTION ADHESIVE

Instant Grab!
Repositionable

• CONCRETE, BRICK VENEER
• TREATED LUMBER
• PLYWOOD, DRYWALL
WATER CLEAN-UP • PAINTABLE

HAMMER ENVY.

Loctite® Power Grab™ may make hammers history. With **NINE TIMES STRONGER** initial grab than the leading brand, Power Grab bonds instantly – without nails or bracing. When time is money, it makes quick work of most any job. No wonder hammers can't keep up.

LOCTITE
Project Solved.

THE END
OF THE
hopefully•he'll•think•it's•just•a•new•dance•move
SNIFF CHECK

New from Secret.
Introducing Secret Platinum Invisible Solid. Its new time-released formula is our longest lasting odor protection ever.

Strong Enough for a Woman.

conflict in needs. Thus both teachers and students want learning and growth to occur, and order, peace and harmony are valued by both as well. All voices are needed in the dialogue and working together with each other we are most likely to find strategies that meet the needs of all. There may be occasions when, because of constraints of time or limitations of imagination, we do not identify a strategy that meets all needs and we mourn the unmet needs when this occurs. But the special holding and valuing of all needs is a constant.

Approval and Self-Esteem—Who Needs Them?

Two other would-be needs that are not on the list of universal needs but often heard in everyday conversation, are desires for approval and self-esteem. Approval—other people communicating that you are a "good" person or have done something desirable or "good"—may seem like a need. We all have needs for making a contribution to life and being valued, appreciated, and seen. But approval in fact is a judgment mixed up with needs. It is a judgment of what other people are thinking of you and your behavior. Can you think of an activity that you engaged in that was very important and meaningful to you, that contributed to your quality of life, but did not necessarily receive the approval of other people? Perhaps it's an action that no one else witnessed. Can you imagine a rich and full life in which you do not receive a lot of approval from others, but you are living in a manner consistent with values that you care about—love, integrity, respect, consideration, community? How satisfying is approval, when it involves being judged by another? Is it possible that such approval might not meet your needs for autonomy, choice, and self-acceptance? If we seek to align our behavior with our own values and needs, rather than the approval of others, we will have a much better chance of meeting those needs and increasing our quality of life.

Likewise, the list of universal needs does not contain the need for self-esteem, because self-esteem includes a judgment—a judgment of ourselves. When I look at myself and I say, "I am a good, worthwhile, important person," I am not describing something I did that brings me pleasure but what I believe about myself and how I think I am as a person. Although the judgment in this case may be "positive," it is nevertheless a judgment—a point along the continuum of 'good-bad' and an example of right-wrong thinking.

Sometimes we behave in ways consistent with our most cherished values and sometimes not, leaving needs unmet. By evaluating how our choices are consistent with our values, we can learn from our choices. But assessing whether our actions meet our needs is very different than judging ourselves for who we *are*. Self-esteem is linked to this kind of evaluation. It is a *moralistic judgment* of my worth as a person. Even positive, moralistic self-judgments, such as "I'm an honest person" create a static view of ourselves and human behavior.

Some needs that are related to the concept of self-esteem are the needs of self-acceptance and self-respect. A deep abiding sense of self-acceptance and self-respect contributes to a quality of life for all people. Self-acceptance is not about judging who I am or believing that I have never done something that I regret because it has stimulated pain in myself or another person. It is about accepting our choices and holding our needs as valuable even when we make choices not consistent with our needs or values. This topic is covered in more detail in Chapter Five.

When we evaluate how well a behavior or action aligns with our needs, we are making a *needs-based* or *value-based* judgment. In contrast to moral judgment, value-based judgment discerns how an action meets needs and is consistent with our larger values. This kind of discernment or needs-based judgment might sound like, "I'm disappointed you didn't make the deadline because I was counting on your work and I value honoring agreements." In this case the value-based judgment is focused on a particular behavior at a particular time and place. A more general, needs-based judgment might be, "When you don't meet the deadline we have for a job I feel angry and discouraged because I want to trust that you will do what you say you will do."

Balancing Everyone's Needs

Every behavior we engage in has the goal of meeting one or more life-fulfilling and universal needs. But sometimes we discover that a behavior has other consequences, leaving other needs unmet, which we may regret. This is why making choices in life can be challenging—we're juggling more than one need and not confident we can meet them all. At other times, we may be meeting some needs and not realize how our actions are not meeting the needs of another group or person.

Let's look at an example. Ruth agrees to meet Muhammad at the library at 7 p.m. to help him with the math homework due the next day, which she understands and he does not. Arriving at the library early she goes upstairs to look for some history books for a paper she's writing. She becomes so engrossed in her research, she loses track of time. When she remembers her appointment with Muhammad, it's 7:30! She rushes downstairs to meet him but he's already gone. She tries to call him on his cell phone, but no luck. The next day she sees him at class and he's very angry. He really needed help and there will be a quiz in class that day. He feels hurt because Ruth forgot about her commitment to help him.

Ruth may feel tremendous sadness and regret that in attending to her own learning, she neglected to fulfill her commitment to Muhammad. She has a high value for honoring agreements, and likes to help and support her friends. Aware of her sadness about missing the appointment, she may mourn that her behavior did not reflect her own needs and values. This sadness and regret, however, does not mean that Ruth needs to judge herself as "bad," self-centered, or absent-minded. It also does not mean that Ruth will feel guilt or shame. Rather, she can acknowledge how she is feeling and the values she would like to have met—for reliability, follow-through, connection, and contribution. If Ruth chooses, she can share with Muhammad how sad and regretful she is feeling and how her own needs for reliability and follow-through have been left unmet by her actions. Often, this kind of honest expression can lead in itself to connection, shared understanding, and resolution. For Muhammad, hearing how Ruth is feeling and what she values, he may feel some ease, connection with her, and relief. In hearing her experience, he may feel renewed trust that his needs matter and that they have some shared reality around honoring commitments and following through on support. Through this process, the needs of both parties can be heard and valued.

Not the Dynamite but the Detonator

One of the most important concepts in Nonviolent Communication is that we are responsible for our own needs and feelings. Other people's actions can contribute to meeting our needs and be the stimulus for our feelings. But ultimately, we are responsible for meeting our needs and our emotional responses when our needs are met, or not. Just as we seek to step out of "right-wrong" thinking, we want to think outside "cause and effect," making a distinction between stimulus and cause.

This concept can be difficult to understand or swallow at first. If you stimulate a feeling in me, aren't you the one causing it? It seems so clear—YOU are the one making me angry! I was just fine until you cut me off on the road or when you made that stupid comment! And the more needs and pain are stimulated, the more seductive it becomes to blame someone else and find them responsible. Because our own emotional responses feel so automatic, immediate, and intense, it's easy to think that someone else has lit the fuse or turned the switch. At these moments, we're really wanting understanding, connection and relief—not to mention probably other "hot" needs to be met.

Yet while a car passing in front of you could understandably stimulate frustration and anger (and desires for consideration, awareness, and safety), that car and the person driving it cannot "make" you feel anything. No one can get inside your head and activate your feelings. More, if you're really wanting understanding from those who have taken actions that are stimulating for you, there is far greater likelihood your concerns will be heard and needs met if you can take responsibility for your own feelings and needs.

As discussed earlier, our feelings occur in response to our experience of our needs being met or not met. While I might be angry or frustrated when I see a car run a red light, these are not the only responses possible. The feelings most up could be fear, sadness, or concern. In each given moment, we can each experience a range of emotional responses. How we respond to particular circumstances is related to our own feelings and needs and our prior and larger life experience. From earlier experiences, some emotional responses can be highly familiar and comfortable for each of us. We each have a history of needs met and unmet, which can be re-stimulated

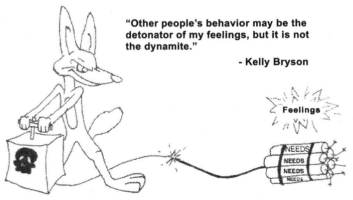

"Other people's behavior may be the detonator of my feelings, but it is not the dynamite."

- Kelly Bryson

Feelings

NEEDS
NEEDS
NEEDS
NEEDS

By Andrew Jung and Meredith Woitach

by what we're experiencing in the present. And the circumstances stimulating our feelings and needs can, of course, change rapidly. To see these principles at play, let's consider the example again of Ruth and Muhammad. Had Ruth met Muhammad, he would have had the opportunity to get the tutoring he wanted. In not tracking the time, Ruth did not meet her own needs for awareness, consideration, and honoring of agreements. Regardless of how Muhammad responded to the situation, those needs would probably be up for Ruth. She values these needs herself. But while we can understand Muhammad's disappointment and anger, these are not the only responses possible. Let's say, for example, that Muhammad had been studying all day and, at the time he was supposed to meet Ruth, he was tired and hungry. He might have been confused and disappointed she was not there, but not angry and, perhaps, even happy and relieved. He could have been thinking, "I wonder why Ruth's not here? But I'm actually glad. I'd hate her to come, only for me to cancel. I really want to eat and rest before the quiz tomorrow!"

One way to test this principle is to consider how you respond to a similar stimulus at different times. I know, for example, that the same stimulus can affect me very differently depending on what else is going on for me that day. If I'm already feeling tired and anxious and someone says something I don't enjoy, it's more likely I'll be irritated. This is especially true if the words remind me of what I'm already stressed about. In contrast, if I'm already feeling self-connected, contented, and at ease, the words might have some "buzz" but I won't feel stung. My response is as much about what's going on for me—and prior experiences and judgments—as what I'm experiencing in the present moment.

Understanding through NVC

Exercise 4, Chapter 2: Separating the Bee from the Sting

Think about a type of stimulus that occurs for you on a regular basis—perhaps words that someone you care about can say, behaviors you see on the road while driving, circumstances at work or school, or even problems with your computer or another electronic device. Now think back to the last three times this kind of incident occurred and how you responded. While your response may have been similar on the three occasions, see if you can identify even shades of difference. Then consider larger circumstances that may have contributed to the quality and intensity of your response.

EXAMPLE:

Stimulus	Response	Circumstances/ Thoughts in Mind
Someone opens a car door when I'm cycling by	Mild irritation, with some acceptance	This is the first time this has happened today; I've not ridden by bike for a week, and am excited about being out and enjoying the weather.
A car turns right in front of me, without indicating first; to avoid being hit, I jam on my brakes	Frustration, anger, dismay	This is the second incident today! In this case, it was a close call! I really could have been hurt!
A truck drives by a construction site where water has collected on the road and, in passing within a foot of my bike, splashes muddy water all over my clothes	Rage and dispair	I really want drivers to see cyclists on the road and have some consideration and care! Why couldn't the driver slow down or wait for me to pass by before driving through the puddle?!?

Now It's Your Chance to Try…

Stimulus	Response	Circumstances/ Thoughts in Mind

Choice, Autonomy, and Responsibility

That we take responsibility for our response to stimuli does not mean that others are not responsible for their actions. We may feel very strongly that a particular action is not life-serving, and feel confident that many, if not most, people would agree with our view. Yet while we may not like what we see, this doesn't mean we have to have a moral, "right-wrong" judgment. By focusing on the particular behavior, and how that behavior meets our needs or not, we are far more likely to get our needs met and see a shift in how we're feeling. No one likes to be judged or blamed, even if they can see how a choice they made has contributed to pain or suffering in others. We want understanding, to be seen for our intentions, and our humanity.

So, we are all responsible for our actions and the extent to which this behavior is consistent with universal human values or needs. We can let people know if a particular action is meeting our needs or not. But *you* are responsible for your own feelings and needs. This doesn't mean you need to change your feelings or disregard them. But it does mean that you have choices about how you will or will not meet your needs, and how you will respond. It means you have choices about how you interpret the world and the behavior of others. This awareness can give us freedom as well as autonomy in how we respond to incidents and events in our lives. It means you have choices about how you interpret the world and the behavior of others. We can see that all people are trying to meet needs, even in behavior that doesn't meet ours.

Exercise 5, Chapter 2: Responsibility, Action, and Response

Think of an action you took that you feel some sadness or regret about, that did not fully meet your needs and/or contribute to the well being of others. Identify the action, the impact or result, how you're feeling thinking about this, and needs met and unmet.

Action	Impact/ Result	Feelings	Needs met by choice	Needs unmet
Decided to go out for dinner and movie	Didn't finish term paper on date agreed	Frustrated, disappointed, annoyed	Rest, fun, connection	Effectiveness, ease, competency

More about Emotional Liberation

Being responsible for our own feelings and needs also means that we are not responsible for the feelings and needs of others. That is their responsibility. Consider the following statement: "When you didn't call me last week I felt lonely, sad, and depressed." If you, the listener, hear this statement and care about the speaker the implication is that you caused them to feel lonely, sad, and depressed. By not calling, you are responsible for how the speaker is feeling. You are a real heel—or at least thoughtless and self-involved. From an NVC perspective, a more accurate statement would be: "When you didn't call me last week I felt lonely, sad and depressed because I was wanting companionship." This statement clearly shows the relationship between the feelings and the need. The sadness comes from wanting company, a need of the speaker. If the speaker hadn't been experiencing a need for companionship, they might have said: "When you didn't call me last week I was relieved because I was needing rest and really wanting a break from all the socializing I've been doing." Note again that the events are the same—in both cases, you didn't call. Taking responsibility for what they are feeling, the speaker is also aware of their own needs. In the second example, by your not calling, the needs of the speaker were in fact met. This had nothing to do with the actions you took.

It is very important to express the needs that are being met in particular situations. The need to enrich the lives of others, to find a purpose or meaning to life through service to others, is one of the strongest (if not the strongest) of all universal needs. But there is always more than one way to meet any given need; needs are not strategy-specific. If someone is wanting connection and companionship, for example, this does not mean that you are the one who has to provide it, or provide it at this moment. Hearing this need from another, you may offer to meet them later in the day or on the weekend; you may also be able to suggest another friend that might be willing to spend time with them now. Perhaps in simply

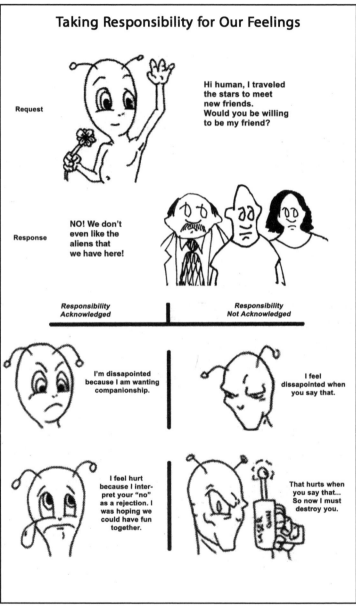

receiving an empathic response from you, the need for companionship will have been satisfied. Holding others responsible for our feelings and needs and having only one strategy (or person) in mind to meet them is like being in a straitjacket—limiting and immobilizing, to say the least.

Integration: Questions and Exercises to Further Explore Chapter 2

A. What does it look like when we take responsibility for our own feelings and needs and state our feelings and needs clearly? For each of the following statements put a "Y" for "Yes" if you think the speaker is taking responsibility, and a "N" for "No" if you think the speaker is not taking responsibility.

_____ 1. "You piss me off when you leave the dorm room unlocked."

_____ 2. "I feel sad when you say that because I want understanding and I hear your words as an insult."

_____ 3. "I feel enraged when I don't see you looking at me when I'm talking."

_____ 4. "I'm disappointed that you won't go to the game with me because I was hoping we could catch up."

_____ 5. "I feel angry because you said you'd help me with physics and then you didn't."

_____ 6. "I'm discouraged because I would have like to have made my swimming times by now for the lifeguard exam."

_____ 7. "Sometimes the little comments my mom makes hurt me."

_____ 8. "I feel relieved that he won the election."

_____ 9. "I feel scared when I hear you raise your voice and use language that I consider profanity."

_____ 10. "I feel grateful that you had an extra umbrella because the rain is getting heavier."

My responses for this exercise:

1. If you put a "Y" next to this item, I do not agree. To me, the statement implies that the other person's behavior is responsible for the speaker's feelings. It does not convey the speaker's own thoughts or needs that cause those feelings. The speaker could have said, "I'm pissed off when you leave the room unlocked because I am afraid my stuff will be stolen and I want my feelings to count for something."

2. If you put a "Y" next to this item, I agree that the speaker is acknowledging responsibility for his or her feelings. The speaker expresses their feeling (sad), and need (understanding) and also indicates that their need for understanding was stimulated by the interpretation or judgment that what the other person said was an insult. But the speaker "owns" the judgment, indicates that they *heard* it as an insult, not claiming as a fact that the other person's statement *was* an insult.

3. If you put a "Y" next to this item, I do not agree. To express the underlying needs or thoughts, the speaker

might have said, "I feel enraged when I don't see you looking at me when I'm talking because I want to be seen and heard."

4. If you put a "Y" next to this item, I agree that the speaker is acknowledging responsibility for his or her feelings.

5. If you put a "Y" next to this item, I do not agree. To express the needs or thoughts underlying his or her feelings, the speaker might have said, "I feel angry when you said you'd help me with physics and then didn't because I have a strong need for reliability and dependability."

6. If you put a "Y" next to this item, I agree that the speaker is acknowledging responsibility for his or her feelings. The speaker is stating the want behind the discouragement— the desire for making the swimming times. Some might disagree since making swimming times can be seen as a strategy for meeting needs for competence, acceptance, inclusion or respect, but to my ears the speaker is taking responsibility.

7. If you put a "Y" next to this item, I do not agree. To express the needs or thoughts underlying his or her feelings, the speaker might have said, "Sometimes, when my mother makes little comments I feel hurt because I want appreciation and acceptance."

8. If you put a "Y" next to this item, I do not agree. To express the needs or thoughts underlying his or her feelings, the speaker might have said, "I feel relieved when I heard that he won the election because I do not trust that the previous administration was looking out for our best interests."

9. If you put a "Y" next to this item, I do not agree. To express the needs or thoughts underlying their feelings, the speaker might have said, "I feel scared when I hear you raise your voice and use language that I consider profanity because I am thinking that I might be in danger and I want to feel safe."

10. If you put a "Y" next to this item, I do not agree. To express the needs or thoughts underlying their feelings, the speaker might have said, "I feel grateful that you had an extra umbrella because the rain is getting heavier and I like to be dry and comfortable."

B. Needs can be seen like layers of an onion, often connected to each other. These needs can often be obscured when mixed with strategies. Choose an object or objective that you are wanting, such as a car, for example. Then complete this equation: "I need a car because I need X…Then go to the next layer: "I need X, because I need Y…." And then, "I need Y, because I need Z…. Keep going until you've reached the primary or core need. Regarding the car, for example, this might sound like:

I need a car so that I can be popular.
I need to be popular so that I can have friends.
I need to have friends so I have companionship.
I need companionship so I won't feel lonely…

In other words, I am want companionship and ease and confidence around not feeling lonely.

Reaching this point, you may also wish to ask yourself, "What if I am lonely..? What will happen? Perhaps if you're lonely you won't feel connected with others or safe.

Doing this exercise, you can see that the car, being "popular," and having friends are all strategies. The core needs might be connection, safety, and community.

Now try this exercise with an object or outcome that you are wanting:

I need _____ so that _____

I need _____ so that _____

I need _____ so that _____

Alternatively:
What if I don't get_____ or _____?

What will happen?

C. Our feelings and needs can be stimulated not only through direct contact with individuals and circumstances but also by simply hearing, seeing, or thinking about events and situations in the larger world. Thinking about particular situations in the world today, what do you feel and what needs are met or unmet?

EXAMPLE:

Situation	Feelings	Needs Met/Unmet
US in Iraq	Sad, angry, worried	safety, consideration, honesty, awareness, care

D. Read the following quotations, the first said by Joseph Goebbels, active in the Nazi party during World War II, and the second by Richard Perle, a member of the current federal administration in the U.S.

"So total war is the demand of the hour...The danger facing us is enormous. The efforts we take to meet it must be just as enormous...The rest of Europe should at least work to support us. Those who do not understand this fight today will thank us on bended knee tomorrow that we took it on!"

—*Joseph Goebbels, February 18, 1943*

"If we just let our vision of the world go forth, and we embrace it entirely, and we don't try to piece together clever diplomacy but just wage a total war, our children will sing great songs about us years from now."

—*Richard Perle, January 31, 2002*

Now answer the following questions:

1. What strategy (course of action) is each speaker suggesting?

2. How do you feel reading about each strategy? What needs are "up" for you (met or unmet) by their words and stated intention?

3. What feelings do you imagine the speakers were attempting to stimulate in their audience? Is this different from the response you in fact have had to their words? If so, why?

4. What feelings do you think were "up" for Goebbels and Perle when making these statements?

5. What needs do you imagine they were/are trying to meet?

6. While spoken nearly 60 years apart, how do both quotations refer to and make use of similar strategies—both in intended impact on the audience (a strategy in itself) and in the strategy suggested (course of action specifically advocated)?

CHAPTER THREE:
Empathy—Not for the Faint of Heart

"Seek first to understand, then to be understood." —Stephen Covey

How Could the Woman I Thought I Knew Be So Different?

Susan, a junior at Binghamton University, was taking a course in Multicultural Psychology when she wrote the following about her "difficult" mother:

> My mother is a very critical person. No matter what I do it's not good enough. She doesn't like the way I dress, who my friends are, who I date, what I do in my spare time, how I keep my room. I am ready to explode. I just don't want to go home any more. It is so unpleasant. Every moment she thinks I am going to get pregnant. She is constantly riding me, watching me, checking up on me. I just wish she would get a life and give me a break!

After learning the basic principles of NVC, Susan decided to try using these new skills in talking with her mother. Aware of feelings and needs, she was able to hear her mother and her concerns in a way she never had before. What she discovered amazed her:

> After talking with my mother for half an hour and listening, really listening, as carefully as I could, I can't believe what I learned about her. I had no idea how scared she is for me. She feels like her life was cut short and not what it could have been because she got pregnant young and never had a chance to go to college. She really does want the

best for me. She worries a lot because she loves me and is scared for my safety. She says that she will always be there for me, but she doesn't want me to 'mess up' the way she did.

After years of conflict and misunderstanding, connecting with her mother in a new way changed how Susan thought about her and her behavior. Susan commented about their exchange, "This was such an eye-opener. Before, I would always put my opinion in and tell her what I felt. And I never really heard her. I see her very differently now. And I am grateful for that. And for her."

What made the difference in how Susan heard her mother and perceived her mother's actions, shifting anger and impatience to compassion and gratitude? As we saw in the last two chapters, connecting with what we are feeling and needing in any given moment can help us connect to what's most alive in others and ourselves. Listening for feelings and needs, Susan was able to hear that her mother is scared and worried. She was also able to understand the underlying need that her mother is so urgently wanting: peace of mind with respect to her daughter's future. She wants her daughter to have opportunities and choices that as a young person she didn't enjoy. When Susan was fully able to understand her mother's hopes and fears, she could finally appreciate what had been motivating her mother's behavior for so many years. She also realized that their needs were not in conflict. Both of them want Susan to have choice and meaning in her life. Both also want to be fully heard and their concerns valued by the other.

Don't Just Do Something. Stand There!

In the example above, Susan reports that she talked with her mother "half an hour" and listened, "really" listened, "as carefully as I could." How do we "really listen" in this way? How do we know when we're fully present to others? Being fully present involves not just eye contact and physical cues—although such behavior can indicate intent. It involves not just listening to the words we hear but the energy and intent behind the words. Listening in this way involves our whole bodies—not just our heads. The primary organ involved in listening is the heart.

Most of us are accustomed to listening just with our heads, to giving and receiving opinions, thoughts, and judgments. Rather than connection, companionship and presence, "head-listening" usually leads to a degree of separation and disconnection. The "symptoms" of this disconnection can include numerous non-empathic responses, such as offering information, analysis and advice. Most often, it is characterized by some form of agreement (yes, this is terrible, what can we do about it?) or disagreement (judgment, dismissal, minimizing, or denial). When we are disconnected in this way, we are not fully present to our own needs and to the experience of the person we're wanting to attend to.

To listen with our whole bodies and get outside good/bad, right-wrong thinking, we need to listen empathically to what is beneath a person's judgment or story. This means not simply responding to the content or ideas that a person is expressing but the underlying feelings, values, and needs. The goal in giving empathy is not to solve a problem, or to get another to change their behavior. The goal is to connect with and to understand at a heart-felt level what another person is experiencing. Often this kind of connection in itself can contribute to clarity and a change in how we and others approach a situation and/or experience.

Helping by Not Helping

How often do you feel fully heard and supported? That someone is fully present with you and your concerns? Based on an experiment I did in a class one day, I would guess that most people rarely if ever get to enjoy this kind of experience. In my class, students were asked how they would respond to the statement, "I've

> "Because I've been a good student so far, nobody takes me seriously when I am worried about a test or something. They say, 'Oh, Davita, you'll do just fine.' They don't get it and I wind up more upset than when I started."
>
> —Davita

got a big test tomorrow and I just don't think I'm going to do very well" if it were made by a fellow student. Table 3-1 shows a number of ways that students responded. As you can see, the most common form of response is what we could call *Advice Giving*. In response to the statement, some students suggested how the person might study, how he might get some rest or relaxation, or what to do if the exam didn't go well. None of the responses explored what the speaker might have been feeling or needing. Rather, the students responding were trying to "fix" the situation.

Reassurance is Not Empathy

The next most common response was reassurance. The speaker was told that their feelings weren't "justified," that what they feared was not going to happen or wasn't true. When we reassure

> "I just hate seeing a guy cry. I will do anything to avoid that."
>
> —Merri

someone, our intention usually is to offer comfort and support. Unfortunately, it often has the opposite effect and closes off the conversation. So, if Davita, in the boxed example above, is worried about a test and I say "You'll do just fine," I have no understanding of why she is worried and what it would mean for her to get a lower grade than she wanted. In giving her reassurance, I am not meeting her where she is in the present moment and her own experience. As such, I am unlikely to connect with her in an authentic way.

Table 3-1	
Your friend says, "I've got a big test tomorrow and I just don't think I am going to do very well." How would you respond? When we categorized the students' responses we found the following:	
A. "Just study as much as you can and then don't worry about it."	Advice-Giving: Most common type of response
B. "Oh, you're smart, you'll do well."	Reassurance: Second most common type of response
The following types of responses were giving less frequently:	
C. "Don't worry. It's silly to worry."	Denial of feelings
D. "There are lots of tests. That one doesn't count much."	Minimization
E. "If you think you have it bad, you should hear about my test schedule this week…"	I can top your story
F. "That's terrible. I feel so bad for you."	Sympathy
G. "Yeah, something like that happened to me last semester, and what I did was…"	Story-telling, comparing stories
H. "Let's go drinking and forget about it."	Avoidance
I. "I will help you study for it."	Offer of assistance
J. "Your problem is you're a compulsive worrier."	Diagnosis
K. "I think you worry a lot because you want to please your parents."	Analysis
L. "You should have studied all along."	Judgment

Sympathy is Not Empathy

Another type of response that students gave was a sympathetic one: "How awful. I feel terrible hearing that." When we see another person—especially someone we care about—expressing strong feelings, this can stimulate sympathetic feelings in us, feelings we may believe are similar to what the other person is experiencing. If we hear someone feels sad, for example, we may also feel sad. This is a sympathetic response ("sameness of feeling" or "feeling together"). When feeling this way, it can seem as though we're heart-connected with the other person. Certainly at these moments, our feelings are aroused. But in offering sympathy, while providing some emotional companionship for the speaker, we are attending to our own needs and experience, not the feelings and needs of the other. In doing so, we are not fully connecting or being fully present to another. Have you ever told someone about a painful experience and found their reaction so strong that you then shifted your attention to supporting them? This is an extreme example, but it highlights that when we listen empathically we want to maintain our attention on the feelings and needs of the speaker, to be open to connecting with the speaker's feelings and needs, not our own.

Story Telling and Comparison Are Not Empathy

Less commonly, students would share a story of their own. Sharing stories can be a form of reassurance and advice giving, through example. It can also be a way of trying to connect with the other person, by showing that we understand what they are experiencing and that we're sympathetic. Intentionally or not, it can also have the effect of bringing the attention back to our own experience rather than keeping the focus (at least for the moment) with the person we're wanting to support. Especially when someone is experiencing intense feelings, sharing an anecdote or comparing their situation is unlikely to foster greater understanding or connection. It shifts the focus to outside them, and can act as a form of minimization or denial.

Exercise 1, Chapter 3: Other Than Empathy

Read the following statements and identify each as an example of fixing, advice giving, comparison, one-upmanship (I can top that story!), analysis, diagnosis, reassurance, minimization, avoidance, judgment, or sympathy. (Some statements may illustrate more than one kind of response.)

A. "Well, why don't I help you get ready for the trip—then you'll have more time?"

   Type of Non-Empathy: _____

B. "Wow, I'm really sorry to hear that. That's terrible."

   Type of Non-Empathy: _____

C. "That's nothing! You should have seen the test I had in Chemistry last year!"

   Type of Non-Empathy: _____

D. "Maybe you're not making good choices because you're not getting enough sleep?"

   Type of Non-Empathy: _____

E. "I would talk to the professor. For sure he'll give you an extension."

   Type of Non-Empathy: _____

F.   "But this isn't as bad as last year. At least in this room you have heat!"

Type of Non-Empathy: _____

G.   "What a jerk! I'd be pissed off too!"

Type of Non-Empathy: _____

H.   "Let me tell you about what happened to me when I drove to Florida, in this old truck, with you know, that guy who was so weird in that English class we took, who called himself Shakespeare. You won't believe this story!"

Type of Non-Empathy: _____

I.   "Just go to bed and don't think about it. You'll feel better in the morning."

Type of Non-Empathy: _____

Putting the Shoe on the Other Foot

However we choose to respond to a person, there is nothing "wrong" with that choice. Sometimes hearing about your experience or how to fix a problem is just what a person wants. Such responses can meet needs for companionship, understanding, clarity, and support. Before choosing a communication strategy, however, you may wish to ask the person you're speaking to if they would enjoy hearing advice or a story of your own, or if they're simply wanting someone to be with them and listen, at least for the time being. Checking first can contribute to meeting needs for autonomy, awareness and choice, which can be especially important when a person is already aroused by their needs not being met. Checking first can help you focus on the other person and their needs in the moment.

In choosing how to respond, it also can be helpful to check in with yourself to see what you're feeling and needing. If you feel distracted or distressed, you may not be able or willing to listen to what's going on for someone else. Or perhaps you've heard this person express something similar before, and you're feeling frustrated and tired hearing what sounds to your ears like the same story again. Without full awareness of why we're making this choice, we may, at times like these, respond with reassurance, advice, or another non-empathic response. Doing so can be a strategy to communicate that we're not interested or available now, and wanting to attend to other needs. In these moments, however, rather than using non-empathy as a strategy, we can be honest and authentic about what's going on for us. "Sue, I'm hearing how anxious you are about your test tomorrow, and I have a paper due at 5 p.m. today that I'm really nervous about getting done on time. I want to focus on that." In doing so, we can attend to our needs for choice and self-care as well as accuracy, honesty, and integrity.

A recent experience, which is very fresh in my mind, gave me some insight into this matter. I was feeling discouraged about some choices I had made and how these choices were contributing to some needs being left unmet in my life. I was feeling sad and shared my concerns with my mother. Her immediate response was to disagree with me. She pointed out examples of what she considered constructive decisions I'd made and how the decision in question had in fact contributed to some "positive" results in my life. As if reading my resume, she then listed all the things I'd done in life. Hearing her, I felt more discouraged and depressed than ever—and frustrated and overwhelmed!

What was happening in this situation? In sharing with my mother what was going on for me, I wanted companionship and support. I wanted understanding, and to feel heard—for another human being to be present with me. I'm guessing that for her, it was very challenging to hear my pain. As a parent, she probably has a deep desire that I feel content with my life. Concerned about my well being, she wanted to foster ease and acceptance but didn't know how. By giving me reassurance, she was in fact responding to her own fear and discomfort.

After expressing my frustration about how I was so wanting companionship—for someone "to just be there" for me—she did listen. I'm sure it was challenging for her. But her simply being present was a great gift. I experienced in her listening a sense of care and understanding. After fully expressing myself, my mood lifted. Perhaps you can think of a time when you were distressed and someone wanted to "change" your feelings. Maybe all you wanted at the moment was their presence. Thinking of times like these can help me have more awareness and choice about how I want to respond to others. Do I want to listen empathically, with my heart? Or will I choose a strategy that may feel easier or more familiar—such as advice giving or fixing—that may not offer the support and companionship I'm wanting to give?

Exercise 2, Chapter 3: Being There

Think of a recent situation where someone you know was stimulated in some way—perhaps angry, sad, or discouraged—and shared with you how they were feeling and you responded non-empathically. What were you feeling and needing at that moment? What do you think their feelings and needs might have been?

Situation (What I heard person say):	My feelings hearing this:	My needs hearing this:	Their feelings:	Their needs:

For Beginners

Most of us, of course, are accustomed to giving and receiving non-empathic responses. At first, it can be very hard not to respond in habitual ways. Especially if we're stimulated by what we're hearing, it can be easy to slip into analysis, disagreement, advice, or other types of thought-based response. For that reason, the sentence frame in the following paragraph can be very useful for keeping us focused on feelings and needs. This focus supports empathic connection.

Sentence Frames for Empathy Guesses

1. Are you feeling (insert feeling word here) because you're needing/wanting (insert need here)?

2. I am wondering if you're feeling (insert feeling word here) because you're needing/wanting (insert need here).

3. Sounds like you're feeling (insert feeling word here) because you're needing/wanting (insert need here).

4. I am guessing you're feeling (insert feeling word here) because you're needing/wanting (insert need here).

5. So, you're feeling (insert feeling word here) because you're needing/wanting (insert need here).

6. Is it that you're feeling (insert feeling word here) because you're needing/wanting (insert need here)?

Note: In some of these examples, inflection in voice tone indicates a question is being asked.

Three things are important to note about these frames. First, they are oriented towards the present. What are you feeling and needing *now*? We want to understand the person's experience in the present tense because that is what is "alive" and compelling for them at this moment. It is what they currently are experiencing.

Sometimes a person's feelings may relate to thoughts about experiences in the past. But if a person is thinking or speaking about a past event, it is because that event still resonates with them now. So any statement we make, even about the past, can be framed in the present tense. This is what the "past as the present" frame looks like:

> The past as the present:
> "When you think (present tense) about what happened _____
> (years, months, days) ago, are you feeling_____ because
> you're needing _____?

Often when bringing up the past, it's an indication of how much intensity and pain a person may be "holding" in regards to a present situation. There's a history of disconnection and unmet needs. This can be helpful to know in supporting them, indicating the depth and intensity of feeling you may wish to "match" when offering them empathy.

Exercise 3, Chapter 3: Bringing the Past into the Present

For each statement about the past below, give a present-tense empathy guess.

EXAMPLE:
PAST: "I failed a test last year."
PRESENT: "Thinking about that, are you especially nervous about this test you have tomorrow? Are you wanting to be seen for all the hard work you've put in this semester?"

A. PAST: "The professor last year was never there during office hours and when I went for help at the writing center, they said there were no times open."

PRESENT: _____

B. PAST: "He dropped all his other girlfriends without warning too. He never told them why. Just said, 'Don't bother calling me anymore.' He did the same thing to me. What a jerk."

PRESENT: _____

C. PAST: "I never made it on the team in high school, either."

PRESENT: _____

D. PAST: "What a loser. He lost a bunch of money gambling two years ago too."

PRESENT: _____

E. PAST: "I was really happy at that other school. Transferring was a big mistake."

PRESENT: _____

A Guess is Just a Guess

The second point to remember is the tentative nature of empathic reflection. We are not analyzing the other person or trying to "figure them out." Only the speaker knows what they are experiencing. We are trying to guess the nature of that experience and confirm whether or not our guesses are congruent with it. This is why we put our empathy guesses in the form of a question, "Are you feeling…because you're needing…?" Alternatively, if we don't use a question, we can indicate openness by raising our intonation: "So, you're feeling … because you're wanting…?" We can also add on a tag question to such statements: "Is that accurate?" "Does that match your experience?" When we ask a question we also needn't worry about getting it "right." The person we are offering empathy to will let us know if our guess matches their experience. Even if it doesn't, just our intention—our attempting to empathize—is enough to create connection. It is our willingness to be fully present with the other person that matters.

To support the person we're empathizing with in getting clear about what they're wanting, it's also helpful to ask content-based questions, such as "Are you feeling sad because you're missing your family and wanting companionship and support?" Such questions facilitate connection and exploration more than an open-ended question such as, "What are you feeling?" or "What do you want?" Common responses to questions like these, such as "I don't know," or "I'm not sure," just leave our conversation and connection at a dead-end.

The question "Why do you feel that way?" is especially to be avoided. This kind of question (asking for a reason or explanation) is likely to elicit thoughts or cognitions rather than a connection with feelings and needs. Sometimes people also interpret this kind of question as having to justify their feelings. When offering empathy, we want to foster acceptance and connection. Our feelings *are* our feelings. There is no need to justify or explain.

Exercise 4, Chapter 3: Asking about Content

Go back to Exercise One in this chapter where a number of non-empathic responses were listed. Think of a situation that might have stimulated the response and list the feelings and needs that you think might be stimulated in the person. Then give a content-based empathy guess for each situation. You may wish to refer to the lists of feelings and universal needs as reference. The first one has been done as an example.

A. Situation: Person with a lot to do before a trip.
    Feelings: stressed, overwhelmed
    Needs: space, support

Empathy guess: Are you feeling really stressed about the number of things you have to do before you leave for the airport? Are you wanting support?

B. Situation: _____

Feelings: _____

Needs: _____

Empathy guess: _____

C. Situation: _____

Feelings: _____

Needs: _____

Empathy guess: _____

D. Situation: _____

Feelings: _____

Needs: _____

Empathy guess: _____

E. Situation: _____

Feelings: _____

Needs: _____

Empathy guess: _____

F. Situation: _____

Feelings: _____

Needs: _____

Empathy guess: _____

G. Situation: _____

Feelings: _____

Needs: _____

Empathy guess: _____

H. Situation: _____

Feelings: _____

Needs: _____

Empathy guess: _____

I. Situation: _____

Feelings: _____

Needs: _____

Empathy guess: _____

Walk on the Sunny Side

A third important point when giving empathy is that we want to identify what the person *wants*, not what the person *doesn't* want. This contributes to clarity and increases the chances that our needs will get met. If you say to your roommate, for example, "I can't stand you blasting the radio!" you may get some change in behavior. He may stop playing the radio so loudly. But the next week, he may have the television going at full volume. Rather than focusing on what you don't want, you have a much better chance of getting what you want by focusing on what is your greatest desire or longing. "I am upset because I need some quiet to be able to study." Or "I am upset because I want you to take into consideration my desire to study in quiet." We then can make a specific request to meet that "positive" need—for quiet and/or consideration (see Chapter Four about requests).

Exercise 5, Chapter 3: Sunny Side Up

For each of the following statements what might you guess the person is feeling and needing?

A. That was the rudest salesperson I have ever met. I can't believe they keep someone like that on staff to abuse customers!

Feeling(s): _____ Need(s): _____

B. It's hopeless. I'm never going to pass this course. It was so dumb of me to think that I could handle 20 credits in one semester and be in the band.

Feeling(s): _____ Need(s): _____

C. My so-called friend is avoiding me ever since I lent him $20. I'll never trust him again. If he can't pay it back or doesn't intend to I just wish he wouldn't lie about it.

Feeling(s): _____ Need(s): _____

D. The stress is really getting to me. I am feeling so pressed—by my parents, my teachers, my job and my girl friend. I can't remember the last time I was able to just relax and unwind.

Feeling(s): _____ Need(s): _____

Short but Sweet

In offering empathy, it's also helpful to be succinct. Don't try to explain or justify your reflection. The goal is to help the speaker understand their feelings and needs. If we focus on the details of a story, it can be easy to "move into the head" and start analyzing. You don't usually need to know or understand all the details to create an empathic connection. And if you use more words, those listening can feel overwhelmed and have trouble tracking all of what you've said. Try keeping your empathy guess to twenty words or less.

Let's look at an example:

Friend: "I can't believe Luke decided to end our relationship and doesn't want to talk about it. I sort of knew it had to end, but the timing is so difficult, what with my mother being sick and everything. He has meant so much to me for so long—I don't know how I am going to manage without him. Everything is just falling apart."

Not as helpful: "So, I am wondering if, as a result of what he said, you are feeling sad because you really care about the relationship you've had and didn't want it to end in this way, especially with all the other things that are going on with you and as long as the two of you have been seeing each other?"

More helpful: "Are you bummed that he left because you're really wanting support now?"

Exercise 6, Chapter 3: To the Heart of the Matter

For each of the following statements make an empathy guess of twenty words or less.

A. "I just came from the bookstore and the books for my courses are over $500! How can they charge that kind of money? It's highway robbery!"

_____

_____?   .

B. "My pants don't fit. I've put on 15 pounds this year. I feel like a fat slob."

_____

_____?

C. "Hey, I just got an 'A' on my physics exam! Whooppee!"

_____

_____?

D. "Sharon, I read your paper and I can see that you put some effort into the formatting and style. However, the writing needs a lot of work. In several places I can't figure out what you are trying to say—it just doesn't make sense!"

_____

_____?

E. "Why can't you come home this weekend? It's your dad's birthday and it's important to him."

_____

_____?

Enjoy the "Talking Head" Show

When you first start offering empathy to others, you may feel baffled and even lost about guessing feelings and needs. At first, it can almost seem like magic—how can you possibly know what someone's deepest emotions and desires are? People don't wear this information on their sleeves. When they're speaking, it's frequently about thoughts, opinions, and, often, judgment and name calling. Finding a feeling or need in all the information tumbling out can be like finding a needle in a haystack.

How do you start? Ironically, in listening for feelings and needs, often the best place to start is with the opinions, thoughts and judgments being expressed. As you may recall, "speaking from the head," means using thoughts, judgments, and cognitions—statements of blame, criticism, labeling, analysis, diagnosis, etc. While this is not the level we want to stay on, these thoughts can provide important first clues to unmet needs.

Often we can find a clue in the root meaning of a word that comes up in a "talking head" show. If a person says, for example, "He's the most unsupportive person I've ever met!," the speaker is probably wanting care and support. While "unsupportive" is a judgment, "support" is a universal need. Similarly, if someone uses the words "dependent" and "uncaring," the needs up for them might be independence and care.

Words not only share roots with each other but also can be seen as belonging to cognitive "families." Awareness of these families and how some words have similar meanings (with connotational differences) can also be helpful in giving empathy, especially if you think about which strategy words are similar to which feelings and needs words. If someone says, for example, "I'm sick of this job! I never get any help!" it's likely the speaker could be wanting support. "Assistance," "help," "guidance," "direction" all refer to particular but related strategies. They are all similar in meaning to the universal need, "support."

In addition to looking at the root meaning of a word and its "family," it can be helpful to look for it's opposite and/or what universal need would "satisfy" the feeling or judgment being named. If someone is screaming, "I can't stand the noise! I just need a break from it," it's safe to guess they're craving quiet, movement, and relief. The opposite of "noise" is quiet, and if you're wanting a "break," you're probably wanting a change in the situation (movement), so you can experience a change in your experience (relief). Similarly, if the names you have for someone are "stubborn" and "pig headed," you may be wanting mutuality, openness, and consideration. If you're feeling hungry, what would satisfy this? Nourishment. If you're feeling tired, you could be wanting rest. If you're bored, you could be wanting stimulation and/or challenge.

Again, when empathy guessing we can't know for sure what's going on for the other person. But watching the "talking heads" show—all the labels, opinions, and judgments that come rushing out—can help us connect with the underlying feelings and needs.

Exercise 7, Chapter 3: Unearthing Needs in Roots and Oppositions

Part One: Look at the following judgments and labels. Based on the root of the word, guess what need might be up for a person using such a judgment. To help think of the needs, you may wish to refer to the universal needs list.

Judgment: Need:

A. caring   _____

B. untrustworthy   _____

C. inconsiderate   _____

D. kind   _____

E. unsupportive   _____

F. disconnected   _____

G. uncommunicative   _____

H. meaningless   _____

I. unclear   _____

J. ineffectual   _____

Part Two: Look at the following judgments and labels. Based on the opposite of each word or word set, guess what need(s) might be up for a person using such a judgment. To help you in thinking of needs, you may wish to refer to the universal needs list.

A. mean, cruel, vicious   _____   _____

B. tired, exhausted, spent   _____   _____

C. anxious, worried, tense   _____   _____

D. selfish, self-centered,
    self-serving   _____   _____

E. cramped, crowded,
    overwhelmed   _____   _____

F. critical, judgmental,
    demanding   _____   _____

G. disgusting, ugly, distasteful   _____   _____

H. meaningless, pointless,
    irrational   _____   _____

I. short-sided, thoughtless,
    unaware   _____   _____

J. finished, perfect, complete _____   _____

Walking in Another Person's Shoes

There's an old saying that before judging another person, you need to walk a mile in their shoes. In offering empathy, this concept is also helpful. Based on what you hear the person expressing, what do you imagine they'd be feeling or needing? Think for example about someone who has a final exam the next day and has not, in their opinion, sufficiently prepared. What would you be feeling in this moment? Take a moment to imagine it. What sensations do your feel in your body? Perhaps anxious, worried, tense? Perhaps the needs most up for you could be effectiveness, ease, confidence, and relief? Placing yourself in a similar situation in your mind's eye, you can imagine a "bridge" from your own experience to that of another. Your experience may not match what the other person is experiencing. But using your imagination in this way, you can begin to guess what their experience might be—and offer them empathy.

Empathizing across Cultural Differences

Within any given language and culture there are numerous dialects and sub-cultures, each with different expectations and levels of experience in talking about feelings and needs. In Jewish culture, for example, it is considered acceptable to share personal feelings somewhat freely and in some detail. In Asian or Native-American culture such sharing may come less readily. With coworkers we may talk less about our feelings than with family or friends. We may notice a difference when talking with those who are younger or older. When speaking with those who are less comfortable talking about their feelings and needs, empathy guesses are especially helpful. Even if not accurate, the content of the guess gives the speaker something to start with and "chew on," to reflect on their own experience.

In some environments, such as at work, you may find it helpful to give empathy guesses about needs only. If you recall, our needs are the driving energy of life; our feelings simply connect us to this energy. Among those who practice Nonviolent Communication, there is the belief that 90% of the power of empathy is associated with empathizing with needs, and 10% associated with empathizing with feelings.

Regardless of who you're speaking to, you'll want to adjust your language and manner of expression to match theirs. Feelings, for example, vary in intensity and flavor. "Nervous" has a far different level of intensity than "terrified" but both words describe being anxious or fearful. In choosing which word to use, you may wish to balance two considerations: What, in your estimation, best matches the person's current experience? Are they just scared or, in fact, terrified? And which word will they be most comfortable hearing, fostering trust and connection? If someone is feeling vulnerable or unsafe, or simply not comfortable talking about feelings, you may wish to guess "lower" on the level of intensity. Using modifiers ("little," "a bit," "very," "extremely," "really," etc.) can also be helpful in adjusting the pitch of your guess. "A little nervous," for example, has a far different level of intensity and pitch than "very nervous."

In a similar way, you can choose words describing needs that go shallower or deeper. In a work environment, for example, you may not want to guess that a person needs "safety," even if you sense this is the need at play. To encourage comfort and connection, you might guess instead that the person is wanting consideration and care. While not getting to the deepest root of a person's fear or pain, connecting in "shallower waters" can still create connection and understanding. What's most important is not the words you use but the intention you hold.

In some cases, where you are just not sure what words would support connection, you might wish to use silent empathy. In silent empathy you are focusing on understanding the speaker's feelings and needs and your intention to connect is expressed by being present, attentive, and listening with your whole body. No words are needed when you are really present and tuned in to the other person. Can you remember a time when someone listened to you intently, with caring? That was silent empathy.

Exercise 8, Chapter 3: Changing Pitch

For each of the following word pairs below representing "high" and "low" feelings in terms of intensity, add other feeling words that complete the range. You can also use modifiers to increase and decrease intensity. Some words may be quite close in meaning.

EXAMPLE: Anxious…Nervous…Scared…Afraid…Frightened… Terrified…Stricken with fear

A. Happy _____Ecstatic

B. Sad _____Seriously depressed

C. Irritated _____Furious

Going Deeper

When giving a person empathy, take your time. As you guess the feelings and needs you will start to hear phrases like, "Yes, exactly" or "Absolutely," or "Yeah, yeah." These responses indicate that the person is really connecting with the needs underlying their feelings. Initially, you are likely to observe a flurry of words as they are eager to explain and clarify for themself just what is going on for them. Continue with the process. You may be amazed by what unfolds and the range of feelings and needs that emerge. Take your time and keep empathizing until you sense that the person feels complete and "done."

Why do we want to keep guessing until the person feels complete? Often, it is only in reaching the "core" need that a person feels fully heard. And they may not become aware of the "core" need until feeling heard about the "constellation" of needs surrounding it. Have you ever seen those Russian doll sets where each doll is smaller and smaller? When you open one doll, another is inside that one, until you reach the last doll, at the center. This is similiar to finding the "core" need. Sometimes we can be using one need as a strategy for another (community, for example, can be a strategy for safety). It is only by empathizing with the first need that we can become aware of what need is related to it or beneath it.

Often when people are upset about something, they will move from one point to the next without stopping. In such cases, it can be very helpful to interject and ask that they pause for a moment, allowing you to connect and offer them an empathy guess. Otherwise, as a listener you can easily get lost in the level of detail, losing connection and clarity. When interrupting, to foster understanding, it's helpful to state what you're feeling and needing. "Can you pause for a moment? I'm feeling overwhelmed with all that I'm hearing and I really want to understand what you're saying." Both parties pausing to take a breath can really help slow things down, contributing to movement and clarity of communication.

When Do You End?

After a while the speed with which the person is speaking will slow and you are likely to observe a calming, easing, or dissipation of tension. This may include a physical shift, indicated by a deep sigh, a change of facial expression, or a repositioning of their body. You might wish to ask at that time, "Is there anything more you would like to say?" You can also follow up by asking, "What's going on for you now?" This is a reminder for the speaker to "check in" with what they are feeling in the moment; it can help them see if they are "complete" with what they have been sharing. Even if you choose to simply sit in quiet empathy, the speaker will let you know when they are done.

Even before you sense the empathy process is complete, it's helpful to pace things and to take your time. Careful attending speeds up the process of understanding.

When Is It My Turn?

When a speaker feels "complete"—that they have finished sharing what's most alive for them, they then often want to hear what is going on for you. There may be a need for shared experience, or reassurance that you are accepting of them and their feelings. If you have been caught in a conflict with the person you're giving empathy to, it is usually at this point—after they feel fully heard— that they will be most interested in hearing what you're feeling and needing. In fact, after receiving the gift of empathy from you, they probably will be eager to hear about your experience.

If the person is not able or willing to hear your concerns, this is a sure sign they're not feeling complete in the empathy they need. If you can, go back to the steps described above, focusing on what's alive in them. If you are feeling too stimulated or fatigued to do so, you may wish to take a break to get some empathy for yourself or to give yourself self-empathy (Chapter Five) before continuing. If your own needs are not being met, it can be difficult if not impossible to give empathy to another. This is a basic principle, "Empathy before Education," that we will explore in the next section.

Empathy before Education: Attending to One's "Cup" Before Filling It with Another

If you have one cup full of water and attempt to fill it with another, the contents will spill over; there simply is not room to hold the contents of both. Similarly, if two people are stimulated— angry, frustrated, or hurt—and one wants to give the other "a piece of their mind," it will be difficult if not impossible for the first to hear the second. Like the cups of water, they are too "full" with their own needs to have the space to "hold" the needs of the other. In Nonviolent Communication, this principle is known as *Empathy before Education.* If we want to "educate" someone about our own experience (our feelings and needs), we want to see that they get the empathy and "hearing" that they need first.

The principle was discovered first hand by a college student, Becky, who'd been introduced to Nonviolent Communication. She found herself in an English literature class where a book about abortion was being discussed. Ninety-five percent of the students opposed a woman being able to choose to have an abortion and she did not. A tense situation ensued:

> The class got into an argument about abortion being murder or not. My standpoint was firmly pro-choice— 'my body, my choice.' Another girl's viewpoint was that abortion is 'baby killing.' 'God makes that choice—not you.' I had a hard time relating to her, or even hearing her for that matter. We were in a heated argument, to say the least, when I finally realized this was getting me nowhere. I decided to stop talking and only listen, but *really* listen— not how I'd been listening before. Before I was listening, but only with my own idea in the back of my head. I was literally waiting for her to stop talking so I could elaborate on my position. Now I cleared my head and heard her completely. I realized she was very firm in her opinion,

which did have some good points that I had not been able to see before. And although I disagreed with her, I had to give her credit for her opinion and allow her to think the way she wanted to.

Becky realized that since the other student felt so strongly, there was no way she would be able to hear Becky's viewpoint and concerns. Putting her own opinions aside for the moment, Becky chose to hear the other student in a way she had not been able to before. What was the result? A shift occurred:

After I listened without speaking, besides her being in shock that I had finally shut up, I think she appreciated my listening and hearing her out. She was then willing to hear me, so I spoke. I explained my ideas and I said, 'I understand and respect your opinion,' which made her happy and allowed her to open up to my ideas. By the end of the conversation, she admitted that perhaps her way of thinking was backward, but that was how she was raised, and she would be open to others' opinions. I was really impressed with how well Nonviolent Communication worked in this situation. I was able to open my own mind and able to do the same with somebody else.

By empathizing with the other student first and fully hearing her concerns, Becky opened the way for the other student to hear her concerns too. This is what we mean by "Empathy before Education." Before Becky could "educate," she first needed to empathize.

Sometimes, of course, our own feelings and needs are so "up" that it's difficult to hear what's going on for another person. In that case we need to get some empathy or self-empathy before proceeding. We need to "empty" our own cup before receiving more.

But I Want to Help!

When empathizing, we are connecting with the person's internal experience and not talking about or doing anything directed toward changing that experience or the outside world. At first, this can be frustrating. We're accustomed in our culture to taking action—to changing, fixing, and taking charge. When someone is in need or in pain, it can be challenging to simply be present with what they are feeling and needing. We want movement and relief. Empathy can seem like a detour or "delayed gratification."

Yet as you gain experience in practicing empathy, you'll see that it is also an effective strategy for creating change. An immediate shift can occur in how we are thinking about a situation and how we feel about it, and how we relate to others. From this connection other strategies may emerge that are far more effective in meeting needs than if empathy had not first occurred. You can of course give reassurance and advice any time you want. You probably will find though that sharing experiences and moving to strategies will be much more effective *after* you have offered empathy.

Why is this so? Empathizing first gives you more information about what's actually happening for your friend, rather than just your interpretation. It's easy to think that we see exactly what's going on in a situation for another person. Sometimes, based on what we know about them and/or our own experience, we may in fact have a clear idea. But human beings can respond to the same stimulus in a variety of ways. We have no way of knowing for sure what their experience is unless we empathize first. We can most support them if we see the situation from their perspective, and walk in their shoes. If suggestions come to mind and similar experiences you wish to share, save these for *after* offering empathy. "Would you like to hear of a similar experience that I had?" "Would you like some suggestions about how to handle the situation?" Once your friend has fully expressed their concerns and been fully heard, they will be more interested and probably grateful to hear any ideas you may wish to share.

Will Other People Think I Am Weird or Talk Strangely?

In the beginning, people may be suspicious of your new way of communicating with Nonviolent Communication. "What is this different way of talking all about? Is this some kind of technique you're trying out on me?" If this kind of question or complaint comes up, you may wish to respond with transparency: "Yes, I do want to improve our relationship, to feel closer, to deal with our conflicts more effectively. It may sound different, but it's my way of wanting to understand better what's going on for you and to express my deepest wishes." In effect, in being transparent, you're sharing the needs you're hoping to meet through using NVC (effectiveness, ease, intimacy, and connection). By doing so, you are already taking a step towards empathy and connection. And hearing the needs you're hoping to meet, the person you're speaking with is more likely to understand and appreciate why you may be trying a new way to communicate.

As you learn NVC and put it into practice, those around you will also see how you are now able to listen more effectively and express yourself. They will probably also notice that you can better stay in a conversation that previously would have broken down into misunderstanding and disagreement. As you gain skill in practicing NVC, you can also begin using a "colloquial" or "street" form that doesn't strictly follow the model but still focuses on feelings and needs (see end of Chapter Four). But empathy is not really about the words—it's about the intention to hear the other, to understand the other's experience at the deepest level possible. And sometimes the best type of empathic response is no words at all. When we do speak, it is often not the words we use but our tone of voice and how we position our bodies, relating to the other person, that most communicates our intent.

A Cautionary Warning!

Rome wasn't built in a day. When starting out with NVC, you may not want to change your way of talking with people with whom you have the most intimate or challenging relationships. You may wish to just *think about* feelings and needs first in these interactions. Practice for a while on those more distant from you—or by giving yourself empathy (see Chapter Five). The problem with your most intimate relationships is that they know you the best and will notice the change in how you are talking. If you have had a lot of conflict, they may not have a lot of trust and may think you are trying to manipulate them to your advantage. Trying to connect in this case is like running a marathon on the first day you start jogging. Give yourself a chance to learn the skills and practice before you try out for the Olympics!

This doesn't mean that you can't start using your new skills immediately. Marshall Rosenberg is fond of saying that anything worth doing is worth doing badly. In other words, if we wait until we can do something perfectly, that day may never arrive! By practicing NVC and putting it to use you will gain confidence and fluency. And just as in learning a foreign language, knowing a little NVC is better than knowing none at all. Even casual contact can benefit from NVC consciousness and skills. If you're nervous about starting out, start with absolute strangers. I have found NVC very helpful when traveling in making my needs clear and in requesting help when dealing with people in "official" capacities—such as in banks, schools, and other institutions.

Finally, it is important to remember that the frames we've suggested here are simply a road map for creating an empathic connection. The four signs along the road are observations, feelings, needs, and requests. (Observations and requests are covered in later chapters.) These steps, when you're conscious of them, can greatly contribute to empathic connection even when you're not speaking and giving silent empathy. But regardless of the words or frames you use, keep the focus on the feelings and needs of the speaker. If you are not willing or able to guess both, the most important to focus on is usually the need.

Integration: Further Exercises to Explore Chapter 3

A. Put an E next to each item if you think that Person Two is responding with empathy to Person One. If you do not think Person Two is responding empathically, write a response that you consider to be empathic, as empathy has been described in this chapter, focusing on feelings and needs.

_____ 1. Person One: "How could I be so stupid, leaving my wallet at the bar?"

Person Two: "Nobody is perfect man; stop being so hard on yourself."

_____ 2. Person One: "Honestly, all the rich city kids should leave this school. Let them go to a fancy private school."

Person Two: "Do you really think that would fix anything?"

_____ 3. Person One: "You aren't Mr. Know-It-All."

Person Two: "Are you frustrated because you want to be acknowledged for what you know?"

_____ 4. Person One: "I think you take me for granted. If I transferred schools and left, how the heck would you live without me?"

Person Two: "That's a lie. I don't take you for granted."

_____ 5.	Person One: "How could you say something so mean?"

Person Two: "Are you angry because you want more consideration and care in how you're spoken to?"

_____ 6.	Person One: "My boyfriend is getting me mad! Whenever I cry he just calls me a baby and walks away."

Person Two: "Do you think he should stay and comfort you?"

_____ 7.	Person One. "I'm so down. I haven't had a relationship for 6 months. I look so fat."

Person Two. "Are you discouraged—wanting someone you can be close with?"

_____ 8.	Person One. "I'm worried about this semester. I'm taking four upper level classes and they seem so hard. I feel like I should change majors."

Person Two: "Are you anxious because you would like the semester to be a bit easier?"

_____ 9.	Person One: "When my family comes to visit me without letting me know I get so pissed. I feel like they don't think I have a social life."

Person Two: "I know what you mean. My parents do the same thing and I could kill them."

_____ 10.	Person One: "I didn't like how you rowed today's race. I wanted to see the stroke rating up higher. It seems like all the training help we did together was useless."

Person Two: "I know you're upset. I just didn't feel in the groove."

My answers to this exercise:

1. If you put an "E" next to this item, I am not in agreement. I interpreted Person Two's behavior as telling Person One how they should think about themself, and as an attempt at offering reassurance. A response I consider empathic would be, "Are you ticked off because you want to take care of things that are important to you?" The feeling guessed is "ticked off" and the needs guessed are awareness and caring, remembering to take care of things that are important.

2. If you put an "E" next to this item, I am not in agreement. I interpret Person Two's question as about Person One's thoughts rather than their feelings and needs. A response I would consider empathic is, "Are you angry because you value respect for all people, regardless of their financial situation?" The feeling guessed is anger and the need, respect.

3. If you put an "E" next to this item, I am in agreement. The guess included the feeling of frustration and the need for acknowledgment, to be seen for who he is.

4. If you put an "E" next to this item, I am not in agreement. I see Person Two as arguing with Person One's judgments, not receiving empathically. A response I would consider empathic is, "Are you hurt and wanting to know that you matter, that you make a difference?" The feeling is hurt and the needs guessed are to matter, to count, to have a purpose.

5. If you put an "E" next to this item, I am in agreement. The feeling is anger and the needs are consideration and care.

6. If you put an "E" next to this item, I am not in agreement. I see Person Two as asking about Person One's thoughts and judgments about what the girlfriend should do. A response I would consider empathic is, "So you're angry and want acceptance for how you express yourself?" The feeling guessed is anger and the need is acceptance.

7. If you put an "E" next to this item, I am in agreement. The feeling guessed is discouraged and the need is for closeness or intimacy.

8. If you put an "E" next to this item, I am in agreement. The feeling guessed is anxious and the need is ease.

9. If you put an "E" next to this item, I am not in agreement. Person Two is saying that he has the same experience and feelings as Person One, but this is not empathy. A response I would consider empathic is, "Are you irritated because you want to make your own decisions about how you spend your time?" The feeling here is irritated, the needs guessed are choice and autonomy.

10. If you put an "E" next to this item, I am not in agreement. Person Two is explaining his perspective, not inquiring about Person One's feelings and needs. A response I would consider empathic is, "Are you disappointed because you want to know that your efforts make a difference in how the team does?" The feeling guessed here is disappointment and the need is contribution and being seen.

CHAPTER FOUR:
Furthering Connection via
Observations and Requests

"There is no more difficult art to acquire than the art of observation, and for some men it is quite as difficult to record an observation in brief and plain language."
—*William Osler, 19th century Canadian physician*

"Cats seem to go on the principle that it never does any harm to ask for what you want."
—*Joseph Wood Krutch*

Mario: You've got to start doing your share around the house. It's not fair that the rest of us do everything. What do you think we are, your servants?

Jake: What are you talking about? I do my share! You're the one always leaving smelly sox around the house. It's gross!

Mario: Yeah, whatever. A few pairs of sox. You never lift a damn finger around here—except to get a beer out of the fridge. You're a freakin' couch potato. Well, we're not going to put up with it anymore. Either you do your share, or you're out!

In the dialogue above, Mario and Jake are arguing about household chores and their desire for balance and fairness. They certainly see the situation differently. But without clarity about what's happened, it's unlikely they'll reach any understanding or agreement.

What exactly has each of them observed about the housekeeping? What are the *observations*?

An observation is a statement about what a person has seen or heard, without any evaluation, judgment or blame attached to it. It's as if you're speaking with a detective about an incident; all that's wanted is the "who, what, and when"—not your reading or interpretation of actions or events. Or you could imagine yourself a fly on the wall or with a video camera capturing the scene. What exactly did that fly or camera see?

Exchanging observations is vital for clarity, connection, and movement in resolving differences. Have you ever been caught up in an argument when you realized that both sides actually did agree? The problem was not in the principles—your values—or even in the preferred strategy for supporting those values. Rather, you'd been disagreeing over terms or how you described a situation, not the situation itself. Most likely, the reason it was difficult to hear each other was because judgment was mixed in.

You may be thinking, "What's so hard about making observations?! I'm a fair and accurate person. I don't exaggerate. I say it like it is!" But even with the best of intentions, judgment can creep in to how we see and describe things.

What does a "clean" observation—free of judgment and evaluation—look like? Let's look at an example. Let's say you were supposed to meet a friend at 2 p.m. and it's 2:15 p.m. before he arrives. You might easily say in such a situation, "You're late again! And you're always late!" At

"When I started paying attention to the judgments I was making, it was almost overwhelming. It's like every time I see someone I'm thinking about how they're dressed, what they're doing, whether I trust them or like them. Or else I'm thinking about me and whether I'm doing something wrong."

—Mary Beth

first glance, this could seem to be a pure observation. But "late" in fact is an assessment. The observation is in the details *behind* the assessment. He arrived fifteen minutes after the time you agreed. Click! That's the photo op—exactly what the video camera caught. Would you consider him late if he had arrived ten minutes after? Or five minutes? Perhaps you would consider this "late" but not consider it worth mentioning. Would five or ten minutes matter to you if it were a job interview, or meeting some friends to go out? You may think this is splitting hairs, but definitions of "late" vary widely between cultures, individuals within the same culture, and even for the same individual in different situations.

There are other judgments in the statement "You're late again. And you're always late." This has to do with the words "again" and "always." In making this statement, you're probably thinking about how he arrived twenty minutes after the agreed upon time for a meeting ten days ago and twenty five minutes after the agreed upon time for lunch a week ago. These are the observations. Do three times in two weeks make an "always?" Would you have used "again" if the last time he was "late" was two months ago? A year ago? A decade ago?

The word "always" and a number of other similar words (Table 4-1) are broad. When you see "always," do you mean he's *never* been on time, not once? If you recall our discussion about right and wrong thinking, one of the primary elements of this limiting world view is that behavior and life are static. You are what you are all the time—it's not what you're *doing*, but who you *are*, that's causing the problem. By using general and evaluative words, you are in fact damning other people (including yourself and those you care about) to a kind of frozen eternity. No one enjoys being stuck in this cold, desolate place. And in a universe of "always" and "never," what room is there for change?

Table 4-1			
Some Words That Imply Judgment			
All	Always	Constantly	Ever
Extremely	Never	None	Often
Rarely	Repeatedly	Too	Very

Exercise 1, Chapter 4: Tracking Judgments

For a few hours in a day carry a small notebook or a few index cards with you. Write down as many judgments as you can that you observe yourself making about yourself or others.

A. What do you notice about the judgments you're making. Is there a pattern?

B. Were there more judgments about you or yourself than others?

C. Were they mostly "positive" judgments or "negative" judgments?

D. Were you surprised by the content or frequency of judgments? Why or why not?

Shifting from Evaluation to Observation

So, what would a "clean" observation look like in the case of being "late"? It probably would sound something like this: "It was my understanding that we'd agreed to meet at 2 p.m. and it's now 2:30 p.m." As if you were the eye of a camera and observing the time and movement of people, this is what you'd see. By using the phrase "my understanding," you are recognizing that you have a particular idea or story in your head about what the two of you agreed to do. Of course, we have no way of knowing if this matches your friend's understanding. This, in fact, could be the cause of the whole mishap! But by starting out with calling someone "late"—in effect, another kind of "name calling"—we are moving away from mutual understanding, not towards it.

There's a third element to an observation you may have noticed—perhaps the most important and dramatic shift of all. When we are making a judgment about another person, we're talking about *them*. "*You* are the one who's always late!" If we're focused on someone else, rather than what's going on inside ourselves (our own observations, feelings and needs) the likelihood of a judgment occurring increases by a quantum leap. A pure observation, in contrast, will concern our experience. It will most likely start with a phrase such as "When I see…" or "When I hear…" or "When I think about…" Even though you may be seeing, hearing, or thinking about an action of another person, by starting out in the first person we're taking responsibility and ownership of what we're observing.

In my experience, fifty percent of all conflicts or more occur simply due to a lack of information or misinformation. Nine times out of ten, people don't clarify or confirm what they're seeing or hearing. As a result, they're drawing conclusions about something that may in fact not have happened (or actually did happen when they thought it didn't). I recently was at a meeting, for example, where I made a few points. Later, someone told me he was disappointed I wasn't included more, especially given how familiar I seemed with the subject. I was surprised. I'd felt very included, especially given that I'd just met the facilitator for the first time. When I shared this, the whole situation shifted for the person who was disappointed. He'd assumed that the facilitator and I had known each other for months! He too then felt excited about the way I'd been included. What had changed? The information he had and how he was seeing the situation.

Exercise 2, Chapter 4: Observation or Evaluation?

Mark each of the following statements as an "O" if you think it is an Observation or "E" for Evaluation, judgment, interpretation, or conclusion. If you mark "E," compose an observation for the situation.

_____A.   "Tina stayed in her house for two days."

_____B.   "Bob fixed my computer last night."

_____C.   "John didn't ask why I called him."

_____D.   "My mother is a giving person."

My responses for this exercise:

A. If you checked this item, I agree that an observation was expressed without having an evaluation mixed with it.

B. If you checked this item, I do not agree, although I understand that others feel differently. In my mind "fixed" is a matter of opinion. I remember one particularly painful situation where I had a dispute with an auto repair center that claimed they had fixed my car and I did not agree. I did agree that they had replaced some parts. An example of an observation without evaluation might be: "Bob worked on my computer last night and I was able to read data from the hard drive when he left."

C. If you checked this item, I agree that an observation was expressed without having an evaluation mixed with it.

D. If you checked this item, I do not agree. I believe that "a giving person" is an evaluation. An observation without evaluation might be: "The past three winters my mother handed out blankets to people who were sleeping on the streets."

Owning Judgments

Shazam: You're driving too fast!
Terri: No, I'm not.
Shazam: Stop yelling!
Terri: What makes you think I'm yelling!

Sometimes it's not easy to convert a judgment to an observation. It requires equipment, for example, to measure the loudness of a voice objectively. A poem or another work of art might be wistful, sad, and moving for us, but how do we give "observables" for the complexity of that experience? And how do we know how fast is "too" fast? When road conditions are icy or wet, driving at the posted speed limit can seem "too" fast.

In these cases it's helpful to "own" the judgment, to indicate that the thing or behavior you see is not what you enjoy or value (or do value). This "ownership" takes your words out of the realm of moralistic judgment and shows your view for what it is: a preference or value. You can "own" a judgment by adding a tag to your statement such as, "In my opinion" or "In my judgment" or "I would consider that (to be) X." So, for example, Shazam could have said, "In my opinion, we're driving way too fast on this road to be safe." Terri could have replied: "I'm confused. I wouldn't consider this 'yelling'." Or when describing a work of art you could comment, "To me, that's the most amazing and beautiful work of the twenty-first century!"

Exercise 3, Chapter 4: Owning Our Judgments

Take each judgment below and rewrite it so that the person speaking is taking responsibility for the judgment they're holding. Try using both feeling words and tag lines.

EXAMPLE:
Judgment: "That's a stupid thing to say."
Ownership: "I find comments like that very irritating."

A. Judgment: "Beethoven's Ninth Symphony is inspirational and uplifting."

 Opinion: _____

B. Judgment: "There's no better sport than women's basketball."

 Opinion: _____

C. Judgment: "Stop bothering me!"

 Opinion: _____

D. Judgment: "Can't you move any faster?"

 Opinion: _____

Expanding the Roadmap

In the last chapter, we suggested a "classical NVC" formula to use as a road map when first using NVC. As you may recall from the introduction, the NVC model in its entirety includes four steps: observations, feelings, needs, and requests (OFNR). Later in this chapter we will be looking at requests in more detail. For the moment, however, our road map looks like the following:

> OBSERVATION(S): When I see/hear/think about _____ (observation),
>
> FEELING(S): I am feeling _____ (feeling), because
>
> NEED(S) : I'm needing _____ (need).

Take Two

How do the first three steps of the model sound put together? Suppose your boss came to you and said, "I can't believe how irresponsible you are! Is it too much to return a phone call to someone?" Imagine if rather than a judgment, your boss offered a clear observation, feeling, and need:

Observation: "I just heard from Mr. Smith that he left two phone messages for you last week and has not heard back."

Feeling: "I'm really baffled as to why you've not returned his calls. And knowing how much business we do with Mr. Smith, I'm also anxious."

Need: "I want the company to be sustainable and I also want consideration and respect to be an integral part of how we do business. Not returning calls to clients doesn't cut it for me."

How does hearing a clear observation, along with feelings and needs, shift how you hear this concern? First of all, you probably have more clarity and understanding about the situation and what's actually happened, at least from your boss' perspective. Hearing what your boss is feeling and needing, you may also have some understanding about why she is so agitated and concerned.

Regardless of where the conversation goes from here, by starting out with a clear observation at least we know what is being discussed and can share the information we have. Perhaps you have information your boss doesn't have such as that you were out sick the week before. Or perhaps you have returned Mr. Smith's calls and you're also baffled as to why he's not gotten them.

Putting It All Together

As we've seen above, NVC-based dialogues begin with observations so that we can feel confident there is a shared understanding of what each person is responding to. The second and third steps of the process, identifying feelings and needs, further this empathic connection. The last step of the model, requests, brings the shared understanding we have fostered to completion.

Observations and requests are like bookends at either end of the process; in many ways, they are similar to each other. Observations involve an objective, concrete description of what you are experiencing; requests, in turn, involve a clear, positive and do-able description of what you'd like to see happen that could support you in meeting your needs. Without a clear request, neither party knows what would contribute to the well being of the other. Especially when you are expressing feelings associated with unmet needs, it is important to include a request in your communication. Otherwise, your communication may feel unresolved and incomplete.

What is the Essence of a Request?

The most important thing to know about a request is the spirit that it comes from. It comes from an intention of really caring about both person's needs. It's not about getting people to do what you want. It's about flexibility with respect to *how* your needs get met while caring that both your needs and the needs of the other are addressed. When we have strong attachments to a particular strategy for meeting our needs, that's when we run into trouble and the potential for misunderstanding and even violence. We have the mistaken belief that only *this* strategy can meet our needs and become desperate if others don't agree. In the end, it is our responsibility to see that our own needs get met.

Victoria, for example, was very upset that she was not receiving the consideration and respect that she wanted from her boss. After receiving a lot of empathy from her friend, and making several requests to her boss, she realized she was unlikely to get these needs met by this person at this time. This was frustrating and disappointing for her. Yet because she valued respect in her life, she choose to consider other strategies to meet this need. She chose to make a request of herself to speak to her boss in a way that was consistent with her own values. She also began to look at other options available to her, such as working with her boss more by email and transferring to a different department.

We can reduce our attachment to a particular strategy by generating many possible strategies for meeting our needs. One NVC practitioner, Gail Taylor, says "there are 10,000 strategies to meet a need." While we may struggle to see that many possibilities, being attached to only one or two strategies can certainly be seen as a crisis of the imagination.

Exercise 4, Chapter 4: Broadening Our Horizons

Felice has had a rough week at school and wants to relax and connect with others on the week-end.

A.   What are fifteen different ways Felice could meet her needs for relaxation and connection?

B. Can you imagine fifty more ways she could meet those needs? How about one hundred?

C. What was it like imagine so many different possibilities? How did it affect your feelings about any one strategy?

What Does a Request Sound Like?

To be effective, requests need to be *doable, positive,* and *oriented to the present.* The first quality, do-ability, means feasibility within the realm of possibility. There's no point, for example, asking someone to go to the moon unless they work for NASA and are scheduled for a flight. We will consider more mundane, closer-to-earth examples of what is meant by "doable" requests below, as well as what makes a request positive and oriented to the present. In effect, all these aspects come down to something that a person can do now that will contribute to the well being of another. We want to form requests that can be fulfilled and are life-enriching.

Specificity Supports Clarity

Why do requests need to be specific? If they are vague, we may be unsure whether or not the request has been fulfilled. And it may seem hopelessly impossible even to try. Let's say for example that Juanita is upset with Mark because he arrives later for their dates than she likes. So she asks him to be on time in the future. What is her definition of "on time" and how does that compare with his? As we have discussed earlier, there are huge individual and cultural differences in the meaning of "late" and "on time."

Beyond definitions of "on time," there's another difficulty with Juanita's request. She asked that Mark arrive on time "in the future." Does that mean for the rest of his life and in every situation? Maybe this is what Juanita would like, but it's impossible for Mark to fulfill such a request. Even with the best of intentions, he may again arrive after the agreed upon time on occasion—caught in traffic or held up at work. Agreeing to such a request would certainly not meet my needs for honesty, ease, consideration, or do-ability.

So what would a doable request sound like in this case? One example could be, "Would you be willing to make a commitment now to arrive within 30 minutes of the agreed-upon time the next time we meet or else call me?"

This request is remarkably different from the first. Juanita is not asking absolutely for Mark to arrive "on time" for the rest of his life. She's also not asking that he always call. Rather, she's asking for a "commitment" that he be willing to call if he's running 30 minutes behind the time agreed. Again, the specificity of 30 minutes is helpful. If Juanita simply asked, "Would you be willing to call me if you're running late?," this would leave us back at square one, since we wouldn't have her definition of "late."

Let's look at another example. Ted's father is angry because Ted has maxed out his credit cards and doesn't have money for textbooks for the spring semester. He says that he wants Ted "to be responsible." What would that consist of? Being "responsible," of course, certainly involves a judgment and interpretation. Might there be differences of opinion between Ted and his father about whether or not he had fulfilled that request? If the request is specific, without a judgment, Ted is likely to be far more willing and able to act on his father's wishes.

Think Positive

When a request is positive, it asks for something we *do* want, rather than something we *don't want*. Why is this important? Again, this has to do with specificity. If I tell you I don't want vanilla ice cream, there may be dozens of other flavors to choose from. It would be very easy for you to bring back another flavor that I also don't like. In contrast, if I ask for chocolate, rocky road, or mint chip, you have a clear idea of what I want. Unless none of those flavors are available, it will be quite doable to meet my request. Let's look at a more complex example. Say you're concerned about tripping and want some order in your room. So you request that your roommate pick her clothes off the floor. If you ask her not to leave her clothes on the floor, next week she might very well leave her books on the floor. But you would have an even better chance of seeing your needs met if you asked her to simply keep the floor clear of any objects.

Exercise 5, Chapter 4: Making Requests Crystal Clear

Part One: To practice identifying and expressing clear requests, place a check mark next to any of the following statements in which you think the speaker is requesting a positive, doable, specific action be done. Compose a request for statements that you do not give a check mark.

_____ A. "I want you to pay attention to me."

_____ B. "I'd like you to tell me what you consider the high point of your day."

_____ C. "I'd like you to be more sure of yourself when you talk."

_____ D. "I want you to tell me why you take drugs."

My responses for this exercise:

A. If you checked this item I do not agree. I do not believe that the phrase "pay attention" clearly identifies the specific action being requested. Instead, the speaker could have said, "I want you to look at me when I am talking and to tell me what you heard when I am finished."

B. If you checked this item, I agree that the statement clearly expresses what the speaker is requesting. Although watching a video camera of a person's day I might not know what the high point is for them, in this request the speaker is implicitly asking the other person to describe what the high point was for them.

C. If you checked this item, I do not agree. I don't believe this sentence clearly requests a specific action. The speaker could have said, "I would like you to consider taking a course in public speaking which I think might contribute to your self-confidence."

D. If you checked this item, I am not in agreement. I am not confident the listener would know when they had completed telling why they use drugs. The speaker could have said, "I would like you to tell me two things that you enjoy about using drugs."

Part Two: Translate each negative statement into a positive, doable request.

EXAMPLE:
"Stop making noise!"
Request: "Would you be willing to turn the radio down to half its current volume and close the door?"

Now you can try:

A. "Can't you give up smoking?"

Request: _____

B. "I don't want you to break any more dishes. They're expensive!"

Request: _____

C. "Jimmy, can you stop climbing that tree? It's bad for it!"

Request: _____

It's about Now

To be effective, requests also need to be for actions in the present, things that the other person can do *right now, in this moment* that would give pleasure to or meet the needs of the other. So Ted's father might ask, "Would you be willing to agree now to talk about your budget for the coming semester and how you plan to stick to it?" or, more simply, "Would you be willing to make a commitment to stay within your budget for the coming semester?" While the budget concerns the next semester (fifteen weeks leading into the future), Ted's father makes requests regarding the budget that can be fulfilled now—a commitment or an agreement to talk.

Hearing the "Yes" Behind the "No"

Even with the most specific, positive, and present-oriented requests, you never know for sure if the other person or party will agree to fulfill it or not. That's what makes it a request.

The spirit of a request comes with the understanding that, as human beings, we enjoy contributing to the well being of others. Few things are more satisfying in life than contributing in this way. The only time when this is *not* satisfying is when we perceive a conflict of strategies: if the particular strategy for meeting the needs of another conflicts with the strategies to meet our own needs. Holding this understanding in our consciousness, when a person says "no" to a request, we can hear this "no" in a new way. We can hear "no" not as a "no" to us and our needs but rather a "yes" to other needs the person is wanting to meet. Because we care about their needs as well as our own, we can empathize with them to understand what those needs might be. Since needs are never in conflict, only the strategies we may choose, we can try to find strategies that work for all.

Exercise 6, Chapter 4: Finding the "Yes" in "No"

Read the following requests and the "no" replies. For each "no," give an empathy guess (Are you feeling ….because you're needing…) and then another request.

EXAMPLE:
"Hey Tom, I'm really tired and have an exam tomorrow. Would you be willing to do the dishes tonight?"
"No—I have a test too!"

Empathy guess and new request: "Hm, sounds like you're also stressed and tired. How would you feel about our leaving the dishes tonight and my washing them tomorrow afternoon, after my test?"

Now it's your turn:

A. "Hi Susan, it's Jill. I hate to ask you this, but I don't get paid till the end of the week and I really want to go see this movie tonight with my class. Could you lend me $10, just till Friday?"

"I don't think so Susan. I'm really tired of lending you money. Why can't you budget your resources better?"

Empathy guess and new request: _____

_____

B. "I have a petition here asking that the state close the Indian Point Nuclear Power plant. This plant is dangerously close to New York City and unsafe. Would you be willing to sign it?"

"I don't like to sign petitions unless I really know what they're about."

Empathy guess and new request: _____

_____

C. "Umm, baby, I'm feeling really sexy. Why don't we skip that concert and just stay in tonight?"

"Actually, I was really looking forward to the concert…"

Empathy guess and new request: _____

_____

Requests Are Not the Same as Demands

If you're assuming the person will agree and you're not open to other options, including their saying "no," you've probably just given a demand instead of a request. And if someone hears a demand, if they sense they're going to be punished in some way for not giving you what you ask, they are more likely to refuse. If they do comply, they may do so with resentment that will affect the relationship in the future. Most people value choice and autonomy, deciding for themselves, based upon their own needs and priorities, what and how they will do what they do. Hearing a demand does not usually meet those needs. Remember, in practicing Nonviolent Communication we're interested in seeing the needs of everyone met, not just your needs or my needs.

Distinguishing a request from a demand is not always as simple as you may think. It's certainly not only a question of the words used. The question, "Will you please put the dishes away now?," for example, could be either a request or a demand. How it's heard and intended might be indicated by the tone of voice used, body language, and the larger context of what's occurred in the conversation. But the real test is what happens if the person receiving the question says, "No." If it is a request, then we don't want the other person to fulfill it unless it gives them pleasure. The needs of both parties are being fully considered and held. Does this mean that if someone says "no" that your needs go unmet? Not at all. It means coming up with strategies that can meet everyone's needs.

Consider the following dialogue between two room-mates, one of whom, Sam, has started studying NVC and is doing his best to make clear observations, identify his feelings and needs and make requests.

Sam: "I'm really annoyed when I see you leaving dishes on the kitchen table after dinner. I want some consideration of the fact that I want to use that space, too. So I'm wondering if you'd be willing to pick up the dishes before you leave the kitchen?"

Tom: "Actually, I'd rather not. I like to relax after I eat, and watch the news. I get to the dishes eventually."

Sam: "Eventually? You mean like by the next night? You're so selfish! Why can't you be reasonable, and care about someone else for a change!"

Initially, Sam seems considerate of Tom and his needs. "Would you be willing,...?" But Sam's response to Tom makes clear that he's not open to Tom's needs and concerns. Hearing what's up for Tom, he falls into judgment: "You're so selfish!" Sam is so attached to a particular outcome to the conflict, he is not, in fact, making a genuine request but a demand.

Alternatively, after hearing Tom respond, "Actually, I'd rather not. I like to relax after I eat, and watch the news," Sam could seek to further connect with Tom's needs. The challenge for Sam is to find out what Tom is saying "yes" to and then, considering his own needs as well, come up with strategy that can meet both their needs. Sam can start that process by empathizing with Tom:

Sam: "So you'd like some time to chill out after eating before you take care of the dishes?"

Tom: "Yeah. It's so hectic—rushing home, getting something together to eat. I just want to relax for a bit. I don't mind taking care of my stuff after. I mean I'm not out to annoy you. I just need some time after dinner. How about I clean up within an hour of leaving the table?"

It would seem that Tom feels his needs are being considered. Having his need for relaxation heard by Sam, he elaborates and clarifies where he is coming from. He also shows concern for Sam and proposes a solution that he believes might meet both their needs. Does this work for Sam? Are his needs being met with the strategy Tom suggests? Let's see:

Sam: "Yeah, that's OK. The only problem is, sometimes you say you will clean up and then you don't. This week I've come down in the morning a couple of times and found dishes here from the night before. That's really irritating for me because I like to have breakfast in a clean kitchen."

Tom: "Yeah, that's true. I sometimes get distracted and forget. Well, why don't you just remind me?"

Sam hears Tom's proposal, but from his observations of Tom's behavior, he sees a flaw in it: sometimes Tom doesn't follow through on his stated intentions. So Tom acknowledges Sam's observation and proposes a new strategy. But Tom's new strategy doesn't work for Sam:

Sam: "Because then it's my responsibility! I'm really wanting some sharing of the responsibility for the kitchen. And I want to be able to trust that we can make an agreement and that you'll honor it."

Tom: "OK. Look. How about this? I'll set the kitchen timer for an hour after dinner. When it goes off I'll clear my stuff. That way I can relax and you get the table clean."

Sam: "That's cool with me. Let's try it."

Sam sees another need that would not be met by the proposed solution—Sam wants each of them to have consideration for the other and to take full responsibility for their own messes and clean-up. He doesn't want to remind Tom to follow through in order to have a clean table. Tom sees that his previous solution might not meet those needs, and suggests a variation that he thinks will. Sam likes the plan and agrees. They have come up with a strategy that meets both their needs around this issue of housekeeping.

At the time two people strike a deal, it may seem like a perfect solution to meet both parties' needs. After a trial period, however, some further "tweaking" based on the experience of both parties might be necessary. If that's the case, then you would begin a new dialogue about what's going on for each of you now.

The Tango of Compassion

This type of dialogue, where at least one person is aware of and consciously cares for both parties' feelings and needs and where the dialogue moves back and forth between honest expression of feelings and needs and empathy, can be seen as a kind of elaborate tango. Especially for those just learning, it can be a challenging dance with plenty of opportunities for losing your step. Statements by one person, especially statements which can be heard as judgmental or critical, can easily stimulate a huge emotional reaction in the other and begin a chain reaction of blame-defend-blame. However, the tools of NVC can help bring you back to seeing the humanity in each person and to finding strategies to care about and meet the needs of both parties. In doing so, you can halt the chain reaction and find a place of mutual connection. The key is in pacing and taking the time to hear each other. When we really care about both sets of needs, we can experience a shift in our needs and how to meet them. Sometimes, it can be enough to just be heard and know that our needs matter. We can also choose to mourn needs not met in a current situation and, seeing their beauty and value, feel some completion and resolution.

> "I tried this stuff with my mother. It sort of worked but then she said something and I lost it. I got so angry, it was impossible to hear her. But once I cooled down, I was finally able to get what she was talking about. In the end, I think listening in this way really did make a difference."
>
> —Stuart

Exercise 7, Chapter 4: Compassionate Dancing

Using the dialogue above between Sam and Tom as a model, think of a recent interaction that was not satisfying for you. "Rewrite" what happened in the situation, using several rounds of empathic connection.

Part One: Describe the situation in one-two sentences.

_____

_____

_____

Part Two: Honestly express what's going on for you using observations, feelings, needs and requests (OFNR). Then write down how the person responds and respond empathically.

Honest Self-Expression: _____

_____

_____

Response: _____

_____

Empathic reply: _____

_____

Try this same process for one-two more "rounds" of empathy.

It's Not Really about Compromise

Many of us have learned that getting along with people requires compromise. "You have to give a little to get a little." "You can't have it one way." "Sometimes you win, sometimes you don't." Behind such statements is the belief that it's not possible for two (or more) people to get what they really want at the same time.

In this book, we take a different approach. We don't recommend compromise and sacrifice. Why not? Too often people give up on their needs quickly. They don't bother to check in with themselves— how do I really feel about this? Will it work for me in a way I can feel good about? Are there some other strategies that we can think of that might meet both our needs? When people make agreements by compromising or sacrificing genuine needs, they may not be able to comply with the compromise, or at least not for an indefinite period. Having needs unmet, they may fall into resentment or retaliation. The apparent agreement will be ultimately undermined, to everyone's detriment. As an old saying goes, when you compromise, each person gets to keep half the resentment.

Exercise 8, Chapter 4: Choice or No Choice?

Part One: Discuss the following questions with another person. You can also respond in writing, in your journal.

A. Think of a time when you agreed to do something that you really didn't want to do. What was it?

B. Did you do it? Did you do it whole-heartedly, with energy and enthusiasm? Or did you do a half-baked job that didn't really satisfy anyone?

C. Did you feel resentful to others whom you felt "left you no choice?"

D. How would the situation have been different if you had had a chance to openly discuss what was up for you about the situation and to be heard about your needs that weren't being met?

Part Two: World history gives repeated examples of what happens when one group of people's needs are met and not another's. World War I, for example, was supposed to be the war to end all wars. But after the war, the German people were left with little economic means to meet their needs; due to high inflation, a wheelbarrow of *Deutsche* marks was insufficient to buy even a loaf of bread. Many historians believe that such conditions contributed to Germany starting World War II. Think of an historical or recent event where, based on what you know about the event, you're confident that the needs of all parties were not met. Then give some concrete examples of how this may have led to resentment and/or retaliation.

Event	Parties Involved	Needs Not Met	Retaliation/ Resentment

The Duck Criterion

"Never comply with a request until you can do so with the joy of a small child feeding a hungry duck."   —*Marshall B. Rosenberg*

We're so used to compromising in our culture and taking second best, how can we feel confident that everyone is *really* satisfied? A key tool in this process is a highly advanced technology known as the "hungry duck" test. How does this technology work?

You can ask someone how they feel about a particular strategy and they might say, "Yes, that's fine by me." But in agreeing to a strategy, do they have the enthusiasm, excitement, and joy of a small child feeding a hungry duck? To make sure, Judith and Ike Lasater, NVC trainers in California, have proposed the "Duck Index" in negotiations. When considering fulfilling a request, parties rate how they feel about fulfilling that request on a scale from one to ten, where ten is "the joy of a small child feeding a hungry duck" and one is "no joy at all." The rating, which may be done internally and silently, or not, provides clarity about the needs of both parties and if the needs of everyone have been met.

If you can't relate to a hungry duck, imagine instead a time in your life when you did an action out of complete delight and choice. There was nothing more at the moment you would love to do. Perhaps you were working on an art project for someone you love, helping a small child with a task, or playing your hardest with your team so you could win a goal. At that moment, you felt content, satisfied, and fully alive—as if you'd just enjoyed the most delicious and nourishing meal possible. It's that kind of satisfaction and energy that we want when an agreement is reached. If all parties involved are not feeling that full, satisfied, delighted, and energetic, then there are still needs to be addressed.

This "delight-not-compliance" or "hungry duck" scale can be especially helpful when negotiating between friends or intimate partners. In these kinds of relationships we may be accustomed, out of wanting ease, harmony and consideration, to taking second best. If we truly want intimacy with those we love and want to be fully present to who we are and what we're wanting in the moment, the hungry duck index can help.

The hungry duck can also be useful in expressing how much one person wants a particular outcome. Let's take a peek at an interaction between Shelley, who wants to go a special lecture tomorrow night for her economics class, and her partner Anna, whom Shelley is hoping will attend with her.

Shelley: "Hey, Anna, you know that economics lecture tomorrow night, the one that I can get extra credit for attending? How about going to it with me?

Anna: "I don't know, I really don't like economics."

Shelley: "How would you rate your feelings about going on a scale of one to ten?"

Anna: "Sort of a three."

Shelley: "Hmm. My interest in hearing this speaker is also about a three. But I want the extra credit points for my grade. That's a nine to me. And I would really like you to come

with me, also at a nine. Having you with me, no matter
how bad the lecture is, would make it a lot more fun."

Anna: "Wow, I feel differently hearing that—especially how much
you'd like my company. And maybe afterwards we could
go out for ice cream. What do you think?"

Hearing how much her attending the lecture would please
Shelley, Anna experiences a shift in her experience. Her enthusiasm
for attending with Shelley genuinely changes, and she offers an extra
strategy that might also meet her needs (going out afterwards for
ice cream). This is different from doing something because Shelley
wants her to. It is not done from a sense of coercion, fear, judgment,
or obligation but out of giving, pleasure, and desire. Suppose Anna
doesn't have a shift in her feelings? Then Shelley might choose to
empathize with Anna's feelings and needs, finding out what needs
she is trying to meet by not going. They both might come up with
a strategy to meet the needs they identify.

The Fist and the Open Hand

In addition to thinking about the Duck Index when making
requests, it may also be helpful to think about a fist versus an open
hand. When making demands, we are in effect not trusting that our
needs can be met. We're making a demand because we have a strategy
in mind that we are convinced will meet our needs, and are
determined at all costs to see those needs met. Anxious and lacking
trust about meeting our needs, we clench up. Our needs and the
single way of meeting them harden up in the form of a fist. "Either
we do it this way, or else." The "or else" can take myriad forms. But
whenever there is a demand or "demand energy" (an urgency and
lack of trust around meeting needs), there will be that fist—even if
there are no physical consequences and we use words only. Demands
are a kind of power-*over* rather than power-*with*; the closed fist
epitomizes that kind of "bullying," fear energy.

A request, in contrast, is an open hand. We're not clenched, holding our hand close to our body in fear or self-defense. Rather, we are extending, reaching our arm and hand out with openness towards another. In our open hand is something we would like to offer. We are offering what matters to us most, and trusting that another will see that need and value it.

> "Can I be strong enough as a person to be separate from the other? Can I be a sturdy respecter of my own feelings, my own needs, as well as his? Can I own and, if need be, express my own feelings as something belonging to me and separate from his feelings? Am I strong enough in my own separateness that I will not be downcast by his depression, frightened by his fear, not engulfed by his dependency?"
>
> —Carl Rogers, *On Becoming a Person*

Connecting through Requests

As already emphasized, the most important goal of an interaction between people is connection. A set of requests called *connection requests* play a vital role in supporting this goal. A connection request checks in about some aspect of a person's present experience—what they are thinking, feeling, needing, or understanding in this moment. This shared experience and understanding helps to move discussions forward and creates clarity as well as connection. Connection requests are especially useful when there is conflict or when strong feelings have been stimulated in either party. Table 4-2 shows a variety of connection requests you may want to try.

Table 4-2

Reflection of understanding, being heard:

"Would you be willing to tell me what you just heard me say now?

OR

"I'm not confident that I'm expressing myself clearly. (It's very useful to express the need that would be met by the request.) *It would mean a great deal to me if you would reflect back what you heard me say. Would you be willing to do that?"*

Request for connection/response:

"Given everything I've just shared with you, I'm wondering what's up for you hearing all this?

Reflection of feeling:

"I am wondering how you feel hearing me say this?"

OR

"Would you be willing to tell me what feelings are stirred up in you by what I just said?

OR

"Hearing this, I am wondering if you're feeling _____?

Reflection of thoughts/evaluations:

"Would you be willing to tell me your evaluations or thoughts about what I just said?"

OR

"Having outlined my understanding of the problem, would you be willing to tell me if you are willing to go along with my recommendations, and, if not, what issues you think need to be resolved?"

Reflection of needs:

"Would you be willing to tell me what you might be aware of needing or wanting in relation to what I just said?"

Reflecting Thoughts

Sometimes, especially if a situation is charged or if you're not sure you've heard someone with clarity, you may find it useful to reflect back a person's thoughts or judgments before offering empathy. This is so you and the other person can feel confident that their words are being heard and understood with accuracy. Reflecting in this way can alleviate one of the most common forms of miscommunication, simply mishearing what another person has said. Such "mishearings" and "misunderstandings" can easily lead to disconnection and conflict. What might you do if the listener reflects back a message very different from what you intended? Consider this example between Jill and her boyfriend, Xiao.

Jill: "When you spent most of last night talking with the other women and didn't spend more than ten minutes with me, I was pretty upset. I was wanting to be with you and to have fun together. I didn't want to leave the party and make a "scene." But I was not enjoying myself. I was hurt.

          I'm feeling nervous about this—our relationship is very important to me and I really want to make sure I'm being clear. Would you be willing to tell me what you just heard me say?"

Xiao: "Well, you're saying that I made you leave?"

Jill sees Xiao fulfilled her request; he told her what he heard. There is a discrepancy, however, between what she wanted to communicate and what he heard. She can now address this, and do so without blame. She also has an opportunity to express herself again, and to see if there is now clarity about what she's wanting to say:

Jill: "Thanks for telling me what you heard. I see that I am not communicating clearly. What I want to say is that I chose to leave. But I really want you to understand what was going on for me, and why I made that decision…"

Rather than saying, "See, you just don't listen" or "But I didn't say that," Jill can simply let Xiao know that what he reflected back does not match what she was wanting to communicate.

When reflecting, it's helpful to use "I" statements and take responsibility for what you're hearing. After all, it's not until we've checked with someone that we can know for sure if what we've heard matches what they wanted to express. Rather than beginning, "You said…" you can start with, "What I'm hearing is…" or "What I heard you say is…" and then reflect back the content. It can also be helpful to state what you're feeling and needing when choosing to reflect back. "I'm nervous about the number of words I just used and am not confident I'm making myself clear. Would you be willing to tell me what you heard me say?"

Putting It All Together—Again

Earlier in this chapter, when discussing observations, we presented the first three steps of the NVC model: observations, feelings, and needs. We've now added the fourth and final element: requests. Here is what the whole NVC model looks like:

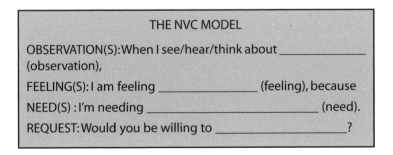

THE NVC MODEL
OBSERVATION(S): When I see/hear/think about _____ (observation),
FEELING(S): I am feeling _____ (feeling), because
NEED(S) : I'm needing _____ (need).
REQUEST: Would you be willing to _____ ?

Let's look at an entire dialogue where every step of the process is put to use. Jane is inviting Akil to a party but Akil is aware that Jane likes him romantically. Akil doesn't want to "lead her on" and is concerned that agreeing to go to the party with Jane would do that. In this dialogue, an informal or colloquial use of the NVC model is used. While you may not see the classic form of, "Are you feeling…because you're needing…" an awareness of feelings and needs informs the discussion and there is a frequent use of observations and requests. At times, when judgments are made, they are "owned" as such.

Jane: "Hey Akil, Doug's having a party Saturday night. Wanna go? I think it's going to be fun."

Akil: "Hmm. Well, thanks for the invite. I'm pleased you'd like to go with me. But I don't think so. Do you want to know why?"

Jane: "Sure. I'm a little disappointed and nervous, but curious."

Akil: "Well, based on how many times you've asked me to go out with you lately, I'm kind of thinking you might like for us to date. Is that accurate?"

Jane: "Well, yeah, that would be nice. We're already hanging out a lot together."

Akil: "I enjoy hearing about how much you like to hang out with me. That matches my experience, and I feel similarly about you. But I also want to be honest, especially because I care about you. I enjoy your company, and, in my opinion, I do think you're good looking. But I'm just not feeling romantically attracted to you. And that's important to me. Jane, this is really hard for me…. Would you be willing to tell me what you just heard me say?"

Jane: "I'm a loser! That's what I hear. Thanks a lot. That's what I really needed to hear today. Just forget it about it." (She turns to go).

Akil: "Wait a second, Jane. I'm really glad you told me what you heard. I really, really value you as a friend and your feelings are important to me. And I see I am not expressing myself clearly. Please let me try again. Are you willing?"

Jane: (Nods agreement.)

Akil: "I really value our friendship and I care about you. Being with you, I really have fun, and I feel supported and understood. But for me, for whatever reason, the chemistry isn't there. That doesn't mean you're a loser. It doesn't mean you won't find other guys eager to go out with you. It just means that I don't feel that way, at least at the present."

Jane: "Great! So I just don't turn you on!"

Akil: "I feel a little sad saying this, because I'm guessing it's hard for you to hear it. You're so wanting that kind of intimacy and connection. But I don't feel sexually attracted to you. And I want to be honest about that. How is it for you to hear that?"

Jane: "Like shit. I get so sick and tired of the old 'let's just be friends' routine. I wonder when it's gonna be different."

Akil: "Yeah, so you're really wanting some hope about enjoying that kind of intimacy and connection with someone?"

Jane: "Yup. I'm pretty discouraged at the moment. Friendship is great, but I also want to relate to someone sexually. It's a different kind of closeness. I want that experience."

Akil: "Yeah, I know what you mean. Sexual expression is definitely a need of mine, too!"

Jane: "Hmmm. Well, it may not be happening for me at the moment, but I'm actually glad we talked. I value your honesty. I actually feel more confident about our friendship, knowing you're willing to talk to me frankly like this."

Akil: "I'm relieved to hear you say that. I've been wanting to
          share this with you for a few weeks now, but was nervous
          about it. I was afraid how much you'd be hurt and
          disappointed—and I care about you."

No matter how you slice it, this is a challenging situation—one
person wanting a sexually intimate relationship and the other person
not desiring one. At the close of the dialogue, Akil empathizes with
Jane's desire for intimacy and sexual expression. He can well
understand it because he has the same needs, but it would not meet
his needs for integrity or honesty to act on those needs in relation
to Jane. Jane's sadness and frustration come from her longing for
an intimate relationship. But by feeling fully heard by Akil, Jane
feels renewed connection with her friend and even gratitude for
the kind of the relationship that they do have. She also then starts
to think about other strategies to meet her needs.

Dogging for Your Needs

Be as open as possible to what strategies you will accept but
don't stop "dogging" for your needs. Maintain a gentle but persistent
attentiveness in bringing your needs to the table, in seeing that they
are attended to.

Want some inspiration for being such a needs hound? No one
does this "dogging" better than my cat! When she wants affection
and attention, she will try to climb in my lap, even if my laptop is
sitting there! If that doesn't work, she will rub her head against my
arm or lie down next to me, purring loudly. She has similar ways of
expressing her needs when she's hungry or feeling bored and wanting
play and stimulation. Unlike many humans I know, she is well able
to "dog" for her needs. And, if her needs are not met in a particular
way, she does not seem to hold a grudge or make any judgments.
She's open to different strategies! If a cat can "dog" for her needs
so well, certainly we humans can too!

In a way, dogging for your own needs while holding concern for the needs of others is like patting your head and rubbing your tummy at the same time. While wanting to hear and meet the needs of others, you don't want to give up on that tummy rubbing. When we're looking to meet all needs, that includes your needs as well. At first, this can seem like a challenging balancing act, especially if we're "up" with our own feelings and needs. In the next chapter, we look at a particular skill, self-empathy, that can greatly support you in staying "on your feet" while engaging in the dance of Compassionate Communication.

A Graphic Overview

A visual summary of the model of Nonviolent Communication is shown on the page 174. As this model illustrates, our senses take in events in the outside world or stimuli internal to us and interpret those events based upon our experience, learning, history, and culture. Some of these interpretations are consciously chosen and others occur automatically without conscious awareness, as, for example, in people who have experienced trauma and have uncontrolled flashbacks when in contact with certain stimuli. As a result of this processing, we experience some needs as met or unmet or we may experience our values as being represented or not represented in our current experience. This causes us to have certain feelings. Drawing upon:

- The stimuli we have been exposed to;
- The interpretations that we make of the processed versions of these stimuli;
- Our experience of our needs as met or unmet and
- The feelings thus stimulated in us

A "chooser" evaluates potential strategies to meet needs and chooses one. The strategy chosen may or may not result in behavior observable to others.

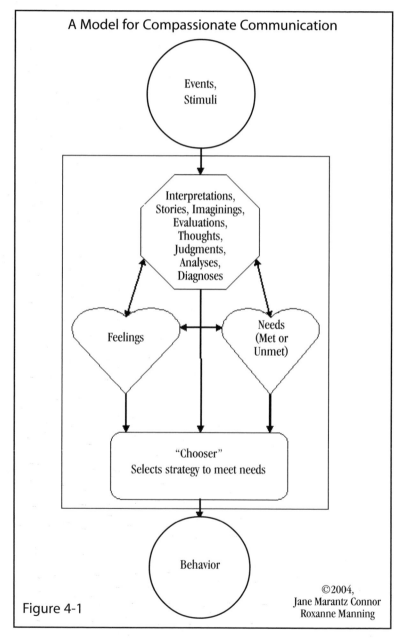

A Model for Compassionate Communication

Events, Stimuli

Interpretations, Stories, Imaginings, Evaluations, Thoughts, Judgments, Analyses, Diagnoses

Feelings

Needs (Met or Unmet)

"Chooser" Selects strategy to meet needs

Behavior

©2004,
Jane Marantz Connor
Roxanne Manning

Figure 4-1

NOTES ON THE MODEL

Events and stimuli:
1. Events and stimuli are frequently external and observable, but can also be internal (e.g., hunger pang)
2. Events and stimuli are interpreted on the basis of:
   - Experience
   - Culture
   - Learning
   - History

Needs:
1. May be experienced as met or unmet, depending on our interpretation of events
2. When we experience needs as met, positive feelings are stimulated.
3. When we experience needs as unmet, negative feelings are stimulated.

Feelings:
1. Positive feelings, stimulated by met needs include:
   - Joy
   - Excitement
   - Contentment
2. Negative feelings, stimulated by unmet needs include:
   - Frustration
   - Fear
   - Sadness

Chooser:
1. The strategy selected by the chooser is that which best serves our needs but is impacted by our interpretations and feelings.
2. The strategy selected by the "chooser" is influenced by:
   - Experience
   - History
   - Learning
   - Culture, etc.

Making interpretations, focusing on feelings and needs and choosing strategies are often internal processes that are not visible.

Feelings, needs and interpretations influence each other.

About "Street" NVC

In Nonviolent Communication we place the greatest priority on connection between people (or between parts of ourselves). We have spent a substantial amount of time elaborating upon the components of Observations, Feelings, Needs and Requests because these components support establishing and maintaining open-hearted connection. However, as we have referred to earlier, there are many times in dialogue that we do not use strict OFNR format—more colloquial expressions are used and, in particular, strategies may be referred to instead of needs.

Since our purpose is connection, we always place primary emphasis on language that supports that connection. Street NVC refers to language that may not fit an OFNR model but is expressed with an NVC consciousness of caring about the needs of all. For example, suppose I have a friend who is feeling grief and outrage about her boyfriend saying that he was only dating her and then finding out that he was also seeing someone else. I might guess that her intense distress is related to a need for more trust and honesty in her life. But if she is talking about how she can't trust this specific person I might initially empathize with how much she is wanting trust in this particular relationship rather than trust in general. Compare these two types of responses:

> Virginia: I can't believe what a liar he is! He swore he was only seeing me and now I know that was all a lie!
>
> Classical Response: Are you furious because you are wanting trust and honesty?
>
> Street Response: Are you really furious? Are you overwhelmed because you wanted to trust that he was being honest with you?

I would move to trust as a general need when she is ready to hear that because it will empower her to realize that her need for trust can be met in a variety of ways and in a variety of relationships—that she does not need to hold this relationship as the only way to meet her need for trust.

Integration: Further Questions and Exercises to Explore Chapter 4

A. More practice - Mark each of the following statements as an "O" if you think it is an Observation or "E" for Evaluation, judgment, interpretation or conclusion. If you mark "E," compose an observation for the situation.

_____ 1.   "Amber often sleeps around."

_____ 2.   "Dan is confused."

_____ 3.   "The student arrived to class late."

_____ 4.   "My brother usually doesn't shower."

_____ 5.   "Denise thinks she looks better in black."

_____ 6.   "My step-mom complains for no reason."

My responses for this exercise:

1.   If you checked this item, I do not agree. I believe that "sleeps around" is an evaluation. An observation without evaluation might be: "Amber has gone home with three different guys this week."

2.   If you checked this item, I do not agree. I believe that "confused" is an evaluation. An observation without evaluation might be: "Last week, Dan said he loved Tanya and this week he says he's in love with Jane."

3. If you checked this item, I do not agree. I believe that "late" is an evaluation. An observation might be "The student arrived at class at 9:10 when the schedule said it was to start at 9:00."

4. If you checked this item, I do not agree. I believe that "usually" is an evaluation. An observation without evaluation might be: "My brother showered four times this month."

5. If you checked this item, I do not agree that an observation was expressed. A pure observation would be "Denise said, 'I think I look better in black'" or "I heard Denise say that she thinks she looks better in black."

6. If you checked this item, I do not agree. I believe that "for no reason" and "complains" are evaluations. An observation without evaluation might be: "At the restaurant last night, my step-mom described something she disliked about each of the dishes that was served, but ate all that was on her plate."

B. Look at the photos on the following pages. First give a judgment about each and then an observation.

Subject of Photo:	Judgment(s):	Observation:

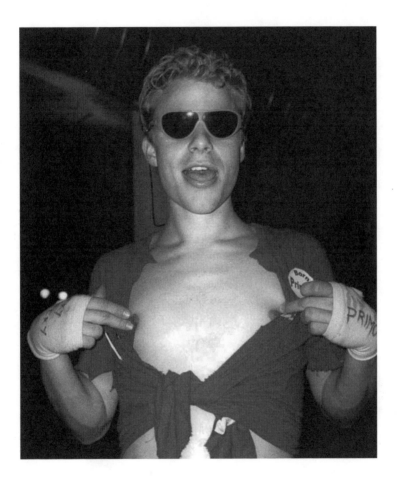

C. More practice - To obtain practice identifying and expressing clear requests, place a check mark next to any of the following statements in which you think the speaker is requesting a doable, specific action be done. Compose a request for any statement which you do not give a check mark.

_____ 1. "I'd like you to respect that I am different from you."

_____ 2. "I'd like you to tell me how you feel about my wanting to break up with you."

_____ 3. "I would like you to commit to doing the chores that you sign up for each week."

_____ 4. "I'd like to understand you better."

_____ 5. "I would like you to show me a little more courtesy."

_____ 6. "I'd like us to go out and have fun more often."

My responses for this exercise:

1. If you checked this item, I do not agree. I don't believe this sentence clearly requests a specific action. The speaker could have said, "The next time you're aware of wanting to comment on a choice I've made, I'd like you to pause for a moment and reflect on what needs you'd be meeting by making that comment."

2. If you checked this item, I agree that the statement clearly expresses what the speaker is requesting.

3. If you checked this item, I agree that the statement clearly expresses what the speaker is requesting.

4. If you checked this item, I do not agree. I don't believe this sentence clearly requests a specific action. The phrase "understand you better" is vague. The speaker could have said, "I'd like to meet once a week for coffee so that I can learn more about you and your perspective on things."

5. If you checked this item, I do not agree. I don't believe this sentence clearly requests a specific action. The phrase "a little more courtesy" is vague. The speaker could have said, "I would like you to ask me to borrow my clothes before you go ahead and wear them."

6. If you checked this item I do not agree. I do not believe that the phrase "more often" clearly identifies the specific action being requested. Instead, the speaker could have said, "I'd like us to go see our favorite band play at the café every Thursday."

Body Wisdom—Requests Versus Demands

The purpose of this exercise is to obtain a bodily experience of the difference when you hear a demand versus a request. The exercise is to be done with a partner. First one person is the speaker and the other the listener, and then you can reverse.

A. The speaker reads the item silently and imagines having a demand energy with respect to the item, experiencing an urgent wish for the listener to comply with what they want, or else! Then the speaker states what they want from the listener coming from this demand energy.

The listener hears this demand and observes the feelings and sensation in their body. Where do they feel them? What are they like?

B. Now the speaker re-reads the item silently thinking about the needs they want to meet and how much they cherish those needs. They want the listener to comply with the request only if it would also meet needs for them, caring for both sets of needs—their own and the listener's. The speaker then expresses the want coming from this request energy. It can be useful to convey this intention by beginning the request with 'Would you be willing to…?"

C. The listener compares the sensations and experience of hearing the same want expressed with demand and request energy and shares with the speaker.

You can either come up with your own personalized want – or select from the following examples.

1. You want your friend to return the five CDs they borrowed from you last week because you want them for a party this week-end.

2. You want your neighbor to turn down the music on their stereo because it's midnight and you want to sleep.

3. You want your instructor to look at a test that you think they graded incorrectly.

4. You want your younger sibling to ask permission before borrowing your clothes.

5. You want yourself to go to bed before 11 p.m. on week nights so that you can feel more rested. (Note: This can be conceived of as a request from one part of yourself to yourself.)

6. You want your employer to arrange for someone else to take your shift this week-end so that you can go to a friend's birthday party.

The next three exercises were inspired by exercises written by Miki and Inbal Kashtan of BayNVC.

"The Broken Garbage Disposal"—Expressing Observations, Feelings and Needs Without Making a Request

The purpose of this exercise is to have a visceral experience of what it's like when a person expresses observations, feelings and needs without making a request. As in the previous exercise, it is helpful to do this in pairs and take turns being the speaker and listener. The listener checks in with their feelings and sensations and reports back.

A. The speaker expresses using observations, feelings and needs (OFN) with no request (R). Express for a minute or two, repeating and elaborating on your observations, feelings and needs.

B. The speaker expresses using observations, feelings, needs and a request (OFNR). You may wish to use a connection request here, or it can be an action request.

C. Reflect on the two experiences. What differences do you note?

You can select from the following situations, or choose one of your own. For purposes of this exercise, if you choose one of your own it is helpful to choose a situation of relatively lower complexity and emotional energy, i.e. not your most painful emotional issue.

1. You are riding in a car with your friend and you are feeling uncomfortable because the speed seems very fast to you.

2. You are feeling worried because the person you are going with has not been feeling well for two weeks and hasn't seen a doctor.

3. You are feeling anxious because you lent your friend $50 two weeks ago thinking they would pay it back by now and they haven't said or done anything about it.

4. Your house-mate's car is blocking your car and you want to leave now.

5. You want the person you are dating to attend the play in which you are doing the lighting.

6. You want to borrow your dad's car for the day so that you can see your friend who lives 50 miles away.

7. You want more hours of work at the fast food restaurant where you have been working for two years.

I chose the title "the broken garbage disposal" above because when I was the listener in this exercise at the Bay NVC Leadership Program and the speaker kept expressing observations, feelings and needs without a request, it seemed as if I were watching the garbage in a broken garbage disposal going round and round with no movement down the drain.

What the ??? Expressing a Request Without a Feeling and Need

The purpose of this exercise is to have a visceral experience of what it's like when a person expresses a request without O, F, N. As in the previous exercise, it is helpful to do this in pairs and take turns being the speaker and listener. The listener checks in with their feelings and sensations and reports back.

A. The speaker expresses a request without an observation, feeling or need. Pause.

B. The speaker expresses a request in addition to an observation, feeling, and need.

C. Reflect on the two experiences. What differences do you note?

Possible situations:

1. Your room-mate invites friends to the room when you want to study. You ask them to leave.

2. You haven't seen your friend for a long time and want to go for a walk together to re-connect.

3. You are involved in a conversation about a sensitive issue with a friend at lunch time and a casual acquaintance starts to join the two of you. You ask this person to join someone else.

4. You are anxious to do well on an upcoming test but missed classes because of a family emergency. You ask a class-mate to borrow their notes.

5. You are very pressed for time and think a friend is going to the library. You want to avoid a heavy fine on the reference material you have borrowed and ask the friend to take it back.

6. You hear that a course you want to take is officially closed. It is a course you have been looking forward to because you have a personal interest in the subject matter. You ask the instructor to let you enroll anyway.

Strategies/Requests for Meeting All Needs

There is no inherent conflict between the needs of two parties but it can be challenging to find strategies and requests that meet all needs. It can be very helpful to practice brainstorming strategies and requests that might meet all needs. Generating a significant number can help to reduce the attachment to any single request or strategy.

It can be helpful to do this exercise in a group because brainstorming is often energized by having more people participate. Remember— with brainstorming the idea is to generate as many ideas as possible and not to evaluate the ideas until the generating phase is complete.

A. Think of a situation of conflict between two people. (One of these could be you.)

B. What are your feelings and needs in the situation?

C. What are the other person's feelings and needs in the situation?

D. Brainstorm as many strategies or requests as you can that might meet the needs of both parties.

CHAPTER FIVE:
Empathy in the Fast Lane:
Self-Empathy and Choice

"In oneself lies the whole world and if you know how to look and learn, the door is there and the key is in your hand. Nobody on earth can give you either the key or the door to open, except yourself."
—*Jiddu Krishnamurti, 20th century Indian philosopher*

"What lies behind us and what lies before us are small matters compared to what lies within us."
—*Ralph Waldo Emerson, 19th century American writer*

In the first four chapters of this book we focused on how to empathize with others. We've advocated a view of the world where everyone's needs can be held with value and consideration, including our own. Yet how does one attend to one's own needs while also attending to others? This is the task we take up in this chapter, considering the practice of self-empathy. As you will see, self-empathy has broad applications; it is useful in responding to judgment, regret, and indecision.

The "Reverse Golden Rule"

Around the world, regardless of language or culture, the golden rule is the same: "Do unto others as you would see done unto yourself." The opposite is also true, what my colleague and professor of rhetoric Lois Einhorn calls the "reverse golden rule:" "Do unto yourself as you would see done unto others." If we are practicing empathy and compassion for those around us, we will want to practice compassion for ourselves. And yet many people find they most frequently speak to themselves with a voice that is critical and harsh.

> "Sometimes I just want someone to listen and be there for me. And then I remember that I can listen and be there for myself."
> —Stephanie

On airplane flights we're told that if there's a change in cabin pressure, to put our oxygen masks on first before helping others. Similarly, if you don't get the empathy you need first, how can you help someone else? In effect, empathy and self-empathy are two sides of the same coin; if we are not engaged in self-compassion and self-care, it is impossible to sustain empathy for those around us. Only when our cup is full—when we're getting the empathy we need—can we be fully available to receive messages from others, including the most challenging messages of criticism, judgment and blame.

Empathy Directed Inwards

As you might guess, practicing self-empathy in many ways is similar to giving empathy to others. The only difference is that rather than focusing on other's feelings and needs, for the moment we turn our empathy "antennae" inwards towards ourselves. We ask ourselves, "Am I feeling _____ because I am wanting _____?" and link our feelings and needs to clear observations and requests. You can complete these steps in your mind, speaking out loud, or writing them down:

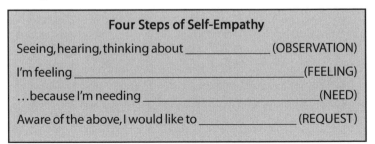

Four Steps of Self-Empathy
Seeing, hearing, thinking about _____ (OBSERVATION)
I'm feeling _____ (FEELING)
…because I'm needing _____ (NEED)
Aware of the above, I would like to _____ (REQUEST)

As with all empathy, we want to focus on what's "electric" (energetic and true for us) in the moment. As such, while we may be concerned with past actions and regret, we talk about our experience in the present tense. You could say, for example, "Thinking about _____ (any past event), I'm now feeling _____." After beginning with this phrase, you would continue through the rest of the model, identifying what you're needing and any request or strategy you may have. In taking these steps, you can become aware of how the past is "living" in the present.

In practicing self-empathy, it can seem odd that we're making a request of ourselves. In talking to ourselves, of course, we don't need to make a formal request, "Would you be willing..." Instead, we can simply become aware of wanting to prioritize or do things differently in our life. We can also come up with a strategy or plan to feel more confident about meeting our needs in the future.

Exercise 1, Chapter 5: Seeing Our Judgments, Creating Compassion

A. Think about a recent choice or behavior you're unhappy about. What judgments do you have of yourself? Write all these out.

B. Now see if you can identify what you're feeling and needing thinking about that choice or behavior. Write these out as well.

C. How does engaging in judgment feel different to you than identifying your feelings and needs?

Self-pity Is a Different Game

"I was brought up to think that you have to be strong and just not let things get to you. Anything else is a sign of weakness."
—Phillip, a student

When people first hear about self-empathy, they can confuse it with self-pity or feeling "sorry for yourself." But these are remarkably different activities. Self-empathy is healing and empowering, focusing on our primary needs in life and how to meet them. It is about taking responsibility for our feelings, not blaming others for them. It is a celebration of who we are, what we most value, and choices that we have. Self-pity, in contrast, involves seeing ourselves as victims, not taking responsibility for our feelings. It is about judging ourselves and taking away our choice and strength.

Let's look at an example. Two friends decide to go to Florida for spring break. They invite their friend Vincenzo to come along too. He would like to go but is taking a temp job during spring break to help cover school costs. Vincenzo feels disappointed, sad and angry about not going. This is the second time he's missed out on a trip like this. Self-pity in this case could sound like this:

It's not fair. How come I can't go? What makes them better than me?

I deserve better. I should have the same chance to go that they do.

There must be something wrong with me that I never go on these trips. Why don't I ever have enough money? If only my parents had more money and helped me out. It'll never change.

Self-empathy, in contrast, regarding the same situation, could sound like this:

Thinking about not going on the trip, I'm really disappointed. I want the choice and freedom to take a trip like this, and enjoy some relaxation and fun.

I'm sad about not being with my friends. I really want to hang out with them and be a part of what's going on.

Thinking about going on the trip, though, I also feel really anxious. I value getting an education and want to meet my economic needs with less stress. I wish things were different in my family—I'd love to have more support on the financial end. But given what I know about my income for the rest of the semester, I wouldn't feel happy, relaxed or secure taking that trip.

In the statements involving self-pity, Vincenzo focuses on what he's lacking. He blames himself ("there must be something wrong with me") and finds the cause in circumstances outside himself—that his parents lack the resources or willingness to help him financially. Vincenzo sees himself and his life as static and unchanging; he never has enough—and never will.

In practicing self-empathy, Vincenzo identifies the needs that are stimulating his feelings of sadness and disappointment—the needs for choice, relaxation, and connection. He appreciates how much he values these qualities and desires them in his life. He also sees the choice he has; by choosing to work and not go to Florida, he chooses to meet his economic needs and his need for learning by paying school expenses. Identifying his needs, he may come up with other strategies to meet them. He may choose to take a day off from work to do something fun with friends, or choose to do something fun and relaxing after work.

Ironically, it is when we are stuck in self-pity that we are most needing empathy. When we pity ourselves, we are likely to feel discouraged and hopeless, even despairing. Finding the cause outside ourselves and engaged in a fixed view of ourselves and the world, we have no confidence that things will change. Through self-empathy, the hope and movement we're wanting can occur. We can focus on what we want in life, mourn needs not fully met, and choose actions that will best serve us. In doing so, we can enjoy self-acceptance, choice, and empowerment.

Exercise 2, Chapter 5: Breaking Free of self-pity

Part One: Re-read the statements above where Vincenzo is engaging in self-pity, imagining that you are him. How is reading and reflecting on statements of self-pity similar or different from self-empathy?

_____

_____

_____

Part Two: Think back to a recent situation when you were feeling sorry for yourself (self-pity).

A.   Describe the situation in one-two sentences:

_____

_____

B.   Engaged in self-pity and thinking about this situation, what judgments do you have of yourself or others?

_____

_____

_____

C. What feelings are you aware of in yourself?

_____

_____

_____

D. What needs are you aware of?

_____

_____

_____

E. How does engaging in self-empathy feel different from self-pity?

_____

_____

_____

Self-Empathy for Our "Mistakes"

"Sometimes I can't believe how hard I am on myself – I don't like the way I look, the way I talk, or the way I laugh. I don't even like the way I criticize myself so much."

—Anonymous student

In addition to self-pity, we all at times can experience self-judgment, regret, and shame. "How could I have done something SO stupid!" At the time, given our needs and the information we had, a particular action may have seemed the best (or only) course to take. In the end, however, it did not meet all our needs or have the impact we wanted. In these moments, it can be easy to engage in self-criticism. We are in pain about our actions and the decisions we made.

Perhaps at times like these you find yourself thinking, "I don't deserve compassion" or "I should suffer for what I did." Such thinking is familiar because it's what we've learned from our culture. Blame-thinking comes from a dominant belief that punishment and suffering are necessary for getting people to do what they "should" do, for learning and growth, and for restoring harmony when people have experienced harm. We may be afraid that if we don't "punish" ourself that we'll make a "wrong" decision again. We're wanting effectiveness, movement, and hope.

Research and other evidence, however, show that punishment and "should" thinking do not lead to long-term change and the kinds of connections that enrich life. This kind of thinking stimulates our needs for choice and autonomy, and can easily lead to resistance and rebellion. No one wants to be told what to do—even if we're the ones telling ourselves! Or, such thinking can lead to submission—to feeling even worse about ourselves, and more discouraged and hopeless. Holding a static view of ourselves, it can be even more challenging to imagine and create change.

In thinking about self-judgment, shame, and blame, it can be helpful to think about the two questions that we started out with in the introduction of this book. What do we want in life and how do we want to get it? We all have needs for effectiveness, competence, meaning, and contribution. But in meeting these needs, do we want to engage in methods that leave other needs unmet—such as for kindness, understanding, and acceptance (including for ourselves)? Self-empathy offers a way for us to determine if our choices are effective or not *and* to learn and grow from these choices in a way that's fully consistent with our values.

Exercise 3, Chapter 5: Recognizing Self-Judgment

Part One: What do you tell yourself that you "should" or "shouldn't" do? Think of some recent and current situations where you might talk to yourself in this way and complete the following statements:

A. "I never should have_____."

B. "I shouldn't be so _____."

C. "I shouldn't always be _____."

D. "I should have known better than to have _____."

Part Two: How do you feel "shoulding" yourself? _____

_____

_____

"Don't 'should' on me!"	—bumper sticker

Rather than "shoulding" ourselves, we have a choice. We can identify the needs we were trying to meet when we made a particular decision. We can also review the needs not met by our choice. Aware of our feelings and needs, we can choose to modify our actions and behavior. Guilt and shame are not necessary in this process. In fact, they only get in the way.

Let's look at an example of how self-empathy, rather than blame, can offer clarity, relief, and change.

198 — Connecting across Differences

One evening Bob and his two friends were feeling restless. After drinking a few beers, they thought it would be fun to see if they could hotwire Bob's father's car. It was a challenge, but they succeeded. Enjoying his friends' company and relaxed from the beers, Bob was distracted and, taking a sharp turn, hit a tree. Fortunately, no one was seriously hurt but the car was totaled. When the police arrived, Bob was charged with driving while intoxicated. Thinking about this situation and the choices he made, Bob feels terrible. Some of the thoughts racing through his mind include:

How could I have done something so stupid? I know better than drinking and driving!

My father already thinks he can't trust me. Now this will only make it worse. After this, he'll never trust me again!

Now it will be impossible to get insurance. I've ruined my driving record for five years. How will I get to work and school without a car?

Later, once he's cooled down a bit, Bob looks at the needs met and unmet by his choice and gets a different perspective. The needs unmet include:

- Trust – His valuing of his parents' trust for him was not reflected in his choice.
- Consideration and Choice – In taking his father's car without checking with him first, Bob was not living in alignment with his own values for consideration and choice.
- Autonomy – In this situation, Bob was influenced more than he'd like by the desires of his friends.
- Ease and Economic Needs – His ability to get car insurance and to drive a car for the next five years is now in question.

- Safety, Care and Community – In Bob's estimation, his decision put the lives of himself, his friends and other people in jeopardy.
- Integrity – He was not living by his own standards of awareness, choice, and responsibility.

Aware of these unmet needs, Bob experiences deep mourning and regret. While experiencing pain about this choice, Bob also examines the needs he was meeting by taking the car. In reflecting on the situation and getting empathy from others, he identifies the following:

- Fun – The need for fun, like all needs, is universal.
- Challenge – He was excited at the challenge of seeing if he could start the car without a key.
- Connection and Companionship – Bob and his friends connected over the goal of going for a ride.
- Autonomy and Power – Bob enjoyed having the choice to go riding, even though he didn't own a car, not going along with societal rules.
- Inclusion and Belonging – Bob was wanting to be a part of the group, wanting to support the group's goals.
- Spontaneity and Aliveness – It was gratifying to live spontaneously in the moment.
- Freedom, Choice, and Movement – Having the car meant the freedom and choice to be elsewhere.

The needs Bob met in taking the car are all understandable, life-serving needs. At the time, he was not anticipating an accident; he was imagining the stimulation and fun of being on the open road with his friends. Subsequent events led Bob to reconsider his choice and see the needs that were unmet. He then experienced deep sadness and regret. But at the time of the decision, those unmet needs were not salient. In situations where we regret a choice we have made, we may mourn that we did not have the information or resources to be aware of all our needs and to meet them in a way that was consistent with our values. Such mourning can be a key part of the process, especially in creating awareness and change. Celebrating and mourning needs met and unmet are two different ways of acknowledging what we most want and value in life. And that awareness can play a key role in making choices consistent with our values. This kind of awareness offers a much greater sense of closure, understanding, and self-acceptance than a simple apology or statement of self-blame.

Exercise 4, Chapter 5: Identifying Needs Met and Unmet by a Choice We Regret

Sylvester decided to take 20 credits this semester so he could graduate sooner. Now he feels overwhelmed and discouraged. Nothing is going well—not his school work, his job, or his relationship with his girlfriend. And he's missing time for relaxation and fun.

A. What needs might he have been trying to meet when he decided to carry 20 credits? _____

B. What needs appear to be unmet by that choice?_____

_____

Exercise 5, Chapter 5: Shifting Self-Judgments to Self-Empathy

Part One: Think of three actions or behaviors you took in the last week that you did not enjoy and/or are feeling frustrated, sad or disappointed about. For each, describe the behavior/what you saw yourself doing (observation), any judgments you have about what you did, how you feel thinking about what you did, and the needs unmet by the action or behavior.

Observation (What I did)	Judgments (Thoughts about what I did)	Feelings about what I did	Needs unmet by what I did
Told my little sister to "shut up" with a volume and tone of voice I did not enjoy.	Mean. Cruel. Bad example. Unfair. Not nice. Out of control.	Sad. Discouraged. Regretful.	Care. Consideration. Awareness. Self-Connection. Choice. Integrity.

Part Two: Looking at each of these situations, would you be as critical of someone else as you are of yourself? If not, why? If you would be less critical, what might you be thinking about the other person and/or the situation that gives you more understanding and compassion?

Part Three: Sitting with how you feel about each situation you described in part one and the needs left unmet, can you think of a request you could make of yourself? Regarding the example above, you might write, for example: "The next time I'm aware of being really angry and impatient with my sister, I'd like to try taking 'time out'—stepping out of the room for five minutes—to cool down and connect with my feelings and needs."

Embarrassment, Fear, and Shame: Dealing with Double Judgment

Sometimes when we say or do things not consistent with our values, we can feel self-conscious, embarrassed, or "sheepish." At these moments, we may not have met our own needs for integrity, awareness, or choice. We may feel vulnerable and prone to fear or shame, wondering what others might be thinking of us. This can especially be true if we fear punishment or "consequences." At those moments, we may be wanting acceptance, understanding, safety, and trust in relation to others. In practicing self-empathy, it can be helpful to look at all our needs, including those unmet by our actions and the needs possibly unmet by being observed and, perhaps, judged.

Let's look at an example. Tim has been considered the "star" of his college basketball team and one of the top scorers throughout the year. After many years, his team has finally made it to the top division championships. He knows that both his coach and teammates are counting on him, as is the whole school. During overtime, in the last minute of the game, he loses the ball and the other team wins. Thinking about losing the game, Tim feels the following:

- Sad
- Disappointed
- Discouraged
- Insecure and uncertain
- Broken hearted
- Shocked
- Dismayed

Thinking about how others may be judging him and what happened, he may be feeling:

- Nervous
- Scared
- Uncertain
- Disconnected
- Vulnerable

In thinking about his needs, he's aware that by dropping the ball he has not met his own needs for competency, effectiveness, and contribution. Thinking about how others might be perceiving him, he's aware of needs for trust, acceptance, understanding, and support. Aware of both sets of feelings and needs, he can be more empowered to connect with others about his fears and get the connection and support he's wanting. He might to say to his coach, for example:

> *"I'm still in shock. I can't believe I dropped the ball at the last minute—especially after getting so many points earlier in the game. I really thought I 'd make the difference for the team this year. I'm also a little nervous—I wonder what you're thinking about what happened?"*

Regardless of what Tim's coach or anyone else is thinking, by asking in this way he can create connection and find out what judgments others might, in fact, be holding.

In my experience, as someone who has struggled with fear of judgment for most of my life, I have found that 99.9% of the time what people are thinking is in fact light years from what I fear. Rather than anger, contempt or judgment, I find understanding and compassion. In the rare cases I do hear judgment, I can empathize with what the other person is feeling and needing. Finding common ground in shared values, we enjoy renewed understanding and connection. By not asking, I never know—and have no opportunity to address misunderstanding that might have occurred.

Exercise 6, Chapter 5: Taming Double Judgment

Think of an action you took that you were unhappy with and that you fear others may also be judging. What are your judgments, feelings and needs in relation to the choice you made? What judgments do you think others might have and how do you feel thinking about these judgments? What needs are "up" for you?

First, describe the situation in one-two sentences:

_____

_____

My judgments of my actions: _____

My feelings about my actions: _____

My needs "up" in relation to my actions: _____

Judgment(s) I fear others may have: _____

How I feel thinking about this judgment: _____

Needs up thinking about this judgment: _____

Self-Empathy for Full Choice: No One Can Take Your Autonomy

In addition to fostering compassion for choices we've made, self-empathy can help us make choices. In doing so, it's helpful to remember that our needs are never in competition. All needs are life-serving and precious. In practicing self-empathy and doing a "needs-meter," we are not pitting one need against another. Rather, we are taking a needs "inventory"—placing all our needs out on the table, where we can see and appreciate them. We can then decide which needs to

> "I could make things the way I want if I could figure out what I want."
> —Andrew

leave unmet (and mourn them) and choose a strategy that can best meet all our needs in the moment.

Here is how you do a "needs-meter:"

1. At the top of a sheet of paper, write down the different strategies you are considering.

2. Below each strategy, write down how you are feeling about each one. In doing so, really sit with your feelings. What sensations and energy do you notice in your body? To help connect with your feelings, you may find it helpful to use your imagination. Visualize taking the course of action you're considering. Imagine going through each step involved in your mind's eye. Imagining the action in this way, what feelings, sensations, eagerness, or willingness do you observe?

3. After connecting with your feelings deeply in this way, consider what needs would be met by taking each action.

4. Once you've completed the above steps, check in with yourself to see if you have clarity or a changed perception about which strategy you'd prefer. If you don't, you may wish to go back and check to see that you've fully identified all the feelings and needs at play.

5. When you are clear about which strategy you would like to choose, check to see if any needs will go unmet. If so, honor those needs. Sit with how much you value those particular needs

and how much you want to experience them in your life. This is an important step to feeling peace and ease about the choice you make.

Exercise 7, Chapter 5: Making Needs-Meeting Choices

Think of a situation you currently are feeling torn about. Then identify two strategies you could take and identify what you're feeling and needing in relation to each. Note that some feelings and needs may be "true" for both strategies. The first row has been completed as an example.

Situation	Possible Strategies(A, B, C)	Feelings-thinking about strategy	Needs Met-by taking strategy
To go to grad school, get a job, or join the Peace Corps?	A. Grad School	Excited, stimulated, nervous, eager	Learning, challenge, growth, community, meaning
	B. Job	Hesitant, bored, accepting, excited	Economic needs, safety, movement, choice, confidence
	C. Join the Peace Corps	Excited, scared, inspired, curious	Purpose, adventure, challenge, learning, growth

Taking Responsibility for Our Choices

Sometimes it's easy to think we have no choice, that there are things we have to do. When I think this way, I remind myself of an old saying: "No one can take from you that which is really yours." Your autonomy—your ability to have choice—is always yours. You may wish in some situations that you had more choices or different choices, but there always are choices. To look at an everyday example, consider the following dialogue:

> You: "I have to go to class because I have an exam."
> Me: "What would happen if you didn't go to class?"
> You: "Well, I would flunk the course."
> Me: "So, you are choosing to go to class because you want to pass the course?"
> You: "Well, yeah, I guess I am."

If you are thinking about reward and punishment, you may feel you have no "choice." If you don't attend class, you will fail. But attending or not is a strategy to meet your own needs. It is these needs—not a demand—that you're responding to when you choose to attend.

Even in the most dire and extreme circumstances, as Viktor Frankl, psychiatrist and author of *Man's Search for Meaning*, observed in the Nazi concentration camps, people exercised choice in how they dealt with their environment. They chose to cooperate or compete with their fellow inmates. It may be challenging to remember the choices we have. If we are anticipating or experiencing needs unmet, it may feel like little or no choice at all. But by practicing self-empathy, we can gain awareness, clarity, choice, and empowerment.

Exercise 8, Chapter 5: Identifying Needs and Choices

The following exercise will give you practice in translating "have to" statements into statements reflecting choices you have and the needs you may meet in your choices.

Statement	Consequence of doing the opposite	Translation into a positive choice statement/Needs Met
I have to go home this weekend or my mother will kill me.	If I don't go home this weekend my mother will be hurt and disappointed.	I am choosing to go home this weekend because I know it will please my mom and I enjoy that. Needs met for contribution, care, connection.
I have to write a paper this weekend.		
I have to go to work.		
I have to call my boy friend.		

Self-Empathy when "Stung" by Others

Self-empathy is helpful not only when dealing with our own inner "bugs" or demons. It also is helpful when interacting with others. When stimulated by what we see or hear another person say or do, it can be challenging to respond with compassion. Our own empathy "battery" is low and so it's hard to be present or caring for another. By practicing self-empathy and becoming aware of our own feelings and needs in the moment, we can "re-charge" our empathy reserve. Gaining greater self-connection and awareness, we can increase our ability to be present, responding with compassion and choice.

> "Sometimes I find myself in a bad mood at the end of the day and I can be really awful to be with—I find fault with anyone and any thing. Usually I don't even know what it was that made me feel so bad or what happened that set me off. But whatever it is, I tell myself I shouldn't let it bother me."
>
> —Samantha, a student

Empathy Choices

One of the most liberating and creative ideas in NVC is that we have choice in how we hear others and how we respond. When a person gives us a message, especially one that we consider critical, there are two choice points:

- Do we focus on the other person or ourself?

- Do we respond empathically (about feelings and needs) or non-empathically (with judgment, evaluation, and blame)?

When combined, these two choice-points lead to four types of possible response:

Four Types of Response (Empathic and Non-Empathic):			
Stimulus:	Focus on:	Non-Empathic Response: Blame, judgment, disconnection	Empathic Response: Focus on feelings and needs
Parent says "Your grades are so low I wonder why you are in school if you're not going to do your best."	Self	Blaming self: "I'm a failure. I don't deserve to be in school."	Empathizing with self: "I'm really sad and pained, urgently wanting some understanding and support."
	Other	Blaming other: "You're so unfair. You don't have a clue what I have to put up with."	Empathizing with other: "Are you upset and worried because you're wanting to trust that I'm going to be OK with the choices I'm making?"

With each exchange in life, these choices present themselves. Will I respond in a non-life connecting way, from a place of criticism and blame? Or will I respond with empathy? How will I direct my energy at the moment, towards another or towards myself? In the course of a dialogue, this focus of attention will repeatedly shift. At one moment, you may be wanting to empathize with yourself; in the next, you may choose to focus on the person(s) you're engaging with.

Exercise 9, Chapter 5: Four Ways of Responding— Awareness and Choice

Read about the following situation and then complete the four types of response possible (focus on self versus other and focus on judgment versus feelings and needs).

At a party, Dan tells a joke about a white man having sex with two "Oriental" women. Peter says "The correct term is 'Asian-American' and I don't think that's funny! It's a racist joke and I'm offended by it!"

What are four ways Dan could respond in this situation?

Give a sample response for each kind of reply:

A. Blaming self: _____

B. Blaming other: _____

C. Empathizing with self:_____

D. Empathizing with other: _____

The Four-Fold Path of Compassion

In any given moment, we can choose to respond with compassion or not. In the preceding table, we saw two ways of responding compassionately: with empathy directed towards our self (self-empathy) and empathy directed towards another (receiving with empathy). There are two other forms we can choose from. We can vocally share our observations, feelings, needs, and requests with another (honest self-expression). And we can listen empathically to others without speaking or responding (offering silent empathy). Overall, the four ways of compassionate response vary in two ways. Is my empathy focused on myself or another? And is it silent or spoken?

Four Kinds of Compassionate Response			
Stimulus:	Focus on:	Expressed	Non-Expressed
Friend says "All men are bastards."	Self	*Honest Expression:* "When I hear you say that, I'm really feeling…because I'm needing… Would you be willing to…?" "I feel sad hearing you say, 'All men are bastards,' because I'm a man and I want to be valued for who I am. How do you feel hearing what I just said?"	*Self-Empathy:* To self or person not feeling disconnected with): "I'm feeling … and needing…!" "Wow – I feel hurt hearing that. I want respect and to be valued for who I am."
	Other	*Empathetic Response:* "So, you're feeling … and needing…? "Are you feeling upset because you're wanting more caring and respect in your relationships?"	*Silent Empathy:* "Sounds like this person is really feeling and needing…" "Hmm, I wonder if she's hurting really bad and wanting more gentleness and caring in her life."

The four possible kinds of compassionate responses (to ourselves or others; silently or voiced) complete the "dance" described as the "empathy tango" in the last chapter. When communicating with compassion, we move back and forth (and back again) between these different "steps," depending on what we guess will most contribute to clarity, movement, ease, and connection.

Exercise 10, Chapter 5: The Four-Step Dance of Compassion

Read about the following situation and then complete the four types of Compassionate Communication possible.

Jennifer is differently-abled and uses a wheel chair. A student group she's involved with is having a party off-campus, and she learns it's being held at a restaurant that's not wheel chair accessible. She raises this concern with the organizer of the event and is told, "It's nothing personal. We want everyone to come. But with the budget and planing time we had, this was the only place that was affordable."

What are the four compassionate ways that Jennifer could respond in this situation?

Give a sample response for each kind of reply:

A. Honest Expression: _____

B. Self-Empathy: _____

C. Empathic Response: _____

D. Silent Empathy: _____

Who's Up Next?

When responding compassionately, how do we decide whom to focus on first, and when? And how do we decide about whether to use empathy, or self-expression? When working to resolve a conflict, we want to go where the greatest "heat" or energy is. Which person or group is most "up" in their feelings and needs? Who is most angry, critical, or defensive? This goes back to the principle of "empathy before education." If one person or party is feeling riled and on edge, it will be difficult if not impossible for them to hear the concerns of anyone else, never mind respond compassionately.

In determining who's the "hottest," you probably will want to check in with yourself first. If you're feeling connected with yourself and in a place where you can empathize with another, you may wish to direct your empathy outwardly, towards the person or group you're interacting with. If not, and you've been triggered by what you've heard, you will probably want to start with self-expression or self-empathy. In self-expressing—stating an observation and what you're feeling and needing—you can attend to your own "fire" first and also foster connection. In practicing self-empathy, you can attend to your own feelings and needs and, in doing so, support yourself in being more present to the concerns of others. Those who practice NVC commonly refer to this practice of silent self-care as "emergency self-empathy." You may not get all the empathy that you'd like at that moment, but enough that you can respond to another with choice and compassion

Even if we're not "triggered" in a conversation by what another person says, in effect we're repeatedly practicing a "short" form of self-empathy when empathizing with others. This "short form" is simply checking in with yourself briefly and repeatedly about your own feelings and needs. Do I still have energy for this conversation? Do I feel engaged? How do I want to continue? Brief, repeated check-ins when connecting with others is like monitoring your pulse rate while exercising. It gives you the optimum work out and, when it comes to empathy, the greatest connection.

The more you become skilled in practicing empathy, the more you will appreciate how related and interconnected different forms of empathy are. Usually in the course of a conversation you will make use of every form of empathic connection: self-empathy, empathy, expression, and silent empathy.

Deepening Our Connection with Ourselves through Our Judgments

Throughout this book, we have talked about how statements of judgment, criticism, blame or analysis do not promote connection between people and frequently stimulate pain. Yet while we don't want to stay with judgments or, perhaps, even use them in communicating with others, they can be very helpful as a first step in connecting with feelings and needs. Being aware of our thoughts and evaluations, we can understand the intensity and quality of our feelings and, through the words we use, gain insight and understanding into what we value.

In voicing our judgments, we can share them with a compassionate and supportive listener who can help us "translate" them into feelings and needs. Or, via self-empathy, we can state our judgments silently to ourselves, out loud, and/or by writing them out in a journal. Once your judgments are "out," see if you can connect a feeling to each one. Then see, based on the words you're using, what needs might be underneath your thoughts and emotions.

Let's see how "unpacking" judgment looks in action, practiced via self-empathy.

Early one morning, Mary Beth is in the bathroom and overhears Lisa, whom she considers a friend, talking about her to someone Mary Beth doesn't know well at all. Lisa tells this person a number of things about Mary Beth's social and sexual life that Mary Beth had told her with the request that she keep it to herself. She also makes a number of statements critical of Mary Beth's maturity and honesty. Mary Beth becomes aware of feeling overwhelmed with anger, rage, pain, and hurt. She decides to explore her feelings and needs further before deciding how to respond.

In private, she shouts out and writes down all the intense thoughts that come to her mind about Lisa and what Mary Beth heard her doing. These judgments include:

- I can't believe she's such a two-faced person.
- She said she was my friend and now she has betrayed me on everything I've said.
- I feel so violated.

- I am disgusted at the thought of people I don't know knowing such intimate things about me.
- People are going to look strangely at me now.
- How could I have been such a fool to trust her.

After writing down her judgments, Mary Beth goes through the list identifying her feelings and needs for each statement. Here's what a few of her judgments on the list might look like. Note that some of the needs come up more than once:

Statement	Feelings: Wanting (Needs)
1. "I can't believe she's such a two-faced person."	Rage: Wanting trust, integrity Disgust: Wanting caring, consideration Fear: Wanting trust, safety, understanding
2. "She said she was my friend and now she has betrayed me on everything I've said."	Despair: Wanting trust, caring Overwhelmed: Wanting integrity, support Hurt: Wanting caring, understanding

After Mary Beth identifies her feelings and needs and sits with them for a while, she can then make a number of requests of herself or other people to support her in meeting her needs. Lisa may or may not be a person to whom Mary Beth makes such a request; Mary Beth can generate many alternatives.

Exercise 11, Chapter 5: Composting Judgments into Live Experience

Based on the situation of Mary Beth and Lisa and the examples above, translate the following judgments into feelings and needs:

Statement	Feelings: Wanting (Needs)
1. "I am disgusted at the thought of people I don't know knowing such intimate things about me."	
2. "People are going to look strangely at me now."	
3. "How could I have been such a fool to trust her?"	

Moving On

Self-empathy can take time to develop. As with giving empathy to others, remember to take time with each step. Allow yourself to sit with the feelings and needs and fully empathize with what you're experiencing. Listen to your body. If you get stuck—unable to fully empathize with yourself or get clear about feelings and needs—you may wish to seek the help of an "empathy buddy"—someone familiar with the steps of NVC and willing to go through them with you.

As we've seen in this chapter, self-empathy has broad applications. It can be helpful in responding to others, in creating the space in ourselves where we can respond with compassion, choice, and awareness. It can also help us in creating kindness and compassion in how we speak to ourselves, when engaging in self-pity, fear of judgment, and addressing "mistakes" we've made. It can be useful in making choices, especially when choosing between strategies where some needs may be met and unmet.

Integration: Further Questions and Exercises to Explore Chapter 5

A. Consider each of the following questions and then complete the chart that follows:

1. Imagine that each of the following happened to you. What feelings might you have? What needs might be stimulated? (Use Table A on page 374 and Table B on page 375.)

2. After completing the chart, take a few minutes to reflect slowly on each need, how much you value and appreciate it, to connect deeply to how much you value that need in your life.

3. Then consider what intention, course of action or "self-request" that you might make.

Event	Feelings	Needs	"Self-Request"
You receive a letter saying that you are not going to be offered the summer internship you had hoped for.			
You get into an argument about politics with a friend who says that your ideas are "stupid."			
You find out that your afternoon lab class is canceled and you don't have to make it up. (Self-empathy is for when needs are being met as well as for when needs are not being met.)			

4. Having completed the exercise above, did you notice a shift in your understanding or experience of the event that happened? If so, describe: _____

_____

_____

B. The daily practice of self-empathy can help us to listen and act with compassion. During the next week, try two to five times to take the following steps when you notice you are reacting to a situation or event. Keep a journal or log of your self-empathy practice. Remember that empathy can be practiced with "fulfilled" feelings and needs met, as well as unmet. As discussed in this chapter, it may also be helpful to start out by looking at your judgments, to unpack what you might be feeling and needing. Here are the four basic steps:

Observation: What is happening (what am I seeing, hearing, thinking about) that is stimulating some response in me?

Feeling: What feelings are being stimulated in me?

Need: What needs and values of mine are not being met at the moment?

Request: What request can I ask of myself (or others) that would meet my needs?

In "logging" the above, you may wish to track the following:

• The names of the feeling(s)

- How you are experiencing them in your body—tenseness, heat, restriction, release, etc.

- Where you're experiencing this sensation—in your head, chest area, etc.

As more feelings come up, empathize with what you're needing until you feel "complete." Note in your journal or log any shift that you experience and when you feel "complete" in your empathy and any strategies that you might be considering.

C. Think back on a recent conflict. Out of the four, possible empathic and non-empathic ways of responding (blame directed outwards, blame directed inwards, empathy directed outwards, empathy directed inwards), how did you choose to respond? What was the result of that choice? How did it meet your needs or not meet your needs? Looking back, how do you think a different response would have led to different results?

D. Choose someone familiar with NVC to be your "empathy buddy" for the week and make an "empathy date." This can be in person or over the phone. At the start of your date, do a quick check in (one to three sentences or about thirty seconds) about what's most "up" for each of you in your life at the moment. Are you angry about a grade you've gotten? Annoyed with someone you're dating? Anxious about paying tuition this semester? After checking in and having a sense of what's most alive for each of you, give empathy to the person who's most up in their feelings. When they're feeling complete, the other person may want to take a turn at receiving empathy. As an alternative, you can also try practicing self-empathy out loud: the person who is "up" in their feelings gives empathy aloud to themselves; you provide coaching and support in this process, especially when they get stuck.

CHAPTER SIX:
Stepping into the Fire:
Enjoying and Responding to Anger

"Anger is natural. It's part of the force. You just have to learn to hang out with it."

—*Tori Amos, pop rock singer*

"For me music is a vehicle to bring our pain to the surface, getting it back to that humble and tender spot where, with luck, it can lose its anger and become compassion again."

—*Paula Cole, singer and songwriter*

In this book we have discussed a wide range of feelings and needs and how to respond to them. There is one "wild card," however, in the pack of emotions that people can find especially challenging to hear and express—anger. Involving judgment and leading quickly to disconnection and, even, physical violence, anger can feel like fire: dangerous, destructive, and difficult to control. Like all emotions, however, anger can also be seen as a gift. In this chapter, by understanding this volatile emotion, we will see how anger can serve us in identifying our values and living authentically.

Only One Person Can Make You Angry

One of the most important things to remember about anger is that no one else can make you angry; only you can. We encountered this idea in Chapter Two—that our feelings are caused not by other people but our needs—and this concept remains pivotal in understanding anger. At first, this may seem a big leap. Blaming others for our feelings is, of course, an integral part of anger. "I'm upset, scared, hurt, or sad, and it's *your* fault for what you did—you shouldn't have done that!" is the primary thinking behind this emotion. Yet while the behavior of other people (or ourselves, in the case of self-judgment) is the *stimulus* or *trigger* for our anger, the way we talk to ourselves about the behavior we see, employing *should thinking,* is, in fact, the actual root *cause* of what we're feeling. Anger is feeling mixed with thoughts and judgments.

Let's look at an example. Felicia doesn't want her parents to know she's dating Tony because he's of a different ethnic background and she's sure they won't approve. Tony is angry about that. The stimulus for his anger is Felicia's behavior—her refusing to tell her parents about him. But the cause is Tony's thinking. He's telling himself, "She should tell them about me. She shouldn't be embarrassed or afraid." Other thoughts might be fueling Tony's anger. He may be wondering how committed she is to the relationship, given she won't let her parents know. Regardless, it is his thoughts about the situation, his *should* thinking, not the situation itself, that is the cause of his rage.

Taking responsibility for our thoughts and judgments, as well as our needs, is the first step in gaining awareness and control in how we respond to anger. If we fall into cause and effect thinking— you *made* me do it, we lose full autonomy, responsibility, and choice. This does not mean we always like the actions of others. As individuals, we also need to take responsibility for our actions and choices. But we also need to take responsibility for how we respond, and see each situation in our lives not as unavoidable cause but simply potential stimulus.

Exercise 1, Chapter 6: Cause or Trigger?

For each of the statements below, mark "S" if you think the stimulus or trigger of the anger is described (if a clear observation is being given). Mark "C" if the cause of the anger is described ("should" thinking, blaming, "cause and effect" thinking).

_____ A. My housemate left food on the counter and now we have ants all over the kitchen.

_____ B. I overslept for my exam and I could have been more careful.

_____ C. The clerk at the store should have given me the batteries I asked for.

_____ D. It is the resident assistant's duty to see that the hall is quiet at night and he's not doing it.

_____ E. I wanted to have sex last night but my boyfriend didn't want to.

_____ F. If I want to go to medical school I've got to study more and get better grades.

My responses for this exercise:

A. In my opinion this is presented as a stimulus for anger because it is an observation of what happened. If the speaker had said "and he shouldn't have done that" after the initial statement, this would be the "cause" of his anger.

B. To me, this is presented as if a cause of anger. The words "could have been more careful" imply a judgment of wrongdoing. A non-judgmental description might be, "I overslept because I set the clock for a time that was one hour after the exam period began."

C. To me, this is presented as the cause of anger; the speaker is blaming/judging the clerk, not describing what happened. It would have been a stimulus if the speaker had said, "I asked for AA batteries and the clerk gave me A batteries."

D.   In my opinion this statement is suggesting a cause of anger. The speaker is talking about what the resident assistant should do, because it is his "duty." An observation of events without judgment might be, "The resident assistant did not speak to the residents about the sound in the hall last night."

E.   To me, this is expressed as a stimulus for anger. There is no judgment. The thought, "Lovers are supposed to please you sexually, that's part of what being in a relationship is about," would be a cause of anger.

F.   To me, this is presented as a cause of anger. The speaker is describing what he's "got to do," not describing observations and connecting to needs. A statement regarding stimulus for anger might be "The pre-med advisor said that students with my GPA are not usually accepted to medical school." If I make a "should" thought about the advisor, the medical schools or myself (e.g. "The advisor should have been more supportive," "Medical schools should be more flexible in admissions," or "I should work harder") my anger will be directed accordingly to the advisor, the medical schools, or myself.

Watch Those Signals!

The second important thing to know about anger is that it's like a floodgate. It's an intense feeling resulting from an overflow of other feelings. When an unmet need stimulates a feeling of sadness, irritation, hurt, or fear within us, we will typically experience these feelings and be aware of them. When the stimulation is intense, however, and the needs "up" are quickly multiplying, we can go on "overload." Overwhelmed, we may be only minimally aware of what we're feeling; we may even go numb. Our feelings may even fall below the range of full consciousness. It is at these moments that we can become aware of an intense feeling of anger and perhaps even fury or rage. Like a siren or blaring red light, anger can be seen as an "emergency" signal that something needs attending to—that some needs are not being met in a big way.

Ironically, the root meaning of "emergency" is to emerge, or become visible. Understanding anger in this way—as an "emergence" of our feelings and needs, can help us understand anger and how it can, in fact, contribute to our well being. Examining our anger and the stimulus that triggered it offers an invaluable way of understanding our values. It acts as a wake up call to pay attention to our needs and attend to them.

Exercise 2, Chapter 6: Getting to the Root of Anger

Part One: Imagine that you are in each situation below and feeling angry:

A. What judgments, criticisms or thoughts of blame might you be having?

B. What might be the feeling you are experiencing underneath the anger?

C. What need do you imagine might be alive in you?

The first one has been done as an example.

Situation	A. Judgment	B. Feeling(s)	C. Need(s)
1. Your roommate comes into your room at a time that you told him you would like to be alone with your girlfriend.	He is so selfish, not caring about my privacy at all. He should think about someone else for a change.	Disappointment Frustration Sadness	Support Consideration Caring Sexual Expression
2. Your teacher announces a surprise quiz and you are not prepared.			
3. You are accused of deliberately setting off a false alarm about a non-existent fire. You are charged with this serious offense on the basis of an eyewitness report. You know that you didn't do it but the police don't believe you.			

Part Two: This week, notice the next time you're angry. What feelings and needs are beneath the anger? In hindsight, were these feelings and needs "backing up" before you noticed or named them? You may wish to write about this in your journal.

The Challenge of Receiving Anger Empathically

"How much more grievous are the consequences of anger than the causes of it."
—*Marcus Aurelius, 2nd century Roman emperor*

Because anger is an intense emotion and involves judgment of wrongness, most of us have difficulty receiving it. With practice, we usually can learn to respond empathically when someone is expressing anger towards another. But it can be a struggle to guess the underlying feelings and needs of a person when we are the "target" of their anger or rage. At such moments, it can be challenging to be self-connected and present. This can be especially true when anger stimulates self-judgment or when we fear punishment or reprisal. We will look at each of these situations in turn.

Facing the Fear of Our Own Judgments

> *"The intoxication of anger, like that of the grape, shows us to others, but hides us from ourselves."*
> —*John Dryden, 17th century English poet and dramatist*

If we agree with all or part of the judgment that is mixed up with the anger, if we are also torn about the actions we've taken, then we can easily move into self-judgment. In effect, in doing so, we're hearing judgment in "stereo"—from both inside and outside ourselves. In such a stimulated state, it can be especially difficult to hear anger; we're overwhelmed. Too distracted by the pain of our own unmet needs, including, perhaps, needs for understanding, acceptance, and shared understanding, it's difficult if not impossible to hear what's going on for the person who's enraged.

This phenomena can occur even when situations are not very intense; no one may be screaming or swearing, but if we're holding the same judgment, it can be difficult to fully hear the anger of another. In my Multicultural Psychology course, for example, students often complain it's too demanding, that there is too much to read and write and too many quizzes. Feeling confident about how I've designed the course, I feel very open to hearing their concerns and, even, their irritation. However, much more often than I enjoy, students will be angry that they didn't receive the grade they wanted. With these encounters, I struggle a great deal and may not be as open as I'd like to their views. Internally, I feel very conflicted about assigning grades; I prefer not to operate in an evaluative or "reward-punishment" system. Assigning grades does not give me the integrity and ease that I'd like. I also doubt that students feel cared for or seen for all the learning and effort they've invested. I also love teaching and want to keep my job. Submitting grades is expected of faculty; I doubt that challenging this norm would be an effective use of my time.

At moments when we're stimulated by agreement, self-judgment or fear, it's especially helpful to pause and self-connect with our own feelings and needs. We may choose to practice self-empathy and then express what's going on for us, speaking honestly and with transparency. Regarding the above situation, for example, I might reflect on how I wished the system was different at our university (and in U.S. higher education in general). I might also reflect on how much I want to contribute to my students' learning, care, and growth. I then might choose to authentically express this to those I am communicating with—owning how I find this conversation challenging and what I'm feeling and needing. In itself, this kind of transparency can greatly contribute to shared understanding and diffuse feelings of anger and contempt.

Exercise 3, Chapter 6: Developing Choice in Responding to the Anger of Others

Part One: Imagine you are in each of the following situations and then answer the following questions:

A. Without thinking about it too much, what might your "automatic" response be?

B. How would you categorize your response? Angry? Withdrawn? Curious?

EXAMPLE: Your boss says to you "You're incompetent and irresponsible. You're fired!"

A. My response might be "You can keep your stupid job!"

B. I would categorize this as an angry response.

1. Your housemate says, "You're not contributing enough to the household expenses. It's not fair!"

   A. My response might be: _____

   B. I would categorize this response as _____

2. Your parent says, "I'm angry that you take us for granted—you're acting greedy and self-centered!"

   A. My response might be: _____

   B. I would categorize this response as _____

3. When you question a bill at a service station the attendant says angrily, "If you don't like it just take your business elsewhere."

   A. My response might be: _____

   B. I would categorize this response as _____

4. Your loved one says, in an angry tone of voice, "How come we always do what you want to do?"

   A. My response might be: _____

   B. I would categorize this response as _____

Part Two: Choose one of the situations above. Identify what you're feeling and needing. Then write out a dialogue where you share with honesty and transparency how you find this situation challenging and the feelings and needs up for you. You may wish to do this in your journal.

The Carrot and the Stick: Fearing Anger in Others

> *"Great anger is more destructive than the sword."*
> —*Indian Proverb*

Sometimes the anger of other people may actually stimulate fear or terror in us. If we have experienced or witnessed physical harm or been punished when people are angry, we may fear this will happen to us again in the present. We may not remember the trauma or be fully aware of it, or understand cognitively how it relates to current events. Yet it can still have an impact. As one person pointed out, the difference between anger and danger is one letter. For some of us, we have experienced this first hand.

Most of us are accustomed to looking to others for approval or acceptance. If someone is angry with us, we assume we've done something wrong. "It's my fault—again!" Caught up with this kind of thinking, we may do whatever we can to "keep the peace," believing, "If they think I'm OK, then I must be OK." We conclude that if anyone feels offended by what we've said or done, then we must change. We don't hold our own value, unconditionally. In doing so, we take responsibility for the feelings of others, using their reactions as a guide for our behavior rather than our own internal values and needs. This concern with pleasing others has been described by the noted therapist Virginia Satir as "people-pleasing."

It's not surprising that many of us have become people-pleasers. Most of us have grown up with punishments and rewards, told that if we do the "right" thing we will be rewarded and, if we don't, made to suffer. We have been rewarded and punished in numerous ways, through grades, treats after dinner, weekly allowances, blame, and corporal punishment (slaps or spankings). As adults, this system continues via pay, promotions, late fees, and traffic violations. Like dogs trained to do tricks, the result is that we look to others as a guide for our choices.

It's also easy to fall into people-pleasing because we've also been taught to take responsibility for others' feelings. From the start of our lives, we have heard people say things like, "I'm angry because you left your toys on the floor!" "He's sad because you won't play with him. Won't you make him happy and share your truck?" "She's furious because of what her boss did." "I'm depressed because you always say 'no.'" When people communicate again and again that their feelings are caused by our behavior, it's understandable that we are confused.

Most of us like to believe we are acting out of autonomy and choice. So accustomed to living in a system of punishment and reward, however, we rarely if ever see how that "system" is informing our decisions. The system is so pervasive, it is transparent—we don't fully see or recognize it. Almost every day we make decisions motivated by fear or societal norms. We may ask ourselves, "What if I get caught? What will my parents say? Would my friends understand?" In contrast, how often do we reflect on what is important to us—what we truly value and how we want to live and behave? In not reflecting on these questions, and not being fully aware of our values, we may not be living in full integrity...or fully living at all.

As a teen, I asked my mother why she'd chosen to have children. She was married just a year when she had my brother at nineteen, and me a year later. She answered that she really didn't know—"It's just what everyone did then: got married and had children." It seems her getting married and having children was a strategy for acceptance and inclusion ("fitting in") and simplicity and ease (not knowing the next step in life). Hearing similar stories from others and reflecting on actions I've taken, I feel sad thinking about how people can make decisions, including what I would consider significant choices, "on automatic" without full awareness or choice. Approval seemingly offers acceptance, ease, and peace. But it comes at a price. It does not support honest or "real" interactions. Learning how to hear and respond to others' anger can empower us to do so.

Exercise 4, Chapter 6: Do You Seek the Approval of Others?

Part One:

A. Read through the following list. Which behaviors are familiar to you? Do you:
- Get very anxious when people yell at you?
- Feel the need to fix things or apologize when people are upset?
- Try to avoid people when they are upset?
- Omit information or rely on a "little white lie" in order to avoid scenes?
- Do things you would rather not to avoid saying "no" to people?
- Sometimes apologize to keep the peace, even when you really don't think you have done anything wrong?

B. Give three examples in your own life when you engaged in people pleasing. You can write about this in your journal.

Part Two:

A. Look back on your life, from your earliest years. Think of five examples of punishment and reward that were used in your "education"—at home, at school, and by society at large. The first one has been done as an example.

1. Grades/ "failing" or "passing" a test

2. _____

3. _____

4. _____

5. _____

6. _____

B. Think about some choices you've made in life, including what you might consider "major" decisions. What informed your choices? Did judgment and/or punishment and reward influence the choices you made?

C. If you were completely unafraid of censure of judgment, what might you choose to do in your life? In considering this question, check to see that all your needs would be met by this choice (including contributing to life and care and consideration for others).

Turning the Tables: Expressing Anger to Others

It's safe to say most people don't enjoy being angry. Physically, anger is a stressful and unpleasant sensation, often experienced as tightness, pressure, and restriction. When angry, we're probably not experiencing connection, ease of communication, understanding or trust. We're urgently wanting movement and relief. For most people, these are crucial needs. In sharing our judgments, we're probably trying to address these values. But when you think about it, how do you feel when someone is screaming at you, telling you that you're the cause of their pain? Does their behavior encourage you to listen—or to disagree and fight back? Sharing our judgments can be appealing, especially if it offers some expression. But how will it support our being heard and getting our needs met?

Isn't Anger Ever Justified?

The more intense our feelings and needs, the harder it is to separate them from their stimulus. It also becomes harder to focus on the particular actions (the stimulus) rather than the person who's provided or performed the stimulus for us. This is especially true in the case of profound trauma, when it can be hard to imagine that the pain we're experiencing is the result of our own unmet needs. Surely if the driver had not run a red light, you would not be in the hospital now with a broken leg, missing spring break. Surely if your partner had not gotten involved with another person and left you, you would not be distraught and alone. In such cases, it is exceptionally easy to have judgments of others. The stimulus or trigger and what you're feeling can seem like cause and effect, clear and simple.

When pain is stimulated in us, especially great and traumatic pain, we may also want someone to blame or "pay for" our distress. We want others to take responsibility for their actions and have a taste of our pain. We may be thinking, "Only if they can hurt the way I've hurt will they understand what I've endured. Then maybe they'll know what it's like and do things differently in the future." At these moments, we're probably wanting mutuality, understanding, and compassion. We also probably have a need for responsibility and awareness, in regards to the impact that a person's actions have had on our lives.

In effect, this way of thinking can be seen as a misguided attempt at empathy. We want others to experience pain or retribution as a strategy to create mutuality, shared experience, and accountability. This kind of thinking can actually lead people to enjoy the suffering of others; they may think they're getting empathy when in fact they're simply contributing to more pain and disconnection, continuing the cycle of suffering and loss. Identifying the choices that both we and others have and have made, and showing the inconsistency between these choices and values we hold, can bring an understanding far more likely to result in the fulfillment of needs, including needs for restoration, harmony, and justice.

Compassionate Communication is not about idealism, kindness, or generosity to others. It is about creating connection and, in doing so, dramatically increasing the odds that our own needs and concerns will be considered and met.

Exercise 5, Chapter 6: Restoration or Retribution

Part One: Read the interview with Marshall Rosenberg in the appendix of this book and then answer the following questions:

A. Why is "deserve" the most dangerous word in the English language?

B. How does the concept of "deserve" motivate and inform retributive justice?

C. Why did the college students in Texas celebrate capital punishment?

D. How is restorative justice different from retribution? What question is it based on?

E. Why is apology "too cheap and too easy"?

F. What is the difference between "life-serving" judgments and "moral" judgments?

G. What "needs" could possibly motivate a person to rape another human being?

Part Two: Think of a situation when you wanted another person to suffer or "pay for" their actions. What were you feeling and needing at that moment? Imagine a dialogue between yourself and the other person, or imagine writing a letter to this person. How might you express your pain—and approach restoration—making use of empathic expression?

Moving through our Anger

In practicing Nonviolent Communication, we don't avoid or suppress our anger. Rather, we seek to identify what's stimulating us and what values are up in the moment. We seek to share this information and make a request to address our needs and concerns. Perhaps you're afraid to express your anger because the only way you know how to do it is with judgment and blame. But beneath that judgment is what really matters most to you. By becoming aware of what you're wanting, you're in the best position to see that you get it—and ask for it in a way you don't regret later.

In responding to your anger, some principles can be especially helpful. Many of these points we've covered earlier; here, we're just reviewing them:

- Take responsibility for your own feelings and needs; distinguish stimulus from cause. Each of us is 50% responsible for what happens in an interaction and 100% responsible for our experience (the feelings and needs stimulated). I am not responsible for how my behavior lands or is received by others—and they are not responsible for the needs I may experience as unmet by their behavior.

- Be open to different strategies or results. When we believe our needs can only be met in one way or by one person we are setting ourselves up for unhappiness, frustration, and possibly violence.

- When tempted to respond with right-wrong energy, also try to remember your goal and purpose—is it to connect with the other person, to address an issue that is stimulating for both of you, or to prove that you are "right?"

- Make use of your judgments. Pay attention to the "judgment show." By listening to the energy and content of your thoughts and opinions, you can more easily connect with your feelings and needs.

- The most vital and frequently missing link to break the chain of judgment and anger is empathy—getting the empathy we need to be keenly aware of our feelings and needs so we can share them vulnerably without any shred of wrong-doing included. Self-empathy is an especially crucial skill in dealing with our own anger and the anger of others.

Playing Ball with Anger

How do all these principles look put into action? A few weeks ago I had a conversation with a student called Patrick about challenges he was facing completing his course work and dealing with his family. His father was seriously ill, had been told he only had a short time to live, and his family was struggling to pay the bills. After making an arrangement about his schoolwork, Patrick sought my input about his 17-year old sister, Samantha, whose behavior was stimulating great anger in him. Samantha was staying out all night, using alcohol and drugs, not helping around the house and, in doing so, triggering distress in their parents. He was furious that Samantha was "causing" so many problems when the family was already overwhelmed. Our conversation went like this:

"I'm so furious with Samantha. I've got to tell her how thoughtless, inconsiderate, and immature she's being. I've got to get through to her."

"Yeah, I see you're really angry."

"You bet I am! How can she be causing so much trouble? My mother's at wit's end and I can't stand to see her stressed like this. Samantha should be helping, not getting everyone more upset."

"You're really wanting Samantha's cooperation and support at this moment, aren't you?"

"Of course I am! We don't need more problems to deal with right now."

"Are you also worried about her getting hurt?"

"Sure. The people she's hanging out with are up to no good. Samantha's a good kid, but she's only seventeen. I really worry about what's happening. She should be staying home and studying, and spending time with my father. That's what she should be doing. I'm going to read her the riot act."

"I'm guessing you're pretty scared about why might happen to her."

"Yeah, I am. And I'm really wanting my dad to be the priority right now."

"I'm hearing how much love you have for Samantha, and how much you'd like to protect her and your whole family from more pain and distress, especially with your father being ill."

"Yes, I do. I really do. I'd really like that…"

At this point, Patrick became a bit tearful and then paused for a moment. After waiting a few minutes, we continued our conversation. At this point, having become aware of what he was needing, Patrick was able to consider the needs of his sister. This is a key step in creating understanding and finding a way forward:

"I'm wondering, how would you feel telling Samantha about the love you have for her and how scared you are for her safety?

"I could do that."

"I think she'd really love to hear that."

"Yes, I think so, too."

"And I'm guessing she's also in a lot of pain about what's happening at home."

"Yes, I'm sure that's true too."

"I wonder if staying away from home and drinking are her strategies for getting some relief from what's happening? And maybe some support from her friends?"

"I don't think so. I know some of the kids she's hanging with. I really don't think they are doing much for her. And she sure doesn't look happy."

"Maybe not. It's possible the strategy of staying out late with her friends is not giving her the comfort and relief she so desperately wants. But it's also her choice—and the need for autonomy, to be the one deciding how you do things, is a really big one, especially at that age. If you come on like you know what she should do, she may choose to do the opposite of what you say as a way of trying to prove to you that she is the one in charge of herself."

"I hadn't thought of that."

"And it might not meet other needs too, such as for trust and respect."

And so the conversation continued. By getting empathy for his anger and unpacking his judgments, Patrick connected with his needs for caring and safety for his sister and came to understand that Samantha had to meet her own needs for caring, comfort, and companionship in her choices. Once Patrick was able to connect to the value of his own needs, he was able to move away from right-wrong energy. He was able to hear Samantha, feel heard by her, and come up with a strategy that worked for both of them, and the family.

How Can I Find Empathy in Anger?

The next time you're feeling angry, try shifting blame for yourself and others to empathic connection. Here are the basic steps:

1. Stop, pause, and take a breath. What are you feeling in your body at this moment?

2. Enjoy all the judgments racing through your head; observe these judgmental thoughts but don't condemn yourself for having them. Allow them to go by and simply recognize them.

3. Identify your own feelings and needs—really sit with them. See if you can feel a shift in your body and/or your feelings.

4. When ready, guess the feelings and unmet needs of the other person. If you're not ready, go back to step three.

Offer empathy, starting with empathy for the other person first, if possible. If you can't muster empathy for the other person, give more empathy to yourself. Express your own feelings and needs, moving back and forth between steps five and six, as needed.

Here are the steps again, fleshed out:

Step 1—Get Centered and Connected

You're probably going to want some breathing room to do this, especially in the beginning when your patterns of responding to anger are entrenched and you have little experience with alternatives. You may wish to absent yourself, or engage in some deep breathing, taking ten slow breaths in and out. Step outside for the moment, or excuse yourself to use the toilet. If you don't feel it's possible to step away, you may want to request a pause— "Can you give me a second?" Use this time to self-connect. If you want additional support in this skill, meditation and mindfulness training can also be helpful in developing the ability to stop, pause, and self-connect.

Step 2—Enjoy the Judgment Show

This is when you say every blaming, critical, other-directed remark you can think of. Don't try to stop the flow, evaluate or judge it. Simply observe it, notice the patterns and rhythms, and underlying themes and common threads. You may even appreciate the creativity, irony, or humor of your judgments. Don't try to stop your "primal scream" prematurely. Let your judgments rush out like water from a dam, the rage and energy completing its natural course. Eventually, it will run down to a trickle. At that point, see if you can translate these judgments into feelings and needs.

The only key here is that your judgments are best enjoyed silently to yourself or at least not aloud in the presence of the person to whom your anger is directed. They won't know, of course, that this deluge of judgment is just a step in offering them empathy. And they probably won't enjoy the show as much as you.

Step 3—Identify Your Feelings and Needs

The wealth of information provided by your judgments makes the identification of your feelings and needs an easier task. What are your judgments, and the feelings and needs behind them? Choose some of the feelings listed in Table A (page 374); try them on for size. Do they fit? Would a more intense word fit? A less intense word? Do the same for the needs listed in Table B (page 375). Feel free to put the need(s) in your own words, or think of needs not on the list. What are you most wanting in this situation? What needs and values are not being met?

Step 4—Time to Swap: Guess the Feelings and Needs of the Other Person

This is a tough one. After giving attention to your own feelings and needs, it's time to guess what the other person is experiencing. Take a deep breath and try to imagine the situation from the other side, knowing that the other person has the same fundamental needs as you do. In what ways are their needs not being met? What, do you imagine, might be stimulated in the other person by this situation? If you're stimulated by their words or actions, give yourself some empathy. Once you have the empathy "oxygen" you need, go back to empathizing with the other person.

Steps 5 and 6—Play Empathy Shuffle!

Being aware of your own feelings and needs, take turns guessing the feelings and needs of the other person and expressing your own. In general, you will want the person who is "bleeding the most"—who is least calm and receptive to input, to receive attention first. When offering empathy to others, begin by making three empathic guesses, waiting for feedback each time. See what is going on in the other person. Stick as close as possible to the model of clear Observations, internal Feelings, personal Needs, and non-coercive Requests (OFNR).

In his booklet *Nonviolent Communication: The Basics as I Know and Use Them*,[4] Wayland Myers describes how he understands this process in three succinct steps:

---

[4] Myers, Wayland. *Nonviolent Communication: The Basics as I Know and Use Them*. Del Mar, CA: PuddleDancer Press, 2002

1. Describe events and my feelings and my needs, rather than my moralistic opinions about them.

2. Illuminate how my needs are producing my feelings and acknowledge that I have freely chosen to do what I am doing/ how I'm responding.

3. Describe what I want next, or clarify my understanding of what they want next, in specific, positive, doable terms.

Remember, the most effective expression of anger does not involve the use of blame. Blame blocks the other person from hearing your concerns. It doesn't matter whether blame is stated or implied. If, "This mess is YOUR fault!," is sensed by the listener, you probably are not going to be heard in a way you'll enjoy or easily see your own needs met.

Want to try this on for size? The exercise on the following page leads you through translating anger and judgment into feelings and needs.

Exercise 6, Chapter 6: Hearing the Life in Anger

Translating anger into feelings and needs takes practice. Look at the following situations and see if you can guess what feelings and needs may be involved for both parties.

EXAMPLE: "You never call me. I'm always the one to call you. You only think about yourself."

Speaker: The speaker might be feeling hurt, sad. His needs might be for connection, trust, caring.

Listener: The listener might be feeling scared or disconnected. She might be wanting her autonomy and authenticity.

A. "I can't believe you didn't give her an X-ray at her last physical exam! Now the tumor is really large and she might die from it! Talk about incompetence!"

B. "My teacher said he would give a make-up test to anyone who missed the mid-term exam. And now he says that I just have to do well on the final. He's not going to give me any break when I went home to be there with my parents when my dad was having surgery. What a jerk!"

C. "When you said that you wanted to use my car for the evening it never occurred to me that you would total it! How could you be so stupid? So careless?"

D. "The security guard at the store stopped me and insisted on searching everything I was wearing. He just wouldn't believe I hadn't stolen anything. What an ass-hole."

E. "How could you copy my homework without even letting me know? That's the most disgusting thing I've ever heard. I never expected it of a person I think of as my friend!"

F. "I don't understand why they invited all the other guys to pledge the fraternity and not me! They are so closed-minded. Just because I come from a small town they think they're better than I am! I'll show them!"

G. "They keep raising tuition and could care less about what the students need! All they want to do is get more and more money. The hell with us!"

Empathy from Hell

Remember, in offering empathy, it is our intention—not the words we use—that has the greatest impact. If you use one of the empathy "formulas" (Are you feeling…because you're needing…") but your heart is not really in it, the speaker will know. Rather than getting connection, you'll get something like, "Just quit with that psychology crap!" or "Why can't you talk like a normal person?" or "I don't need you to tell me what I'm feeling!" "Hollow," heartless empathy is so unpleasant to receive, it's often referred to as receiving "empathy from hell." In some ways, it's worse than getting no empathy at all.

If you find yourself giving empathy from hell, it's probably because your own needs are not being satisfied in the moment, perhaps for spaciousness, movement, ease, or caring. Perhaps you've chosen to empathize with another without first attending to yourself, and you may be the one most in need. Perhaps in the midst of the conversation, you became afraid or disappointed that your intent was misunderstood. And fear, if not stated or addressed, is often interpreted as aggression—the very opposite of an empathic response. Even if you're attempting to focus on the needs of another, if you have feelings and needs that are up for you, you will be distracted and unable to be fully present. If someone lets you know your empathy is not real or genuine, it may not be.

In those situations you need to fill your empathy cup. Take a moment to check in with your own feelings and needs and give yourself emergency self-empathy. If you can't get the self-connection and presence you're wanting, you may wish to postpone your conversation until you can get the empathy you need.

A second situation that frequently elicits the cry of "fake empathy" is when you are first learning to be a more empathic listener. Here you are, working your hardest to communicate more effectively. And what does it bring you? More grief! You have your empathy "antennae" on and they are not strong or sturdy enough to get the connection you're wanting. You're trying so hard to listen and care and instead all you're getting is dissatisfaction and static.

What to do? As always, honesty is the best policy. Explain yourself. "I really want to improve the quality of our communication and am trying out different ways of talking and listening. Could you bear with me for the moment, even though it's a bit awkward?" You may also want to get some empathy for your attempts at communicating in a new way. Changing long-established communication patterns is not "a piece of cake." You may need to get your recognition and "purple-heart" for all your efforts from someone else, at least at first.

Exercise 7, Chapter 6: Moving from Hell to Heaven

Do a role play with someone familiar with NVC. Here are the steps to take:

- Offer an empathy guess to your partner. "Are you feeling….because you're needing…?"

- Your partner responds as if you've just given "empathy from hell." "What's that jargon you're using…"

- Take a breath and self-connect. What are you feeling at that moment?

- Respond to your partner—with honest self-expression and/or further empathy.

- Switch roles.

- When both of you have had a turn playing each role, discuss the experience. How was it for your partner to get "empathy from hell"? How was it for you to practice self-empathy and respond? What did you learn from this exercise?

The Connor Compassionate Communication Index

When I first started learning NVC, I was extremely excited about it. More than anything, I wanted to use it with my husband, whom I cherish. But we'd been communicating for years in ways that had become entrenched. Sometimes we were communicating better than ever and really excited and hopeful about it. Then we'd have a conflict, one or both of us would be emotionally triggered, and we would return to old patterns. Losing our new-found intimacy, the feelings of pain and loss were even greater. Because the closeness was greater, losing it was greater too.

At times of conflict, my husband became in my eyes a huge enemy, the person who could wound me the greatest and destroy my happiness. The impact on our communication was devastating. I realized that I needed to slow things down and also have some patience with myself. After a number of such painful episodes, I developed what I call the "Connor Compassionate Communication Index." During any difficult conversation I monitor how I am feeling about the other person on a scale from one to ten. A rating of ten means this person in my eyes is God's gift to humankind. A rating of one means I'm seeing this person as my worst enemy, as Attila the Hun or Hitler.

When my feeling for the person drops below a seven, I stop talking. I may leave the room, the house, or hang up with a quick, "Sorry, gotta go now." I know meaningful connection won't happen until my scale rises. In the early days, I would just wait and the scale would rise by itself as time passed or after I received empathy from an empathy buddy. As I became more skilled with self-empathy, I could raise my Connor Index quite quickly, sometimes without even leaving the room.

Exercise 8, Chapter 6: Working the Index

The next time you notice yourself getting angry or annoyed, stop and apply the Connor Compassionate Communication Index. On a scale of one to ten, how much are you seeing the person you're interacting with as an "enemy"? How does this awareness inform the choice you make—to step away or continue to engage?

Angry at the World—and Changing It

Friends and family aren't the only ones who can trigger anger in us. Even interacting with a stranger can be stimulating, especially if tapping into needs "up" or unmet before. Let's look at a real example and self-empathy in action.

Riding my bike meets a lot of needs for me, including care for the environment, physical movement, and fun. On my bike, the City feels intimate and familiar. I love stopping on the Manhattan Bridge, watching trains pass by and all the barges and tugboats on the East River. I feel fully alive and content.

Riding my bike has also been a huge source of pain. Almost everyday, I experience incidents that do not meet my needs for consideration, care or safety. People open car doors without looking. Drivers pass me and take turns across my path without pausing or signaling. Cars drive within a foot of my bike, almost hitting me. Some drivers shout things from the road—such as, "Get your fat butt out of the way!"

How do I respond to such conflict? For years, I responded in violent ways. I shouted comments back, banging my fist on car windows or hoods. I wanted physical safety but in fact was increasing my vulnerability and risk. I knew something had to change. I started learning NVC decided to put it to the test.

Owning Anger

"He who angers you conquers you."
—*Elizabeth Kenny, 20th century Australian nurse*

I started out by considering the cause of my anger. In my case, it was clear—the drivers were irresponsible and selfish! I was caught up in blame thinking. But as we've discussed, no one else can make you angry. I knew other cyclists saw dangers on the road but weren't reacting as I was. I realized I needed to look at my own behavior. I also value integrity. I knew at times that I too was doing things on the road that I would consider careless or absent minded. With each incident, I would blame myself. "Don't be such a hypocrite!" "Can't you cut anyone a bit of slack?" When I got angry with others, I would accuse myself, "Why do you over-react so much!" My own inner critic was at fever pitch. Rather than turning blame inwards or outwards, of course, I had another option: empathic connection.

At first, I tried to empathize with the drivers. I guessed that they also had needs for movement, spaciousness, safety, and ease. Seeing a cyclist on the road, they probably felt nervous or crowded. But empathizing with what I saw as the "enemy" wasn't working for me; it was intellectual, all in my head. I was in too much pain myself. This was a clear case of needing "empathy before education." Aware of this need, I got help from empathy buddies and started practicing "emergency self-empathy" every time I was triggered while cycling.

Empathizing with my own needs, it was clear that I was desperately wanting safety, consideration, and ease. I wanted to be seen—literally, on the road. But I also wanted to be seen for how I was contributing to life. According to my way of thinking, I was supporting the environment by riding my bike, not using fossil fuel or making noise (as cars, busses, and trains do). I wanted to be seen and appreciated for that contribution, and the responsibility and awareness I was taking. I also value life and want reverence for it, especially for those that I would consider more vulnerable. And I want everyone's needs to matter. Looking at what's going on in the world, I feel deep pain. In hundreds and even thousands of situations, I see people using "power over" and acting out of "might makes right." Each time a stimulating incident happened on the road, I was reminded—in a flash—of all these larger situations I see in the world. This was compounded with my own shock and fear, and needs for caring, safety, and consideration in the moment.

Phew! So many needs! It took me months to get clear about them all. In the process, I realized how riding my bike was a strategy to feel hope about the world, and trust. I was so wanting hope, and each time my needs for consideration or safety were not met, I felt terror and despair. The story in my mind went something like this: "If I can't even be safe riding my bike, what hope is there for the rest of the world? How will we change energy consumption? End global warming—and the war?!" Like activating a volcano, all this larger, "global" pain and fear would erupt with even the smallest "local" incident or event.

I also realized that what I was wanting on my bike was completely undoable. There was no way I could feel confident that every driver on the road, each and every day, would have the awareness I was wanting—and willingness to act on it. I then felt genuine compassion for all the drivers I'd interacted with. They thought they were passing a cyclist, when, in fact, they were passing a loaded pack of dynamite just ready to detonate! Without even knowing it, I was making impossible demands.

The more I became aware of my own needs, the more I became aware of doable strategies to meet them. I increasingly found routes that met my needs for safety, including through a lovely park that I'd never noticed before and some quiet streets in Little Italy. I started using hand signals, which I'd never bothered with, had never seen other cyclists using in New York, and didn't think would make a difference. But based on how I've seen drivers respond, I'm convinced that signaling increases visibility, consideration, and safety.

Now I think it's funny that I didn't think of these strategies before. In my opinion, they're so simple and obvious! But I was so focused on blaming others, so adamant that the drivers *should* make room for me on the road, that I never thought of other options. It was their "fault" and their responsibility to fix. Once I got clear about my needs and mourned those that could not be met, I was able to focus on the needs that I could meet in this particular situation. I felt excited and empowered. Not only had I gained understanding and movement about what had seemed a hopeless situation, I had met needs for awareness, responsibility, choice, safety, and ease.

In addition to changing my cycling habits, I continue to practice what I call "aggressive" self-empathy. If I get angry on the road, I take the time to really sit with my feelings and empathize deeply with them. Sometimes, if I'm really triggered, I'll pull off the road and take some "time out" sitting with my judgment and the pain motivating it. When I do choose to engage with drivers, I express myself very differently. I've learned that before making any comments, that human connection is crucial. I don't start with an accusation or even an observation, but a question, "Hey, how are you doing?" If I'm not willing to greet a fellow human being, that's a good sign I need some "aggressive" empathy before opening my mouth.

When I do engage empathically, I find the outcome to be dramatically different. Just last week, I used my NVC skills with a driver who'd cut in front of me on the road. He was shocked and dismayed when I told him what happened. On his own, he volunteered, "Next time I'll really look before pulling out." My needs for connection and care were fully met.

I still have no control over the actions of others, including drivers and what they do on the road. I still don't always like what I see and would love more care and consideration. And there are, of course, times I still act in ways not fully consistent with my values. But my needs for safety, confidence, and choice are so much more satisfied now—not to mention spaciousness and ease. Self-empathy and choice in how I respond to anger has been a lifesaver for me—the best kind of "reflective vest" that this cyclist can have.

Exercise 9, Chapter 6: Empathy in Action

Think of a situation that's been stimulating for you more than once. This might be a "small" thing—such as your partner or roommate not replacing the toilet paper when it runs out or leaving dirty clothes on the floor. Practice self-empathy and/or get empathy from a friend. What, for you, are the "core" needs being stimulated? How do these needs speak to your vision of the world, and how you desire to live with and interact with others? You may wish to write about this in your journal.

Moving On

For most people, anger is a challenging emotion to deal with, whether expressing or receiving it. In understanding anger, however, and practicing empathy, we can learn to harness the energy of this passionate emotion and better connect with others and ourselves.

Integration: Further Questions and Exercises to Explore Chapter 6

A. Think of a time that someone was angry with you.

1. How did you know they were angry? What did they say or do?

2. What needs were stimulated in you by this anger? Were you feeling anxious, afraid, or sad?

3. What thoughts, judgments, or "shoulds" did you have about this person and/or in relation to this person's anger?

4. What would you have liked to request of yourself or the other person in relation to this person getting angry?

B. Think of someone you are feeling very angry with. Write this person a letter, explaining how you are feeling in OFNR (observations, feelings, needs, and requests). Your first draft may include judgment and blame—that's OK. Let it out, empathize with what you're feeling, and then go back to writing your letter of empathy.

CHAPTER SEVEN:
When Communication Isn't Possible:
The Protective Use of Force

Nonviolent Communication fosters understanding and connection between people. But what if in a particular moment communication isn't possible? And what if, at such moments, basic needs are not being met and life not being served?

Imagine for example you're at a noisy party where people are drinking a lot. Two guys who are drunk begin to fight and refuse to stop. What would be consistent with an NVC approach? To let them fight it out, at the risk of injury to one or both? To physically intervene to restrain them? To toss water on them with the hope of startling them and getting them to stop fighting? To call the police?

In such cases, where there may not be the capacity, time or willingness to communicate, we may want to use what's known as the "protective use of force." When using force in this way, the intention is not to hurt or injure another but to protect that person or someone they might be trying to harm. It also presupposes that we have a willingness to resume a dialogue when the immediate risk of harm has passed (and it is feasible to do so). Like all force, protective use of force involves the will of one person over another, yet it is starkly different from punitive force or violence. Protective use of force does not involve and is not motivated by judgment, blame, or condemnation. It is not used for punishment, retribution, or revenge. Although protective use of force may look similar to actions done for punitive purposes, the distinction becomes clear when we examine the motive behind the force

In what cases would force be protective? Imagine that you see someone about to attempt suicide or take a dangerous act, such as driving while intoxicated. Given the time you have and the obstacles to communication, taking physical action—restraining the suicidal

person or retaining the car keys of the person too drunk to drive—
would be life serving. While you might want to empathize with
your friend and find out why they're contemplating such an act, if
someone's about to swallow pills or jump from a bridge it is probably
not the time. Once the person is safe, there will be time for such
connecting.

With a person who's inebriated, making an empathic connection
is difficult if not impossible; you can connect with them later when
the immediate danger has passed. You may wish to let the person
know why you're taking the action you're taking: "Tom, I'm
concerned about your safety. Knowing how much you've drunk
tonight, I'm driving you home."

In the case of the two drunken students fighting at the party,
were they broken up for the purposes of "teaching them a lesson"
or because there was concern that they might hurt each other? Was
the restraint intended for the purpose of protection and safety, or
punishment? This is what distinguishes protective force from
punitive force.

Mixing Oil With Water

Even when people take action to protect others, it often is
tainted with judgment and condemnation. Although it may start
with life-serving intent, as soon as judgment or blame enters in, it
no longer can be considered life-serving and protective. Let's say a
parent sees a young child approaching a hot stove; the parent does
not want the child to get burned. What choices does the parent
have? She or he could resort to judgment and blame. The child
could be told, for example, "Jimmy, don't be such a bad boy! Mommy
told you to stay away from the stove!" The child could also be
punished or threatened. "If you go near that stove once more, I'm
going to smack you!" "I told you to stay away from the stove and I
mean it!" In each of these cases, there is probably genuine concern
for the child's safety. Most of us know no other way to communicate

or meet our needs than resorting to criticism, threat, and blame. But in each case, there may also be other needs on the table besides a desire for protection and preserving life. It could be that the parent also wants ease, consideration, and to be "respected" and heard. These needs, not a need for safety and protection, can sometimes be found behind statements such as "Don't be a bad boy." "You listen to me, or else!" Protective use of force is not a strategy to meet other needs, such as for consideration and respect. Its primary use and intent is to protect and serve life.

What would protective use of force look like in this situation? Rather than engaging in punishment or blame, the parent could simply scoop the child up or block their way to the stove. You could also choose to shut the stove off and cover the elements that are hot. Another option could be to engage the child in another way, especially with play (a need all children have). Or you could simply place the child in another room, perhaps behind a gate. While not stating feelings and needs or using NVC phrases, each of these acts can be seen as acts of compassion. You are acting out of needs for nurturing, care and concern, not out of intention to criticize, punish or blame. At another time you may wish to use words to connect with the child and express your concerns.

Isn't Violence Sometimes Necessary?

Many people believe that violence is a "necessary evil" and sometimes can be used for good. When parents hit their children, they may say, "This is for your own good" and "This is hurting me more than it's hurting you." When governments lead nations to war, citizens are told this is a necessary "sacrifice" to "keep the peace." The vast majority of statues and monuments in our public parks celebrate past wars, all supposedly fought for high and noble purposes such as freedom, national security, and democracy. Many religions tell us to "turn the other cheek," but some of the same traditions tell us "an eye for an eye and a tooth for a tooth."

Vengeance and compensation are seen as fair, acceptable, and even desirable. It is only then that the other side "will learn a lesson" and that "wrongs can be righted." It's safe to say that every war, at least those recorded in human history, has involved enemy images of other human beings and right-wrong thinking. Key to this thinking is the belief that "good" ultimately prevails; that God is on the "right" side—that is, our side.

Educated so completely in this belief, some people maintain that punishment is sometimes justified and more effective in teaching people to behave differently than other methods. Teachers, parents and persons in positions of authority especially hold this view. This long standing and pervasive belief drives much in our society, from corporal punishment to prison sentences and fines. In many cultures, force, obedience, and punishment are held in great esteem; to not use them is seen as detrimental or dangerous, especially with children. "Spare the rod, spoil the child," is an old saying that supports this view.

Research, however, has consistently shown that the punitive use of force is not effective in changing human behavior. It may seem to work but in the long term it backfires. It has negative side effects, such as resentment, retaliation, and revenge, and a very poor record of success for actually meeting human needs. Certainly cases do exist where if not for physical punishment applied by a parent, an offspring might have gone down a different, less desirable path. Yet for many people, the application of punitive force leads to resentment, hostility, and ultimately, aggression against others.

When we are considering use of force and especially violent force, there are two questions we may wish to ask ourselves: *What do we want people to do? And why do we want them to do it?* Do we want others to act in a manner consistent with their values? Or do we want them to act or not act because of fear, judgment, or punishment? And if fear or punishment is the primary motivator, what can we expect their behavior to be when they aren't being watched or observed? I know of situations, for example, where parents have told their children not to smoke and most definitely not to smoke in the house. Usually with these rules, there are consequences for breaking them. But what do the children do? They simply smoke when the parents aren't around. Is this what their parents were hoping to achieve?

In the end, when parents and others use punishment to teach children "right" from "wrong," the children's attention focuses on the external consequences of behavior—the rewards and punishment—not the intrinsic value of the behavior. The results can be very different than what you're wanting, and not necessarily healthy or life-serving. Kelly Bryson in *Don't Be Nice, Be Real* talks about an example where Pizza Hut offered children coupons for free pizza every time they finished a book. As a result of this incentive, the children searched for the thinnest books they could find. The reading was only being motivated by the reward of the pizza, not for the sake of reading itself. He suggests that the long-term consequence of this "reward" system is a bunch of kids who are overweight and hate to read.

Similarly, in the case of punishment, if the reason for not hitting is that a bigger person might hurt or punish you, the smart-thinking child (and all children are smart thinkers) would conclude that the thing to do is to fight when others can't see you. The child will learn that's it's OK to hit other children—as long as you're stronger or bigger or as long as you have words to justify what you've done: "He hit me first!" "I was teaching him a lesson." "I was showing him who was right!" Is this the outcome you're wanting? Probably not.

Acting Out of Empathy, Not Punishment

How can you know when you're using protective use of force? Here are the questions to ask yourself when considering it:

Are you feeling angry, indignant, or scared? Is criticism or judgment passing through your mind? How does your body feel?

If you're concerned for another's well being and danger is imminent, you may feel urgency and the rush of adrenaline. But this sensation has a different quality to it than the urgency that comes with anger or revenge. If you're not feeling centered or fully present in the moment, use the feelings and judgments coming up to help you focus. If you have time to self-empathize, see what needs are behind your feelings and desire to use force. Attempt to connect with the other person on an empathic level, then choose the course of action that will best serve your needs, including for care and protection of others. There are four specific criteria to consider when considering the use of force:

- Is there an imminent risk of harm?

- Have all options for dialogue been exhausted? (This does not mean that we are exhausted, but that the other party is not available for dialogue.)

- Is the intention behind using force to protect another from harm?

- Once immediate risk is prevented, are you willing to resume dialogue?

The simplest way to check about your motivation in using force is to ask yourself, "Is my heart open at the moment? Am I acting out of compassion?" If you perceive danger, dialogue is not possible, and you're acting "from the heart," you are most likely acting in alignment with protective use of force.

More Protective than a Gun: Protective Use of Force in Action

Suppose you are walking down the street and someone tries to attack you. Should you just try to talk with them compassionately, or should you physically protect yourself? There are numerous real stories where compassionate connection has been more effective than a black belt or a gun. The Quakers, who do not believe in carrying weapons, share many such stories. A woman in one of our workshops described the following experience.

One day Lauren, who was 19 years old and of limited means, was walking through a wealthy neighborhood. An unshaven young man dressed in tattered clothing grabbed her and said, "Give me your money or I'll kill you." Instead of freezing or panicking, she was able to focus intently on what was happening. She looked the man calmly in the eye. "I don't have any money," she said. "And why would you want to kill me?" He didn't answer. "Why would you want to kill me?" she asked again, with curiosity. The man, unable to respond to this question and clearly surprised by it, simply turned and left.

In a similar true story, an elderly woman was walking home with her groceries. She became aware that a man was following closely behind her, and sensed that he might be intending to rob her. Rather than trying to run away or confront him, she turned around and greeted him warmly. "I'm so glad you came along!" she said. "I'm really needing help with these bags." With that, she handed him one and they proceeded to walk back to her apartment. At the door, she took the bag from the man and thanked him, offering him some money for his help. The man refused and went on his way.

As these stories illustrate, empathic connection can be highly effective in the face of violence or the threat of it. Acting out of compassion even when their own safety was threatened, the two women were able to respond as full human beings, inspiring the potential assailants to act out of their own, fullest humanity. Consistent with this anecdotal evidence, studies have shown that those using nonviolent means in response to violence have a much higher success rate in surviving than those resorting to violence.

262 — Connecting across Differences

Many of us might find it difficult to respond with such equanimity as the people in the stories above, especially if new to practicing empathy. You will need to judge yourself what will best meet your needs, including self-care and care and concern for others.

No Contact, No Violence

A final alternative in Compassionate Communication that one can consider using is withdrawal, silence or non-communication. Sometimes a relationship may be so deteriorated, trust may be so low, and hope for improved relationship so minimal, that the best alternative may be to conserve energy and resources by not communicating and withdrawing. This, too, can be done in the interest of preserving and protecting life, health, and well being and can be considered a different form of protective use of force. Hanging the phone up on someone or not answering the door can certainly seem like aggressive acts. But if the person you're severing contact with is stalking you or threatening physical violence, such actions may in fact be life serving. Such acts, if done compassionately and without judgment, may meet your needs for safety and care.

Integration: Questions and Exercises to Explore Chapter 7

A. Choose a war or international conflict that you're familiar with, either from studying history or from your own experience and/or knowledge of current affairs. Then answer the following questions:

1. Would this incident or some aspect of it qualify as a protective use of force?

2. Why or why not? What other needs or intentions might have been at play other than serving life?

3. What, if anything, could a protective use of force have looked like in this situation, and how may the results have been different?

B. Read the interview with Marshall Rosenberg, "Beyond Good and Evil, Creating a Nonviolent World," that appears in the appendix of this book. Then answer the following questions:

1. How would you describe "restorative justice" based on Marshall's description of it?

2. Why is Marshall less concerned with physical acts of violence?

3. Why does Marshall oppose capital punishment? What protective use of force does he suggest instead?

4. How was a protective use of force used by people demonstrating? How did they change their message, and how was it ultimately effective?

5. According to Marshall, what was the cause of the 9/11 attacks on the World Trade Center? How could these attacks have been avoided? How does a lack of empathy lead to increasingly violent acts?

6. Did the U.S. attack on Iraq qualify as a protective use of force? Why or why not?

7. Marshall comments, "We are getting to a point where our best protection is to communicate with the people we're most afraid of. Nothing else will work." Based on the context for this statement in the interview, why does

Marshall think this is the case? Do you agree with him? Why or why not?

C.   Consider the following situations. What could the protective use of force look like in each context? (Remember that protective use of force is also about the intention of our actions—this cannot necessarily be seen). The first one has been done as an example:

1.   Situation: A child is playing near a hot stove.

Protective Force: Ask the child, would you like to play with some blocks in the other room with me?

2.   Situation: A child is running out of a yard and onto a street that has traffic.

Protective Force:

3.   Situation: One person is threatening to hit another.

Protective Force:

4.   Situation: You are a passenger in a car that is being driven at a speed you consider unsafe. You have already made several requests for the driver to drive more slowly.

Protective Force:

Chapter Eight:
Thanks, but No Thanks

"You're the best ever. No one tops you as a friend."

"Your gift was great! Perfect—and so thoughtful!"

"You're such a good boy when you pick up your toys. I love you so much when you're being good."

"I really admire you. You're so smart, ambitious, and popular. And you have such honesty, loyalty, and generosity. I wish I could be like you..."

Imagine the above was being said about you. How would you feel? Many people would say "super" or "great." Who wouldn't? After all, you're hearing words of gratitude and respect. What could be more delightful?

Yet these statements, while expressing pleasure, are all judgments—evaluating the listener and their behavior. While most of us prefer praise to blame, judgments, regardless if approval or disapproval, are forms of "right-wrong" thinking, on the "good-bad" continuum. Such thinking, regardless if "positive" or not, supports our valuing other's opinions in assessing our own behavior. And such statements provide little or no information about what we've actually done (or not) to contribute to another's well being.

Looking at the second appreciation above, for example, what does "great" mean? While stronger in degree than "nice" or "good," it doesn't tell us what exactly pleased the speaker. Did the receiver of the gift feel seen or appreciated? Will the gift contribute to ease, creativity, or fun? Without hearing a clear observation and the needs satisfied, it's impossible to know why the gift was so wonderful.

In the last example, a compliment, the speaker refers to the person being smart, ambitious, and popular; honesty and generosity are universal needs. But what actions contributed to these needs being met? When no clear observations are given, even "honesty" and "generosity" are judgments. We don't know what the speaker is seeing, so we're depending on their interpretation of what is honest and generous, or not.

While we may get some enjoyment out of them, compliments are all about approval. Different things contribute to different people feeling happy. When we try to please everyone, we are likely to please no one. Suppose you meet someone who will be happy if you sell illegal drugs for them? Cheat on a test? Have sex with them, whether or not this is something you want to do? On what basis will you decide what to do? If our only guide is whether or not it pleases other people, if we are automatically looking to the reactions of others as the basis for our choices, we can lose our sense of our selves and what meets our needs.

Gratitude for giving, when expressed judgment-free and in relation to needs met, is the great motivator and ultimate "power-fuel" of life. When we use gratitude in this way, and not as a strategy for other ends, such as acceptance or approval, there is great meaning and pleasure in giving to others. Giving is "reward" in itself. It is this kind of gratitude—how to hear it, give it, and, when necessary, say "no thanks" with integrity, that we explore in this chapter.

Exercise 1, Chapter 8: Grateful for Judgment?

Part One: Think of three compliments and/or expressions of gratitude that you recently heard:

1. _____

2. _____

3. _____

In each of these cases, were you completely clear about what actions you'd taken that pleased the speaker? In each statement, what judgment was stated and/or implicit? You can write about this in your journal if you like.

Part Two: Think back on your life to when you received positive feedback or compliments. Did this judgment influence you in any way? Did you make choices and/or change your behavior that was not in full integrity with your values?

EXAMPLE: My high school science teacher gave me a lot of compliments so I ended up taking more science classes, including advanced courses on anatomy, dissection, and histology. After about two years though, I realized I wasn't even that interested in science! I'd been taking all these classes just because I was hungry for appreciation and to be seen, and because someone was telling me I was "good" at it. I shared this with my science teacher and I could tell he was hurt and disappointed. I wish he'd given me a different kind of feedback, but I know he didn't know how.

The Power Juice of Gratitude

As we've explored throughout this book, needs are the compelling motivator of all life. When we contribute to another's well being, we're contributing to meeting their needs; this is why helping and supporting others is so satisfying. When we do things to enrich our own lives, we have an immediate feedback system, our feelings, that tells us whether or not we have succeeded in meeting our needs. But when we take actions to contribute to others, we have no way of knowing if we have, in fact, been successful—unless they tell us. Receiving gratitude is the only sure way we can "test" if our behavior (intentional or not) has been a contribution.

Sometimes, especially when people know each other well or where the context is clear, a simple "thank you" or a smile will suffice. But through receiving "needs-based" gratitude, we can better understand a person and what they most desire. We can know how our choices meet needs, and have clarity for decision-making now and in the future. Most gratitude leaves us in the dark. Giving "empathic gratitude," including observations, feelings and needs met, is a way of turning on the lights.

Exercise 2, Chapter 8: Giving—the Pleasure Principle

Think of something you did recently that you're confident contributed to the well being of another.

Part One: Thinking about this action, how do you feel? What sensations do you notice in your body? How does this sensation feel different than when you're angry or sad?

Part Two:

A. What was this action that you took? Describe it in one-two sentences.

B. What needs were you hoping to meet in taking this action?

C. Were these needs met? How do you know?

D. What observations and/or feedback do you have from/of the other person that confirms that you contributed to their well being?

E. What in their feedback and/or response leaves you unclear about whether their needs were fully met or not?

Part Three: Have you ever taken an action that you were sure would contribute to another only to find it wasn't being received as a contribution? This can especially be true for gifts. One time, for example, I made a treat for a friend only to find out that she was allergic to some of the ingredients. Think of an action that you took to help or contribute to another that did not, in fact, meet needs, all or in part. How did you know needs were not being met?

Use OFN Often

In giving life-enriching gratitude, and making clear how an action has contributed to another, we simply use the first three steps of the NVC model—Observations, Feelings, and Needs (OFN). Here's how these steps look when speaking about gratitude:

(O for Observation)
What did you specifically *observe* that you appreciated?

(F for Feelings)
What *feelings* did this behavior stimulate in you?

(N for Needs)
What *needs* in you did this behavior meet or support? What values do you hold that are consistent with this behavior?

These steps are probably familiar to you at this point in the book. But in expressing gratitude, there are a couple of points to keep in mind. Most often with gratitude, the feelings up will be "appreciative" or "grateful." But it also may be accurate to say that you're feeling warm, touched, or moved, or another feeling. You can check in with yourself to see what is actually "true" for you in the moment. In looking at the steps above, you also may have noticed that one step in the NVC model is missing: requests. Because gratitude is a celebration of needs satisfied, there usually is no need for a request—unless you want further connection and/or to know how your gratitude has been received.

Let's look now at a few examples of "low octane" gratitude (simply thanking someone) and then the same appreciation translated into high impact OFN:

THANKS: "Thanks for always being there for me. You're the best friend ever."
OFN: "I was really moved when you picked me up at 3 a.m. at the bus station last night. Your care and support really means a lot to me, especially given how ill my mom is."

THANKS: "Your present was terrific. I can't thank you enough."
OFN: "The gift certificate you gave me for that new restaurant is just what I needed! I wanted to celebrate finishing my thesis but my boyfriend and I are low on funds. Now we can celebrate in style! I'm really excited."

THANKS: "You are the best boy ever. I love you so much when you're being good."
OFN: "I'm really appreciating that you put your toys back on the shelf. Now there's some order and ease in walking around the room!"

THANKS: "I appreciate our friendship tremendously. You are someone I really admire—your honesty, loyalty, and selflessness."
OFN: "I'm really touched that you're willing to lend me some money, especially knowing you don't like the choice I'm making. I feel so supported and cared for, and trusted."

In looking at these examples, you may notice they don't follow very closely the "formal" NVC model. The word "needs" is not used and only in some cases will you find universal needs explicitly mentioned. Yet in each of these gratitudes, there is a clear observation given—be it about a gift certificate for dinner or being picked up at the bus station at 3 a.m. A feeling is mentioned—be it appreciation, excitement, or being moved. And, even when not named directly, a need is clearly met and alluded to—be it celebration, care, safety, ease or, support.

Try reading these out loud. Did you find the OFN gratitude more satisfying and meaningful? In the OFN versions, you may have enjoyed greater understanding and connection since you could clearly see the impact on the experience of the receiver, connect with what they're feeling, and appreciate the needs met. This gives a full picture, and shared understanding. You may have also been surprised by what you learned, since how our actions contribute to others can sometimes be in ways other than we expected. Regarding the gift certificate, for example, a student on a limited budget might certainly enjoy it. But hearing how the student just completed her thesis and was wanting to celebrate, adds a whole new level of richness and value to the gift.

Perhaps most importantly, OFN gratitude is always stated in the positive. When giving gratitude, of course, we're talking about fulfillment and "up" experiences. Yet ironically, when giving praise, people often use negatives. In the case of the boy picking up his toys, for example, the parent might say, "It's great you picked up your toys—it was so messy in here!" Or if someone turns down the music they were listening to, the person who'd requested it might say, "Thanks. That was really giving me a headache." In referring to what was wrong with the situation— "messy" and "headache"— we don't have the same clarity, satisfaction, or connection as in hearing about the needs met. Stating our needs in the positive— such as for order, safety, or peace—increases the chances that our needs will be understood, acted on, and celebrated with us. It also increases the chances of them being met in the future, since those around us know what we *want* (rather than what we don't).

Exercise 3, Chapter 8: Guessing the Need

Part One: Imagine that each of the following statements were made to you. What needs do you think might have been met for the speaker in each expression?

Statement	Possible Needs Met
A. "Thanks so much for your work on the carnival."	Support, creativity, caring
B. "Your presence at my birthday party meant a lot to me."	
C. "You've been a great friend."	
D. "I've always loved your spirit."	
E. "You do so much for me. Thanks a lot."	

Part Two: Think of three judgment-based gratitudes you recently made. Then translate them into OFN:

A. Judgment-based: _____

   OFN Gratitude: _____

B. Judgment-based: _____

   OFN Gratitude: _____

C. Judgment-based: _____

   OFN Gratitude: _____

Part Three: Take the following "negative" praise and put it in OFN "positive."

A. Negative Praise: "I'm so glad you cut your hair. It really didn't suit you."

   OFN "Positive" Praise: _____

B. Negative Praise: "My mom's really relieved that you left that dead-end job."

OFN "Positive" Praise: _____

C. Negative Praise: "This room looks a lot better since you painted it. It was really dreary before."

OFN "Positive" Praise: _____

What about Compliments? Aren't They Good?

> *"The way you played the piano was incredible! You're a fantastic musician."*

> *"You are SO smart. You can do anything."*

> *"You're the best athlete in the whole school. I wish I could score the way you do."*

Many people think that compliments such as these help others feel appreciated and can boost confidence and self-esteem. Yet if someone feels good hearing positive judgments, are they supposed to feel bad hearing the negative? Should we determine what we think of ourselves and our choices by relying on the judgment of others? Often, in giving compliments, we want connection and shared understanding. But judgment-based compliments, like appreciation of the same ilk, focuses attention on the *speaker's* opinions, not on what the recipient did or did not do. They provide little or no information about what exactly happened that impressed the speaker. For example, what does "perfectly" mean? "Perfect," like any judgment, can mean different things to different people.

As judgments, such appreciation also places the recipient in a no-man's-land of static, unmovable permanence. No one plays the piano "perfectly" at all times. No one knows everything. Often judgment-based compliments can leave us feeling uncomfortable because we suspect the speaker's opinion might be different if we'd been seen at another time. We don't want the responsibility of trying to live up to a global statement of praise. We are much more comfortable when we know what specifically we did, in the moment, that left a positive impression on the speaker.

As with gratitude, to create judgment-free compliments we can use the OFN model. What did we see or hear that contributed to our well being? How do we feel thinking about this action, and what needs were met? Again, a request will probably not be necessary, unless we're curious how it is for the other person to hear our appreciation and praise.

In giving OFN gratitude and compliments, you may wish to refer to it as simply "feedback" since, in doing so, we're consciously not engaging in evaluation or judgment. Rather, we're giving "back" about how others' words and actions have contributed to our lives. It is in this exchange (giving and receiving—and letting others know what we've received) that the real delight of contributing to others is experienced.

Exercise 4, Chapter 8: Live Feedback—in OFN

Part One: Look at the examples above of judgment-based compliments and translate into OFN. The first one has been done for you as an example.

Judgment: The way you played the piano was incredible! You're a fantastic musician.

OFN Feedback: I feel so energized hearing you play. I'm excited by the speed as well as the clarity and interpretation of the notes. I also love how you varied the theme at the end. Bravo!

A. Judgment: You are SO smart. You can do anything.

    OFN Feedback: _____

B. Judgment: You're the best athlete in the whole school. I wish I could score the way you do.

    OFN Feedback: _____

Part Two: Think of three compliments that you've given or might have given recently that involved judgment. Translate each of these "judgments" into OFN, to "live feedback:"

A. Judgment-based compliment: _____

    OFN Feedback: _____

B. Judgment-based compliment: _____

    OFN Feedback: _____

C. Judgment-based compliment: _____

    OFN Feedback: _____

Twice Judged—Not Praised?

There's another thing to watch out for in judgment-based compliments: the judgment can go both ways. As seen in the third example above, sometimes when a speaker is complimenting another, they're also directly or indirectly judging themselves, via comparison. When someone says, "I wish I were just like you…" or "I wish I had it that good…" or "I wish I had done that…" they're speaking about their *own* behavior and needs unmet by the choices they made. The speaker is simply using your performance (or at least their interpretation of it) as a mirror for what they see as their own deficiency. In such cases, how have your actions contributed to another? Is it really enjoyable to hear "inverted" compliments of this kind? Rather than being a celebration, such "compliments" are in fact coded messages about unmet needs.

Compliments as Strategy

In addition to being a form of self-criticism, compliments can also be used as a way of not being present, and attempting to influence the mood of another. Have you ever noticed that if you're feeling sad or discouraged, that some people will try to cheer you up using compliments? They might say, for example, "Don't let one low grade get you down—everyone knows how smart you are, that you're the best in the class!" How satisfying or consoling is a compliment like this? While you may hear the intention behind such a statement, potentially meeting your needs for understanding and support, such "compliments" can be a way of trying to negate and fix how you feel and rarely are effective in building confidence. Rather than being told that your feelings are unfounded, it is far more satisfying to have the gift of another person's presence and care.

Compliments—or Coercion?

Contributing to the well being of others is one of the most primary and satisfying human needs, fostering connection, trust, and meaning. There is a subtle but crucial distinction, however, between doing something because we want reward, approval, or payoff, or because we are responding to our own inner need to contribute to another's well being. Judgment-based compliments and appreciation can easily blur the lines. In the third appreciation at the start of this chapter, for example, is the little boy picking up his toys because he wants to please his mother and be considered "good"? Or perhaps he knows from experience that if he's not "good," what might happen—that he might be screamed at or punished? Or is he picking up his things because he understands how it contributes to his mother enjoying order, consideration, and safety? This goes back to the question we've considered before: What do we want people to do and why do we want them to do it? If we give judgment-based compliments and appreciation, the motivation for people's actions can easily come from fear or a desire for approval or reward—not contributing to others and enjoying shared values.

De-Strategizing Praise

What can you do if you suspect praise is being used for another purpose than appreciation and celebration? Regardless of the strategy—be it punishment and reward, comparison (negative self-judgment), or attempting to influence your feelings, you can go back to OFNR. You can offer empathy for needs unmet (in the case of negative self-judgment). You can check what needs the speaker is attempting to meet (if using reward and punishment or giving praise in an attempt to "cheer" you up). Sometimes you may wish to guess to yourself as a form of silent empathy what those needs might be. In doing so, you can gain clarity and understanding about what might be motivating the use of gratitude for other aims in the moment.

Any strategy we use is an attempt to meet needs. Many of us are so accustomed to using gratitude for other purposes that we may not be fully aware that we are doing so—and not understand how gratitude used in this way is not, in fact, a celebration. By giving an empathic response in these moments, we can renew connection and find out what needs, in fact, are being celebrated or mourned.

Exercise 5: Chapter 8: Praise as Celebration, Not Strategy

For each of the following statements where praise is being used as a strategy for something other than celebration, give an empathy guess to foster understanding and connection. The first has been done for you as an example.

A. I can never get things right. I wish I were good at things, the way you are.

Empathy: So hearing about my grade on the test, you're feeling discouraged? You'd also like to be effective in that way?

B. You're such a good girl that you did your homework. And now you can go out and play.

Empathy: _____

C. I wouldn't worry about losing that game. Everyone knows you're the best on the team, and that our school is number one.

Empathy: _____

D. You look so beautiful in that outfit. I wish I could wear dresses like that—they just don't suit me.

Empathy: _____

OFN Feedback in Action: Enriching Lives, Empowering Choices

Let's look at a real example of these principles in action.

About a month ago, I was observing a teacher and a teacher's aide in a small class for students having difficulties at school. I noticed both teachers frequently praising the students saying, for example, "great job," "super," "fine work." The head teacher told me the children were used to receiving a lot of criticism and very little praise. She wanted to build their self-confidence. I valued her intention and was moved by what I saw as her caring and dedication. I also was concerned that the way she was praising the students was encouraging them to rely on her judgments rather than developing their own internal sense of what they valued.

At one point the teacher's aide was telling a boy, John, that his poster showing how lungs work was, "great, just great." I asked him, "Is there something you like about your drawing?" He said "No." I then said that I liked the symmetry—the pair of lungs was balanced—and I asked the aide what she liked about it. We started talking about what we liked and soon John was pointing out what he appreciated about it too. If we had not had this conversation, I'm guessing John would have had no idea what he had done that was so "great." Now he could see for himself, and was in a position to believe it, and act on it again in the future. This was also far more effective in building up his self-confidence and trust.

Uh, Thanks!

Related to not expressing gratitude with clarity, in our culture we have learned to say "thank you" when we don't really mean it. From an early age, we're told to "say thank you!" when receiving a gift regardless if we like it or not. When young, I don't think I was asked even once if a gift or action had in fact met my needs. Instead, I was supposed to be "polite" and grateful for what I'd been given. I'm sure that demanding such "gratitude" was an effort towards creating connection between me and others, and to fostering appreciation. But how can we feel connected with another if there is not honesty and authenticity? How can we appreciate gifts and contributions if there is not integrity around how they have in fact contributed to us and our lives?

The Power of the Observation – A Story of Two Great Cellists

"My great wish was to hear Pablo Casals. One day my desire was almost fulfilled and I met him. But ironically, it was I who had to play. It was in the home of the Von Mendelssohns, a house filled with El Grecos, Rembrandts, and Stradivaris. Francesco von Mendelssohn, the son of the banker, who was a talented cellist, telephoned and asked if he could call for me; they had a guest in the house who would like to hear me play.

'Mr. Casals,' I was introduced to a little bald man with a pipe. He said that he was pleased to meet young musicians such as Serkin and me. Rudolf Serkin, who stood stiffly next to me, seemed , like myself, to be fighting his diffidence. Rudi had played before my arrival, and Casals now wanted to hear us together. Beethoven's D-Major Sonata was on the piano. 'Why don't you play it?' asked Casals. Both nervous and barely knowing each other, we gave a poor performance that terminated somewhere in the middle.

'Bravo! Bravo! Wonderful!' Casals applauded. Francesco brought the Schumann Cello Concerto, which Casals wanted to hear. I never played worse. Casals asked for Bach. Exasperated, I obliged with a performance matching the Beethoven and Schumann.

'Splendid! Magnifique!' said Casals, embracing me.

Bewildered, I left the house. I knew how badly I had played, but why did he, the master, have to praise and embrace me? This apparent insincerity pained me more than anything else.

The greater was my shame and delight when, a few years later, I met Casals in Paris. We had dinner together and played duets for two cellos, and I played for him until late at night. Spurred by his great warmth, and happy, I confessed what I had thought of his praising me in Berlin. He reacted with sudden anger. He rushed to the cello, 'Listen!' He played a phrase from the Beethoven sonata. 'Didn't you play this fingering? Ah, you did! It was novel to me...it was good...and here, didn't you attack that passage with up-bow, like this?' he demonstrated. He went through Schumann and Bach, always emphasizing all he liked that I had done. 'And for the rest,' he said passionately, "leave it to the ignorant and stupid who judge by counting only the faults. I can be grateful, and so must you be, for even one note, one wonderful phrase.' I left with the feeling of having been with a great artist and a friend."

—From *Cellist* by Gregor Piatigorsky

Even as adults, we sometimes receive a gift that is not consistent with our taste and values. Sometimes a person does something that was intended to meet a need, but did not land how it was intended. How do we respond in such situations? This topic generated a lively discussion in one of my classes recently. Should you lie and pretend to like the gift, return it, or pass it on to someone else? Should you not let someone know that their "help" was not helpful? Could you just express your appreciation of the beauty of the intention behind the gift? Each of these strategies, of course, could meet different needs—including for consideration and ease. But if we share with honesty and care how we're truly feeling and if our needs have been met or not, this in itself can be a contribution, fostering intimacy and understanding.

An incident several years ago illustrated this for me. At that time, I came across a doll that I thought my brother's daughter, my niece, would love. While I don't see them often because they live on the West Coast, I know he's a specialist in Russian Studies and this doll was dressed in a traditional Russian outfit. My niece was also of an age that I associated with liking dolls, and I thought this one was adorable. With eagerness and excitement, I bought the gift and sent it to her. Some time later I spoke to my brother.

"Did Monica get the doll? Did she like it?"

"Well, yes, she did get it. We appreciate the thought that went into it and why you thought of us. But actually Monica has never liked dolls. We gave it to someone who does. I hope you don't mind."

I felt sad and disappointed that my "perfect" present, which was purchased and sent with the intent of providing pleasure, did not reach its mark. In the discussion that ensued, though, I learned some new things about my niece, what kinds of things interested her and what didn't. I also appreciated my brother's honesty and trust; as a result, our relationship was strengthened as we got to know each other better. My disappointment shifted to feelings of connection and appreciation.

Polite or Real?

When people talk about being "polite," it's often in the context of not wanting to "hurt" others' feelings. But, in my experience, when there's authenticity, understanding and connection, feelings associated with unmet needs, such as hurt or anxiety, quickly shift. Regardless, do we want to "fake" our responses to people? Do we want to smile when disappointed, or say "yes" when we mean "no"? Or do we want authenticity and realness, including genuine connection and gratitude? If we're not fully aware of needs met and how our actions have contributed to others, how satisfying, in fact, is it to hear appreciation? It's almost like getting a huge box wrapped up with a bow only to find it's empty inside.

We all also desire, of course, to have care and consideration for others. When concerned about others' feelings or how your honesty may be received, it's helpful in such moments to be aware of all of what you're feeling and needing, and perhaps share it with others in all its complexity. If you're feeling hesitation and concern because you care about someone's feelings, for example, you can name this. You can then also share that you value honesty and integrity, and that you want authentic connection. You may also wish to mention all the needs met and unmet in their offering a gift or assistance, such as care and consideration, and to honor what you see as their intention. We can honor needs met while, at the same time, be honest and authentic.

Exercise 6, Chapter 8: "No Thanks" as a Gift

Part One: Think about a gift you received that you did not enjoy. What needs did the gift not meet for you? Did you tell the person how you felt? Why or why not?

Part Two: Imagine saying "no thanks" in OFN for each of the following situations. As part of your response, try expressing some gratitude for needs met and/or what you see as their intention in giving:

A. A friend offers to help you study for a test but you wouldn't find this helpful.

No: _____

B. Your professor invites you to do independent research with him because you did so well in his class, but you are not particularly interested in the type of research he does.

No: _____

C. A friend asks you out on a date but you're not interested in her in that way.

No: _____

The Appreciation Shortage

Appreciation, when genuine and needs-based, is like liquid gold. It energizes the whole giving and receiving system, facilitating needs being identified, celebrated, and met. Yet if gratitude is so energizing and satisfying, why is there not more of it in our lives? As the old saying goes, why is it that most people focus on the glass being half-empty rather than too full? Perhaps that's because when our needs are met, we feel contented, satisfied, and fulfilled. In contrast, when our needs are not met, this is so unpleasant we're more expressive and proactive. This can lead to not celebrating what we enjoy in life and focusing on what we're lacking.

Perhaps this explains the lack of appreciation most people seem to feel. Ask yourself: Do you feel appreciated for what you do at work, school, and at home? Do you feel that your effort to contribute to the well being of others is seen and recognized? Do you know if your contribution has hit the mark and been experienced as the contribution you intended it to be? Sadly, most people do not feel that their actions are seen, acknowledged, or appreciated. What a missed opportunity!

Enjoying Praise

Many of us have been told that we shouldn't let compliments "go to our head" or allow ourselves to become too impressed with ourselves. Some people find it very difficult to accept a compliment or an appreciation and will try to deny or minimize the speaker's words by saying things like "Oh, it's not really anything" or "I really did a terrible job; it's not good at all" or "I was just lucky." There can be various reasons why we find compliments difficult to hear. But much of it is probably related to compliments usually occurring as judgments. Being judged, even "positively," can lead us to also judge ourselves and/or compare ourselves to others, often negatively. As discussed above, when we judge positively and/or hear an affirming judgment from another, we can experience "performance anxiety," and the prospect of later disappointing the same critic.

For years, I struggled with receiving compliments and still can, if they're judgment-based. I also enjoy knowing, of course, how my actions have been a contribution. I've now learned to ask people for more information and I'm very much enjoying the results. Not only am I enjoying more appreciation, I've also come to appreciate how many needs a single act can contribute to meeting!

After a poetry reading recently, I tried this experiment. Each time a person thanked me for reading my work, I asked them to name one need met for them. Repeatedly, both the speakers and I were surprised by the results. Not one person named the same need and, after reflecting a moment, each seemed satisfied and surprised by what they'd identified. Thinking in this way gave them a whole new appreciation of the reading and what it meant to them.

Translating "bare bone" compliments into needs was like opening a fortune cookie!

In teaching and giving workshop presentations, I often ask the same question: "Would you be willing to tell me one thing that you found helpful about the talk?" The answer helps me to translate a general statement of appreciation into a more useful OFN statement. Similar to the poetry reading experiment above, it gives me numerous "fortune cookies" to open and learn from. And I also learn more about others—what they value most and makes them "tick."

I try to respond similarly when people tell me they don't like my presentations, although they are usually more specific in those instances anyway. The assumption seems to be that if we're giving people "positive" feedback, then no further details are necessary. The reality is that whatever another person has done, feedback with clear observations and needs met or unmet is extremely helpful. Often people talk about "constructive criticism" as that given with details and care. OFN feedback can be seen as "constructive compliments"—information that aids and supports you in further meeting your own needs and contributing to others. Hearing such "praise," you will find yourself wanting to give and receive gratitude more since it actually has content and is "positive" and "constructive" in the best way possible.

Exercise 7, Chapter 8: Naming the One Thing

Think about three things that you're really excited about and/ or enjoy. This could be a person you admire, a work of art or music you love, or an activity you like. For each thing, think of one aspect, in OFN, that is satisfying about it.

1. _____

2. _____

3. _____

Exploring the Appreciation Shortage

In order to understand more deeply the feelings and needs underlying the scarcity that most of us experience regarding appreciation, I asked some of my students to write an appreciation using *O, F,* and *N,* that they would love to have received from a particular person.

One student wrote that she would have loved her father to have given her this appreciation:

> When I saw that you had scored more goals than any other girl on the soccer team this year I was very happy and proud. I value you developing your skills to the best of your ability and I am grateful to have been a part of it by our practicing together. This met my need for seeing you develop and grow into a strong and healthy person. It also gave me hope that you might get a soccer scholarship to college which I desperately want for you because I believe college will enrich your life and I don't earn enough to pay your college expenses.

Another student wrote that he would have loved his former girl friend to have said this:

> When I think about the times you have held me in your arms and listened to me talk about my problems with my family and with school, I feel so warm, supported and cared for there are tears forming in my eyes. My needs for caring and love are well met when you do that.

I then asked them each to guess the needs the person was wanting to meet by *not* expressing appreciation in this way. The first student wrote:

I think he was afraid that if he told me how he felt that I wouldn't work so hard and do so well. I also know that talking about feelings is difficult for him. He might have been afraid that I wouldn't think he was strong and a 'real man.' I know he also had a lot of shame about not earning more money and perhaps he thought that talking about this would make him feel worse and make us think less of him.

The second student wrote the following:

I'm thinking that my girl friend didn't want to let me know how much my love meant to her because she was afraid it would threaten her independence and autonomy, which she also valued highly.

In these and other similar stories I hear, fear is the most common thief that keeps people from expressing the appreciation they feel. Perhaps they fear being vulnerable, or how others may judge them. Perhaps they fear even speaking about their feelings, or how their gratitude will be heard by the person receiving it. Many of us are simply not accustomed to talking about gratitude; we're accustomed instead to "tough love"—showing how we "care" through criticism and demands. Sometimes the only time we receive positive feedback, it comes with a disclaimer: "You're doing X better now, so now you need to do Y."

In addition to fear and lack of gratitude "fluency," people often think their needs are in competition. How can the father earning low wages express his appreciation of his daughter without revealing his sadness and regret about not earning the money he'd like? How can the girlfriend express her gratitude while also meeting her needs for dignity and autonomy? When we really understand them, however, needs, are never in conflict; there is never a scarcity in expressing what we most value in life. The strategies we choose to meet one set of needs can sometimes conflict with strategies to meet other needs. But the needs themselves are not in competition. The need for encouraging a child's athletic development, for example, is not in conflict with the need for seeing and valuing one's own contributions and integrity. The need for autonomy is not in conflict with the need for connection. You can't be connected to someone in a meaningful way if you are not given the space to be a separate person.

How do we navigate between what can seem competing feelings and needs, and name our gratitude, even if fearful? One way is to connect with all that we're feeling and needing in the moment and, if we wish, be transparent about the complexity of our needs. Before expressing our gratitude, we might want to mention other "layers" of feelings also alive. In the case of the soccer-playing daughter, for example, the father might have said:

> I feel sad thinking about how little I earn and my ability to pay for your education. And I'm also really proud of how well you play soccer, and how I've supported you in learning to play. I'm so happy and relieved to know this might help you financially to get through college.

The girlfriend might have said:

> You know I really value my autonomy, so I feel a bit self-conscious and even nervous saying this, but I want you to know how much I appreciate all your support. I don't think I've ever enjoyed so much tenderness and caring.

When being transparent in this way, you will probably want to make a connection request, asking how your words are "landing" or being heard. Especially when we're feeling vulnerable, connection and shared understanding are even more crucial.

When people give value-based appreciation or compliments without judgment involved, it is much easier to hear and digest what they are sharing with us. Rather than resorting to false humility or denial, we can join in their celebration of needs met, both for ourselves and for them. Ultimately, this becomes a celebration of shared values and mutual care.

Exercise 8, Chapter 8: Appreciation You Would Love to Have Received

A. Write an appreciation that you would love to have received from a particular person. Be sure to include:

   1. What specific behavior of yours did the person *observe* that they appreciated?

   2. What *feelings* did this behavior stimulate in them?

   3. What *needs* in them did your behavior meet or support? Which values did they hold that this behavior was consistent with?

B. Stop now and write the appreciation:

   Observation: _____

   Feelings: _____

   Needs: _____

C. Now that you have written your appreciation, consider what feelings and needs stopped or prevented this person from giving you this appreciation. Try to put yourself in this person's shoes.

Review the list of needs, if that would be helpful. You may wish to write about this in your journal.

Exercise 9, Chapter 8: Living with Gratitude

Try practicing empathic gratitude every day for a week. Each day, in the morning or evening, make a list of five things you are grateful for (observations) and then what you are feeling and needing.

Observation: Last night you drove us 50 miles to see a play that I wanted to see.
Feelings: Warm, tender, thankful
Needs: Support, fun, companionship, connection

Now you try it:

Observation:	Feelings:	Needs:
1.		
2.		
3.		
4.		
5.		

Appreciating Ourselves—and Our Choices

It's safe to say that most of us don't get the appreciation we'd like from others. But it's also likely that we don't give much appreciation to ourselves. Because we're the ones contributing to meeting our *own* needs, it can be easy to take our *own* efforts for granted. Yet it's only in expressing self-gratitude that we can become fully aware of what we're doing that's effective (or not) in meeting our needs. In this way, self-gratitude offers a highly enjoyable and stress-free way of engaging in "behavior modification"—focusing on and reinforcing the actions we find most life-serving and valuable. Of course, we're not always happy with the choices we make. But I have found that choices I regret in some ways (due to unmet needs) in other ways I now celebrate (due to needs met). Awareness of both helps me fully celebrate and act on my values; the gratitude really helps with self-acceptance, ease, and balance.

In many ways, for example, I am still sad that I left Ireland where I lived for years and still dearly love. In leaving, I did not meet needs for clarity, understanding, self-care, awareness, and choice (in how I made the decision to leave). No longer living there, I've often had needs "up" for beauty, meaning, connection with nature, and shared values (among many others). As a result of leaving, however, I have, over time, met needs for learning, self-development, and self-acceptance; I also met my partner, who contributes to meeting many needs in my life! I almost certainly would not have met her if I'd not returned to the United States.

I can now express gratitude to myself about this once painful choice I made. When I think about how I coped with leaving Ireland, a place I loved so much and which met so many needs for me, I am amazed by my passion for life, my determination, and resiliency. Having survived that, I am confident I can survive any thing! Expressing gratitude to myself in this way is very satisfying. It gives me appreciation, confidence, self-acceptance, and peace. Ultimately, both mourning needs unmet and celebrating needs met is about celebration: honoring what we most value in life and what contributes to our well being.

Exercise 10, Chapter 8: Celebration and Mourning

Choose a situation or decision that you in some ways regret but that you now also celebrate. Make two lists, one of needs unmet and the other of needs met. If the needs unmet are "up" for you,

292 — Connecting across Differences

empathize first with those. Then write a gratitude to yourself for the needs you have met in response to the same situation. How does it feel to express gratitude to yourself in this way?

Situation: (observation) _____

Needs not met: _____

Needs met: _____

Gratitude to yourself: _____

Living in Gratitude

The spirit of value-based compliments and appreciation and how it involves being fully ourselves, honoring others, and serving life, is summed up well by Marianne Williamson:

> Our deepest fear is not that we are inadequate. Our deepest fear is that we are powerful beyond measure. It is our light, not our darkness that most frightens us. We ask ourselves, Who am I to be brilliant, gorgeous, talented, fabulous? Actually, who are you *not* to be? You are a child of God. Your playing small does not serve the world. There is nothing enlightened about shrinking so that other people won't feel insecure around you. We are all meant to shine, as children do. We were born to make manifest the glory of God that is within us. It is not just in some of us; it is in everyone. And as we let our own light shine, we unconsciously give other people permission to do the same. As we are liberated from our own fear, our presence automatically liberates others.[5]

_____

[5] Marianne Williamson, *A Return To Love: Reflections on the Principles of A Course in Miracles*, Harper Collins, 1992. Chapter 7, Section 3

Needs expressed, especially in terms of appreciation, are difficult if not impossible (as long as genuine) to have too much of. I hope you will practice expressing appreciation every day, both appreciation of yourself and of others. It is one of the best ways to foster compassionate relationships and to become fully aware of what you most value and desire in life, and want to experience more.

Integration: Questions and Exercises to Further Explore Chapter 8

A fundamental assumption of NVC is that there is joy in giving. The following exercise is designed to help you explore that part of yourself which is nourished by giving to yourself and to others.

A. During the next week deliberately and consciously choose to do one thing for yourself that meets your needs, be it for fun, stimulation, rest, or self-care. It could be a material gift, such as an article of clothing, a concert ticket to your favorite band, a special food item or something else that you find pleasurable. Or it could be a non-material present, such as a leisurely bath, meeting up with a friend you've not seen for a while, taking time to read a book, or going for a jog, walk, or swim— something you would enjoy.

Before deciding on your "gift," you may wish to do a "needs inventory." Make a list of all the needs that are most "up" for you now. After empathizing with those needs, see what "gift" comes to mind to meet those needs. Then, after giving yourself this "gift," see how you're feeling. Are you feeling gratitude and appreciation? What needs have you met, such as self-care?

B. Now, do something for someone else that you are confident would give that person pleasure. Choose something that you would genuinely enjoy doing and/or giving and that would meet needs for you as well, such as needs for expression, meaning, authenticity, and integrity. This action could be as simple as calling a friend or family member you've not connected with recently, to let them know that you're thinking about them. Or it could involve helping a friend prepare for a test, assisting your parents with some yard work, or helping at a local food bank. How did you feel during and after doing this action? What needs seemed to be met by your actions? If you experienced negative feelings, what needs seemed to be unmet, including your own?

C. How did the two experiences compare? In what ways were the feelings stimulated similar or different? Which stimulated stronger feelings? Were the needs met or unmet similar or different?

PART TWO

PART TWO
INTRODUCTION

In the first part of this book, we looked at the basic principles of Nonviolent Communication and how practicing NVC can lead to a greater empathic connection with yourself and others. In understanding these principles, we've seen that the grand motivator of human behavior (and the behavior of all life) is the compelling desire to meet primary needs, be they physical (for the survival of our bodies) or non-physical (for the enrichment and development of our lives). No needs are "good" or "bad"; "right-wrong" thinking simply gets in the way of the understanding and connecting with what we and others most want and need to feel fulfilled.

In part two, you will find extensive, real-life dialogues showing NVC at work. Based on actual experiences, these dialogues illustrate how NVC can be used for self-empathy, empathizing with others, and mediating.

Keep in mind that in actual dialogues people may repeat themselves, go at a slower pace, and/or need more "rounds" of empathy than we include here. Also remember that empathy is not solely about words—silence, body gestures, and facial expressions all support empathic understanding.

CHAPTER NINE:
Putting it to Work at Home:
Practicing Self-Empathy

In this chapter we look at two, extended examples of self-empathy at work. In both we see how self-empathy can foster self-understanding and constructive change.

The A-Student Drop Out

Because of low grades, Joseph was facing suspension from school. During the fall, he spent more time partying than studying. In the spring, he started out studying more. But his parents often asked him to help with family problems and he felt he couldn't say no. That everyone "pull together" and support each other are strong values in his family.

In high school, Joseph had been on the honor role and he was the first in his family to attend college. Given how proud his parents were of him, he was even more embarrassed about the situation and felt he was letting his family down. He also felt it was impossible to tell them about it or ask for help.

Some of Joseph's Self-Judgments:

- "I can't believe I wasted so much time partying and drinking during the fall semester. I should never have pledged for a frat. I really dug myself into a hole. How could I have been so stupid!"

- "The teachers here are such assholes. They really pile on the work without caring about the students at all. They never think that we have a life outside school and other responsibilities."

- "I wonder if I am just not good enough to go to college. Maybe I just don't have the ability or discipline?"

- "Everyone else seems able to manage. What's the matter with me? I'm such an idiot!"

- "If I flunk out my parents will really be pissed at me. I won't be able to face them."

Shifting Self-Blame to Self-Compassion

Joseph can't help of course that he's feeling discouraged, concerned, and perhaps even scared. His college career will most likely impact his entire future. But rather than letting his inner critic tear himself to shreds, he has a choice. He can choose to empathize with what he is feeling and the two parts of himself that are involved in the present conflict. He can choose to show the compassion for himself that he would show to another person, a friend in a similar situation. It's important for Joseph to remember that he chose to do a lot of partying the first semester to meet important needs. If Joseph can learn to empathize with his choices and understand his needs, he will be more likely to make choices in the future that meet them more effectively.

Joseph and I had the following conversation:

"Joseph, when you chose to party in the fall, what needs were you attempting to meet?"
"Well, I wanted to relax, have fun, chill."
"So, you were interested in enjoying yourself, having a good time."

"Yes."

"And what else?"

"Well, I'd just broken up with my girlfriend from high school. I wanted someone else to go out with."

"So, you were looking for intimacy, a close, caring relationship?"

"Yes."

"And some expression of your sexuality, too, I imagine."

"Obviously."

"And what about the school-work. How were you feeling about that?"

"In high school you had to go to class. That isn't the case in college. So many of the classes were boring and when I didn't feel like going, I just didn't go."

"So you were enjoying having a choice, making your own decision whether to go or not, not because someone said you had to."

"Exactly. But when I did go, I felt lost because I'd missed so much material. It seemed I could never catch up. Eventually I just stopped going altogether."

"So it sounds like there were some important needs you were trying to meet in your first semester. You were interested in developing your social relationships, having fun and feeling comfortable in the things you did to occupy your time. These needs are ones we all have. Can you accept that and cut yourself a little slack for the choices you made?"

"I guess so."

"I'd like you to take a few minutes and really savor how much meeting those needs adds to the quality of your life. Imagine doing some of the activities you did this last fall, and see how you feel thinking about doing them—not how you're feeling now, judging them."

"OK."

(A few minutes later…)

"That part of you that chose to meet your needs for relationship, fun, choice, etc., I would like to call that part of you the "Chooser." And I'd like you to appreciate and even commend the Chooser for helping you get those needs met."

"Alright. I can do that. But I'm still pissed with myself for the choices I made!"

"OK, but now I'd also like you to empathize with the other part of yourself, the part that regrets the choices you made, that wishes you'd chosen differently. Let's call that part of yourself the 'Educator.'"

"OK."

"Your 'education department' has been saying some pretty harsh things about you. The director of your education department even called you 'stupid.' What do you think that's about?"

"Well, I'm just pissed and angry. Because of what I did last fall, I may have to drop out of school. That was so reckless! And now I may be suspended. What will my family think? And what a screw-up, to lose out on this chance to get a college degree. I wanted so much more for myself!"

"So the Educator wants you to have this opportunity for learning, for achieving some of your personal goals with respect to education?"

"Yes, and my whole family is counting on me to succeed, to help out the family when I get a job, so that my brothers and sisters can go to college."

"So the Educator cares about contributing to the well being of your entire family."

"Yes, and I was always one of the 'good students.' It's really hard to lose that image. I'd always been at the top of my class! I even got a scholarship."

"So you enjoy the recognition you've had for academic success?"

"Yeah, of course. Who wouldn't want to be successful, and seen as smart and hard-working?"

"Is that something you value, or is it something you're doing just because it makes other people happy?"

"Well, a little bit of both, I guess. I don't want to disappoint my parents, but I also value doing well in school. I like it when I am learning and feeling confident with the material. It just seems so much harder to do that now."

"So, at the moment you're feeling disappointed and discouraged, and maybe even confused because you want that feeling of accomplishment and learning again but aren't sure how to get it now?"

"Yes, I am. And I am also scared about flunking out. The stakes are too high. You know, I'm from a rough section of the city. I have a lot of friends who have dropped out, are using drugs and into other stuff. If I'm suspended for a semester and go back home, I'm scared that I'll never get back to college. There's no one else where I live into getting an education, thinking ahead. Going home is the worst thing I could do right now."

"Wow. That sounds terrifying. It's not just about your grades but your safety—and your entire future."

"Yeah, and I just don't know what will happen—and what I'll do if I end up in that situation."

For many of us, learning to be compassionate with ourselves is much harder than being compassionate with others. We may confuse self-pity with self-empathy. With some support, Joseph was able to have empathy both for the needs underlying his choices and for his longing to succeed in school. Empathizing with both parts of himself, the 'Chooser' and the 'Educator,' enabled him to move forward effectively.

Because Joseph also felt a strong need to complete his education, live in a safe environment, and continue learning and growing, he wanted very much to find strategies that would be more supportive of those needs being met, as well as enjoying choice, autonomy, and fun. We spent some time brainstorming alternatives and he took initiative in requesting the assistance of some friends, teachers and a counselor in identifying a number of other resources. Once Joseph was clearer about what his needs really were, including his needs for support, hope and inspiration, developing a flexible plan was not difficult.

Learning to Live with Who You Are

In the case of another student, Steve, his practicing self-empathy led to an increased acceptance not just of specific behavioral choices but of his whole identity and self. Steve was a 20-year old college junior whom I met at a meeting of Parents and Friends of Lesbians and Gays (PFLAG[6]). He came to PFLAG wanting help deciding what, if anything, to tell his parents about his being gay. Steve knew he was attracted to boys from when he was five years old. But he grew up hearing negative comments about gays at home, school and church and his parents were very conservative on matters of sexuality and sexual orientation. He hated lying to his family about who he was dating but was scared that if they found out, they might "kick him out of the family" or stop supporting him financially at school.

Steve was also stirred up because he had recently fallen in love with another student. Bill, Steve's lover, was a year older than Steve and was very comfortable being "out," including to his parents. Bill was critical of Steve for being "closeted." He wanted Steve to be accepting of himself and for their relationship to be celebrated, not hidden.

Steve and I had a long conversation. He started out describing the crux of his problem, and how critical he was feeling of himself:

---

[6] Visit www.pflag.org for more information

"I am so upset with myself for pretending to be someone I'm not. I want to tell the whole world about how happy I am with Bill and stop living a life of lies."

"So, what's stopping you?"

"I don't want to hurt my parents. I don't think they'll ever accept me as a gay person and I'm scared of losing their financial and emotional support. They might even try to turn my younger brother and sister against me thinking I'm a 'bad influence.' There's no way my being gay would be OK with them."

"Sounds like quite a dilemma. You must be feeling really torn, and stuck."

"Yes, talk about being stuck between a rock and a hard place. I am so upset about this and angry with myself. I'm just a coward—like a mouse! Yet knowing my parents, and especially their religious beliefs, there's no way they could deal with this."

"You're a coward, huh? Maybe you're being a little hard on yourself?"

"Yeah, maybe. But other people are out. Why can't I stand up?"

"Hmm. Look, I'd like to encourage your taking a more caring, compassionate approach to how you're thinking about yourself. Would you be willing to do some exploration around that?"

"OK, I'm willing to try…if it will help."

All right, this is what I would like you to do first. Tell me, one at a time, what some of your thoughts are, what you tell yourself, regarding this whole issue. Just let 'er rip!"

"That's easy. I'm telling myself lots of stuff: 'You're such a coward, pretending you're like everyone else when you're not. What are you afraid of? Don't you have any backbone? You're such a hypocrite! Bill's got strength. And here you are sleeping with him, going out on the town, and yet hiding what's between you, even to your own parents! That's not fair to him either.' I'm so happy with Bill—the happiest I've ever been. I don't want to hide that—from anyone."

(Steve pauses here.)

"Is that all?"

"No, I say other stuff to myself too. I ask myself, 'Why do you have to be gay anyway? Why can't you fit in like everyone else? Why do you want to break your parents' hearts—and go against everything you've been taught, at your church, and your entire community?' My parents will be so embarrassed. Being gay is seen as terrible, as disgusting. I hate myself. I don't deserve what I have—Bill or my family. And why would anyone want to be around me, so fake and dishonest?"

"OK. Now, for each one of those judgments I would like you to identify the feelings and needs behind it, and write down empathy guesses that you could use to empathize with yourself." (Steve's work is shown on the following page.)

After Steve completed this step, we continued.

"I notice that you have quite a range of feelings and needs associated with this issue. Part of you wants to be open and honest about who you are and share the excitement that you have in discovering and accepting yourself. Then there's another part of you that wants to protect yourself from those who you're certain won't be supportive. You also want to protect your parents. You're wanting consideration for them, knowing their beliefs and struggles."

"Yes, that's true. So, now what do I do?"

"What I would like you to do is to read each of the empathy guesses that you wrote, slowly, carefully, and thoughtfully. Don't go on to the next one until you have thought about and absorbed the preceding one. Just sit with what you've written. Enjoy the clarity and the positive qualities of all the needs you've identified. Cherish how those needs contribute to enriching your life.

With the 'honesty,' for example, reflect on how much you value honesty in your relationships. Remember how much you appreciate the trust that often develops when people are completely honest. Recall a time of honesty and how much you value the ease of

STATEMENT	FEELINGS	NEEDS	EMPATHY GUESS
"You're such a coward, pretending you're like everyone else when you're not. What are you afraid of?"	Pain Frustration Fear	Honesty, Openness Ease (relief from stress) Safety	Are you in pain because you're wanting to be open and honest? Are you frustrated because you so much want things to be easier for you? Are you afraid for your safety?
"Why can't you be like Bill? He's got strength. Something you will never have."	Pain Hurt Sad	Efficacy Power Choice	Are you in pain and hurting because you want efficacy and power? Is it that you are sad because you so much want to have more choice in your life?
"Why do you have to be gay anyway? Why can't you fit in like everyone else? Why do you want to break your parents' hearts?"	Sad Anxious Distressed	Acceptance Caring Support	Are you sad and anxious because you crave acceptance and caring? Are you in a state of distress because of your need for support?
"Being gay is really an awful, disgusting way to be. Stop being gay!"	Anguish Repulsion	Acceptance Understan-ding	Are you feeling anguish and repulsion because of a big need for acceptance and understanding?
"I hate myself. I don't deserve to live."	Desperatio-n Terror	Self-accept-ance Hope	Are you feeling desperate and terrified because you yearn for self-acceptance and hope?

communicating when honesty is just a 'given.' Slowly review each empathy guess, taking the time to really absorb the meaning and beauty of each one. I want you to have compassion both for the part of you that craves openness and honesty and the part that cherishes safety, support, and caring for others."

"Is that all there is?"

"Well, it's a step. Practice it regularly. It does help. And if you hate writing things down, shout or speak them aloud. What am I thinking now? What am I feeling? What am I needing? Take your time. Really appreciate what you want, what it means to you, and how it contributes to your life."

"Yes, thanks. I'm getting a sense of that. I feel a little less stressed."

"Good. I'm glad."

"At first, it may seem strange, but it is very empowering. The more connected you become to your needs, the more you'll be able to develop ways to satisfy them. As you know, needs are generalized wants. They are not tied to a specific time, place, person, or manner for fulfillment."

Self-empathy often involves connecting with at least two different sets of feelings and needs, each part oriented towards a particular thought, judgment, or strategy. And if those strategies are in opposition to each other (such as being "out" and avoiding rejection) it can feel as if we're in an impossible bind. To get free of this strait jacket, we need to temporarily put strategies aside and focus on the underlying needs we're attempting to meet. Once fully aware of what we're feeling and needing, it becomes ten-fold easier to discover numerous strategies that we'd not seen before, to be at peace with the decisions we've made, and discover strategies that can best meet all our needs. When we are able to empathize with our "dark" side, the part of us that does things we don't agree with, aren't proud of, or don't enjoy, we become free from guilt and shame and can fully consider the choices available to us.

CHAPTER TEN
Sharing the Wealth:
Empathizing with Others

In this chapter, we will look at a tense situation between a student and a teacher and how practicing empathy led to greater understanding and a mutually satisfying solution.

Putting Empathy to the Test

One day at my office a student stopped by, Samantha, who'd been in one of my classes where we studied NVC. I could tell from her expression she was excited. Throwing her backpack down on one of the chairs, she told me, "Hey, teach, thanks for all that Compassionate Communication stuff. I just spoke with my professor. NVC got me an extension on my final paper. It worked!" Hearing this, I was also curious if Samantha had enjoyed the quality of communication with the professor. She assured me that she had.

Samantha went on to explain that two ten page papers were required for an English class she was taking this term. All went well with the first paper but a week before the second paper was due, her father became ill and she went home to take care of her brother and sister while her mother was at the hospital. She returned to school the day before the paper was due. By the time she got back, there was no way she could get it done on time. She decided to talk with the professor about it.

In the past, Samantha found professors unwilling to make exceptions; she in turn found herself becoming angry and resentful, and judging them. Seeing that this resulted in the professors' hardening their position, this time she wanted to be open to what the professor was wanting and to hear her concerns.

The first thing Samantha did was to practice self-empathy. She focused on her own feelings and needs, and got some understanding of what was going on for herself before approaching the professor. She also got some empathy from a friend. As Samantha put it, "I tried to have my empathy tank on 'full.'" In doing so, she appreciated just how rough this semester had been for her. Her father's illness had really added a lot of stress to her life. "When I looked at the needs list that you'd given us, the ones that I could really relate to were ease, comfort and relief. Boy, did I want that! Secondly, I wanted support and assistance from the instructor in order to have the time I needed to write the paper. I wanted some understanding." She also became aware that she wanted the professor to see that she was "genuinely making an effort and not just making excuses." She was wanting some understanding, and to be seen. This awareness ultimately informed what she decided to share with the professor.

She also imagined what the professor's needs might be, and guessed that the professor "might want some understanding and appreciation for her efforts with the class, and her intention in keeping to deadlines." She reminded herself that the professor was a person with feelings and needs, too. This, of course, was "a tall order" for her. As she admitted:

> In truth, I'm so used to thinking of teachers as 'good guys' or 'bad guys,' those who are nice to students and those who aren't, that I just don't think of them as having feelings and needs the way my friends and I do. In fact, I was just sort of forcing myself to act like I believed this in order to give it a chance, and just to see how it worked.

With this leap of faith, she knocked on the prof's door, entered the office and started talking.

At first, when Samantha said she wanted an extension, the professor was curt. She reminded Samantha of her policy: All late papers lose a letter grade. At this point, Samantha was a little upset:

I was thinking, 'Boy, is she rigid! What's the point of talking to her? She's not going to listen.' Then I gave myself some empathy, and remembered how much I wanted support and understanding. I thought about what you said about feelings and needs and decided to give it another chance. I figured I didn't have anything to lose. What, I wondered, might be her feelings and needs right now? I guessed, 'Are you annoyed because you want respect for the policies you set up for the class?' This seemed to be dead on. She told me, 'Yes, and I want to be fair to all students. If I gave you an extension, I would have to do that for everyone.'

Samantha did not especially enjoy this last point:

Hearing this, I was thinking, 'But I'm not everyone! I'm just me!' And then I remembered what you said about trying to give at least three rounds of empathy before expressing how you feel. So I tried again, 'Are you saying you want to treat everyone fairly? That equality and fairness are important to you?' Again, this seemed to be exactly on target. 'Absolutely,' she told me. 'And besides, I don't think I'd really be doing you a favor by letting you hand in work late. When you get out in the real world, you can lose your job over deadlines. That's more important than a grade.'

Samantha was amazed hearing this. "I'd never thought of that before. It actually made sense. She wasn't just being rigid—she was concerned about my well being and my success. She felt responsible for that." At this point, Samantha noted it was actually getting easier to empathize with the teacher.

Feeling confident about how things were going, Samantha decided to give one more round of empathy:

The next thing I said was, 'So you want me to honor agreements and consider it a big thing to miss a deadline?' The professor also agreed with that. She told me that helping me to understand the consequences of my choices, regardless of the reason, was part of her job, too. So then I guessed, 'So you want me to take responsibility for my choices? You see that as part of your teaching and my learning in the course?' And again she agreed.

Again, Samantha found this information surprising:

I don't know if I agree with her strategy of having a lateness penalty, but I was bowled over to discover there was a positive motive behind her behavior. I mean, she really seemed sincere about this and caring. She takes her job pretty seriously! At this point, I thought I understood much better where she was coming from. She values responsibility and fairness and also students' taking responsibility for their actions.

At first, Samantha found this hard to hear because she didn't think she had a choice. Going home, given the circumstances, was something she *had* to do. "My mother told me she needed me and that was that. They have done so much for me—how could I let them down when they needed me? It just didn't seem possible." But after talking with the instructor, Samantha realized that she did have a choice:

My family really needed me and it didn't seem like I could resist. But it wasn't like someone had put a gun to my head. Even though my family and I would have felt a lot of distress, I could have said 'no.' But in our family, when one member is needing help, we all want to help out. I value that strong support. I can count on that too and it's

something I don't want to change about them or me—
even if this choice did wind up costing me a grade on my
paper.

Realizing she had a choice, Samantha also realized she wasn't sorry
that she'd gone and helped out. Clearly, her choice met some
important needs for her.

Feeling confident that she'd fully heard the teacher, Samantha
checked with the prof one last time to see if there was anything
else she wanted to add. Samantha commented, "I asked this because
I remembered what you said, teach, about continuing to give
empathy until the person says they are 'complete.'" Hearing from
the prof that she had nothing else to add, Samantha asked if she'd
be willing to hear where she was coming from and the professor
agreed. Samantha was really pleased. "I never thought she'd care
about my view, but she really seemed a lot more relaxed and open
after I'd heard her out." In giving her perspective, Samantha wanted
to emphasize that she accepted responsibility for her choice and
the consequences. "I told her how I respected her values, which
were not really different from my own."

After speaking about how she also values responsibility and
fairness, Samantha continued by explaining how her circumstances
were, she believed, quite different from other students:

> My father had a heart attack last week and my mother
> needed me to watch my younger brother and sister while
> she was at the hospital with my dad. I chose to help my
> family because they really needed my support last week.
> My brother and sister were very upset about my parents
> being gone and I was able to comfort them in a way no
> one else could. I don't regret choosing to help my family
> as I did and I was prepared for the lower grade, if necessary.
> But I'm hoping you can understand the choice I made

and that you might be open to my handing the paper in late, given the circumstances.

At this point, seeing that the professor seemed to understand Samantha's point, Samantha made a request. She asked if the professor would be willing to let her hand in her paper five days late without penalty. Samantha concluded by saying that she would really appreciate her support on this. At first the professor paused and said she needed to think about it:

> She said that she likes to be consistent, to treat everyone the same, and not diverge from policies that she spells out. But then, after thinking for a moment, she agreed that she could see that my circumstances were unusual and that it sounded as if I really did want to follow them as best I could. And then she told me that if I got the paper to her by next Thursday, that she'd accept it without a late penalty! I told her how excited and relieved I was, and grateful I was for her understanding.

Samantha then shared with the professor how much she cares about both her education and her family and that it hasn't been easy to juggle both.

Samantha concluded her story by expressing her gratitude to me, for what she'd learned about communicating with others. "So you see I am really grateful to you and what you taught me. It really helped in getting the extension I wanted. This course and this empathic listening has been the best yet—it's even helping me with other professors!"

Samantha was clearly excited about the extension but I was wondering if she'd other needs met communicating in this way. She confirmed that she had:

I could see her more as a person after we talked. Sometimes a person will do what you want but they do it begrudgingly, with a patronizing manner. If she'd talked to me with hostility and suspicion, as in 'What are you trying to pull?' or 'Do you think I really believe that story?' I would have been glad to get the extension but I would've had a bad feeling. But I could also see that her heart was in the right place. She was trying to hear me and my concerns and figure out a way of dealing with them. I really felt like I was closer to her when we were done talking because we both disclosed what was going on inside of us, and what mattered.

Samantha and I concluded our conversation by my sharing how happy I was for her and grateful that she'd told me about her success.

No Guarantees

Connecting with another person does not guarantee you'll get what you want. In fact, going into a conversation with the goal of getting "your way" is contrary to the spirit of Nonviolent Communication. The idea is to create a quality of connection where both parties care about the needs and concerns of the other. Not surprisingly, when the teacher felt heard, she was able to hear and care about Samantha's needs.

In Samantha's case, her willingness to view her teacher as a person with feelings and needs, not just as an authority figure, was central to the two of them hearing each other. When one person has the power to make decisions impacting another, it's easy for the person on the "lower rung" to believe their needs don't matter and not "dog" for them. In such situations Nonviolent Communication can be especially liberating and empowering, giving us the tools to see that the needs of both parties are held with mutuality, balance, and care.

CHAPTER ELEVEN
Helping Others to Live with Each Other

Using Nonviolent Communication in mediation is not very different from using NVC to empathize with others or yourself. The same steps are involved: observation, feelings, needs, and requests and working to see that each party hears the other. In this chapter, we will see how a resident assistant successfully mediates a conflict between roommates using these skills.

Meredith, the Mediator

My name is Meredith. I'm a resident assistant in Smith Hall dorm where most of the students are freshmen. When I was a freshman, I found adjusting to college pretty difficult and my "R.A." was a big help. I thought I'd enjoy doing the same for others and, for the most part, that's true. But sometimes situations come up that are pretty challenging.

One thing that's been a big help is learning about empathy and Compassionate Communication. I really use it a lot. It helps me listen, and not give advice and reassurance as much as I used to. I know now that simply being with a person, and hearing what's going on for them, can help the most.

A month ago, a conflict arose in my dorm where my NVC skills really came in useful. I'm also glad I'd taken courses on diversity issues. That helped me understand how different people can see different things in the same situation.

Here's what happened. Shakira, who is African-American, was living with Kelsey who is European-American. I knew they weren't good friends, but it seemed they were happy enough as roommates. But about a month ago, they had a big blow-up—something to do with Kelsey having friends in the room when Shakira was trying to

318 — Connecting across Differences

sleep. They both requested a room change saying they couldn't live with each other anymore. Unfortunately, at this point in the year, it's almost impossible to get a room change. So, I thought maybe I could use my compassionate listening skills to help them work it out.

I decided to listen to each of them separately first, giving them empathy for what they were going through. What I've read, and found true in my own experience, is that when people feel really heard and that their needs matter, they're much more open to hearing what's up for someone else. I figured that if that went well, I'd see if they were open to sitting down and talking with each other.

Before talking with either of them, I started first with self-empathy. I know that in order to be sensitive to others and their needs, I must be aware of what's going on inside myself. I realized I was feeling pretty nervous because I was really wanting to help both of them and wasn't sure I had enough skill to pull it off. I care about both Kelsey and Shakira and have never had a problem getting along with either of them. I also became aware of feeling sad that they're fighting so much. It reminds me of conflicts I've had with my sister. To better understand how I was feeling about that and how it reminded me of the situation in the dorm, I even did some journaling. I wrote freely from my gut, just getting it out of my system how much I value connection in personal relationships and how sad I felt about the conflicts at home. I just stayed with this sadness for a while and became aware of how much I want harmony with those I know.

When I got to talking with Shakira and Kelsey, I was really glad I'd done all this preparation. It definitely helped me stay in the present with what was going on with them. When some of my own needs were stimulated by what they were saying, I would just notice that about myself and then go back to paying attention to what was on the table with them.

I started with Kelsey. The conversation went something like this, with Kelsey describing the situation from her perspective and then my responding.

One Side of the Coin

"My roommate, Shakira, is impossible. She doesn't want to be friends with me, doesn't like my friends, and has a fit every time I bring my friends to the room. For me, college is more than just about studying. I hate it that she gives me a tough time when my friends are over and want to have some fun."

"Are you frustrated because you'd really like Shakira's co-operation when you're wanting to have fun?"

"Absolutely. Last Thursday night, for example, three of my friends came over after we finished barhopping. We were just talking and hanging out. She gave us these dirty looks and the silent treatment, and acted like we were public enemy number one."

"Are you upset because you want her to accept your friends' presence in a positive, or at least neutral, way?"

"Well, yes. And can't she see that we're not trying to disturb her? We were just having a little fun. We weren't hurting anyone."

"So, you'd like her to understand your intentions, and that you want to be considerate of her too?"

"Yes. It's OK with me if she brings her friends over here, but she never does. I think she just wants to spoil things for me since she's so miserable herself."

"Are you concerned because you want to see her enjoying herself too?"

"Yeah, well sure, I do think it would be good for her to relax a little and have some fun. College isn't just about studying. I want a life, and I think she'd be happier if she chilled out a bit too. We may not ever be best friends, but I do want to work things out."

"Is there anything else you'd like to say about what's going on?"

"Well, yes. I don't think our racial differences—she's African-American and I'm white—has anything to do with what's happening, but sometimes she brings it up as if it does. And I find that pretty irritating and insulting. I'm not a racist. Regardless of her background, I'd still want to bring my friends over and have some say and choice in what I do in my room. We do share it—it's not just her room. She seems to forget that sometimes."

'So it's important for you to have some choice and autonomy and be seen as an individual. You really want some understanding for what your concerns are?"

"Yes. I was brought up to treat everyone fairly and I think I'm pretty color-blind. I'm certainly not racist, which is what she's suggesting."

"Is it important to you that people be accepted and appreciated for who they are, regardless of their background?"

"Yes, exactly. Of course I do. That's only fair. I think most people would want that."

"And you want to be seen for that intent?"

"Yes, of course. I feel hurt that she thinks I'm racist. That has nothing to do with this situation, and I wish she'd see that."

Equal Air Time

Next, I went to talk to with Shakira. Similar to Kelsey, she started out describing the situation from her point of view and I offered her empathy.

"That girl is driving me nuts. Kelsey and her friends act like they own the place. Any time of the day or night they come bouncing into the room, never asking permission or anything. It never occurs to her that I might want some time to study or just a place to be by myself and think a bit. There are loads of places they can hang out and party. But our room is the only place where I can go for a while and chill out, alone."

"So are you upset because you want some consideration for your desire to have rest and quiet sometimes?"

"Exactly. The other night was the last straw. I had just gotten to sleep because I was trying like mad to get this paper done for class the next day. I was almost done and decided to go to bed and get up early to finish it. I was really tired and couldn't concentrate any more. Then Kelsey and her friends come rolling in and forget about sleeping! I was so pissed and stressed. I didn't say anything because I was brought up not to 'make waves.' And I also figured, what good would it do? She doesn't care anyway. I finished the paper in the morning, but the paper I turned in was not what it could have been—thanks to Kelsey and her friends."

"So you're really wanting some awareness of how your experience is affected by Kelsey's choices? You want Kelsey to care about your needs too?"

"Yes. By this age she should know better and not be so selfish. She should have more consideration and respect, and be sensitive to that when the lights are out and I'm in bed, I'm obviously trying to sleep. I'd never come in, turn on the lights, and throw a party if she were in bed! That's basic respect. And she doesn't have any."

"You'd really like her to figure out that you're wanting to rest and support you in that by keeping it quiet in the room?"

"Yes. I mean, she's so oblivious to her racial privilege, I really have to bite my tongue sometimes. Just partying the way she does! I have to work extra hard because people are expecting me to fail— they don't give me the benefit of the doubt. If she keeps me up and I turn in something below average, then it's just what people expect—it's just confirming their stereotypes. If she turns in something bad because she's out partying, it's OK because they'll be like, 'She's just having an off day—we know she can do it.' I tried to explain this to her once but she's clueless. She's told me on more than once that she thinks she's color-blind. Right! Like she thinks I'm green or something? She just hasn't noticed that I happen to be Black? Yeah, right!"

"Do you want some acknowledgment from Kelsey that racial differences exist and influence the choices you make and the opportunities you both have?"

"Yes! This color-blind stuff only works if you're the one who's privileged. If you're not White, you learn real quickly that you can't be color-blind because other people sure won't be. And it's not that I think it's only about racism. There are a lot of other differences because of who we are and where we come from, good stuff, like music and culture. If you're color-blind, you don't see that either. Those differences are important too. Why hide it or deny it?"

"Your race and cultural heritage are a big part of who you are and you want to be seen for that, and it to be celebrated?"

"Yeah, of course. I'm very proud of my community and my family. We all stick together and really help each other. I've had so many racist incidents in my life—I don't even want to think about it. It's because of my family and my community that I get through. I'm proud to be who I am, and my determination."

"And you want to be seen for who you are? And you'd like some awareness on her part, and some understanding about how race is impacting your relationship?"

"Absolutely. Race is a big thing in my life. And it is in hers, too. She just doesn't see it. She likes to think that color has nothing to do with our relationship, with the assumptions she makes and how she acts. I'd love to have her and her friends turn Black for a week and see how that affects them! See how they get followed in the stores, see how teachers think they can't do anything right! Then I'd like to see her say that a person's race doesn't mean anything today—including in this room!"

"So you really want some understanding about how your experiences are different?"

"Yes. My friends don't want to come over here because it's just too uncomfortable. They don't want to be stared at and treated like talking to them is part of a social experiment. We just want to chill, and we find better places to do it than here."

"You're really wanting some comfort and acceptance?"

"Yes. I mean, I kind of know what she's feeling. I used to feel really uncomfortable being the only Black student in a room, but coming here I had to get used to it because most of the students are White. I can understand she feels weird when she's the only White person in the room. But if she'd just settle in, and try to get to know me and my friends, she'd discover that we're not so bad. She just has to get over her discomfort, and see us like anyone else."

"So, you're really wanting some connection with her, and more comfort between her and your friends."

"Yes, exactly. I don't hang out a lot with her friends. But at least I try."

"And you'd like the same consideration and effort?"

"Yeah, of course. I don't think that's asking too much."

Bringing It All Together

"I thought this part went really well and I was excited about having Shakira and Kelsey hear each other. I was really hopeful about helping them and really scared, too, because I certainly didn't want to make the situation worse than it was. I knew it would be important for them not to feel criticized or judged as 'wrong' by the other person. I asked each of them if they'd be willing to talk to each other with my support as a mediator. They both said "yes" and we set a time."

During the mediation, at times it was hard because there was a big difference between what each of them said and what the other heard. I really had to slow things down, asking them to pause and to translate judgments into what each was feeling and needing. It was a real challenge to get them away from "I'm right, you're wrong."

"To start, I explained I was going to listen to what was up for each of them in the situation. Then, when all three of us seemed clear about everyone's needs, we would see what solutions might work. They agreed with this plan. Below are some of the hard spots in our conversation that I later wrote down."

Me: Shakira, can you tell Kelsey what it is you want from her, how you want her to behave?

Shakira: Sure. I want her to stop acting like she owns the place. We share this room together—and she seems to forget that.

Me: 'Acting like she owns the place' is a 'don't want.' It's hard for people to do a 'don't.' Can you tell her what you do want?

Shakira: Hmm. That's harder. Well, I guess I want her to be more considerate and respectful of me and my feelings. If I'm already there when she comes in and I'm reading, resting, studying, or sleeping or whatever, I don't want her having a party. She at least could check with me first, and not assume it's OK.

Me: OK. That's clearer. Kelsey, would you be willing to say back what Shakira wants in this situation? I want to make sure we're all hearing each other.

Kelsey: Sure. She wants to have everything her way. She doesn't think I have any rights to the room. Whatever she's doing, I'm supposed to work around it—even if there's no where else to go.

Me: OK. Thanks. I'm glad you told me what you heard. I heard something very different from Shakira. I heard her say she wants respect and consideration. Is that right Shakira?

Shakira: Yes.

Me: Kelsey, I know it may be hard, but I would really appreciate if you would say back what it is that Shakira wants. Would you be willing?

Kelsey: (After a very long pause.) She says she wants respect and consideration.

Me: Good. Thanks. Shakira, what else are you wanting from Kelsey?

Shakira: I want her to quit pretending that somehow we're the same race and that race doesn't make a difference. It makes a difference in my life and it makes a difference in her life, she just doesn't realize it.

Me: So you want some understanding that your experiences are very different from hers and that you have a lot of pain about racism that you've experienced?

Shakira: (Softly.) Yes. I would.

Me: And I am wondering if you also want to be seen as a person who is proud to be a Black female and proud of her accomplishments?

Shakira: Yes, that too.

Me: Kelsey, would you be willing to say what you just heard Shakira say now?

Kelsey: Yes. She wants to blame everything on race. She thinks only Black people suffer from racism.

Me: Thanks, Kelsey. Shakira, does that work for you? I thought I heard it differently. I heard you wanting understanding that in your experience race has made a big difference in your life. I heard you say you wanted to be seen as struggling with racism, but also proud of who you are and your accomplishments. Is that it?

Shakira: Yes.

Me: Kelsey, Would you be willing to let us know what you heard?

Kelsey: Shakira would like me to understand that race has made a big difference in her life, but she is proud to be a Black woman.

Me: Shakira, does that capture it?

Shakira: Yes.

In another part of the conversation I tried to get Kelsey to explain what it was she wanted from Shakira. That exchange went something like this:

Me: Kelsey, what is it that you want from Shakira?
Kelsey: Well, I want her not to scare my friends away when they
          come to the room.
Me: Can you put that into a positive statement – what you *do*
          want?"
Kelsey: (Pause.) I want her to be accepting and welcoming to
          my friends when they come to the room.
Me: Shakira, can you say what Kelsey wants?
Shakira: She says she wants me to act like I'm best friends with
          her friends. I am not a phony. I just won't do that.
Me: Thanks, Shakira, for telling me what you heard. I heard
          something different. I heard her say she wanted you to
          be accepting and welcoming towards her friends when
          they come to the room. Is that it, Kelsey?
Kelsey: Yes.
Me: Shakira, can you say what it is that Kelsey wants?
Shakira: Yes, she wants me to be accepting and welcoming to her
          friends. But I am not going to be welcoming to anyone
          at midnight when I have a paper due the next day!! What
          about what I want?
Me: Is this about the respect and consideration you want?
Shakira: Yes.

The conversation went on like this for about an hour. We got
pretty clear about both of their needs for consideration, respect,
acceptance, and inclusion of friends. They also agreed that they
had different needs with respect to quiet and talked about ways to
accommodate those differences, such as using the lounge area after
11 p.m.

The part of the conversation having to do with their different
experiences with racism was very challenging. At one point, the
conversation went something like this:

Shakira: I can't stand the way Kelsey says she's color-blind and that race isn't important. Race is a really big deal in my life and if she were Black, it would be in hers, too.

Me: So you want some understanding that your experience with race may be different from hers?

Shakira: Yes.

Me: Kelsey, can you say back what Shakira wants on this issue?

Kelsey: She thinks that only Black people have problems, that my life is so easy because I'm White. And that's just not true.

Me: Is that what you want Shakira?

Shakira: No. I just want you to understand that my life has been different from yours with respect to the race issue. You haven't experienced the discrimination that I experience every day. No one follows you around in stores or asks if you use Food Stamps because of the color of your skin. I would love for you to be willing to learn about this. Or at least accept that you have a lot of advantages because of your whiteness.

Kelsey: You want me to understand that it does make a difference that you're Black and I'm White?

Shakira: Yes. Because White people are the ones doing most of the hiring, teaching, and the running of businesses, the courts, newspapers and TV stations, I have to learn a lot about how White people see the world if I want to survive. I'd like you to put some effort into knowing how Black people see the world. Take an interest in the music I listen to, the kind of movies I see. There are cultural events on campus and in town that speak to the Black experience, but I don't think you've ever attended any. I don't think I've ever seen you read a book by an author of color. Why don't you get your head out of the sand? Then you might know what I mean.

Kelsey: Well, to be honest, it never occurred to me to do that.

Shakira: I know. That's what I mean by White privilege. You don't even see it, but you only have to learn about how your own group thinks, feels, and behaves. Because you're in the majority, you don't have to think about what it's like for everyone else.

Kelsey: It's not that I'm unwilling. I'd like to learn more about your experiences. But it's awkward. Often when you bring your friends around, I'm the only White person in the group. I don't even know if I'm welcome.

Shakira: I know it would be hard at first. It was for me when I came here. I had to face the same challenges, being the only Black person most the time, including in some classes.

Kelsey: And I want you to know that I grew up in an all-White suburb and attended a school that was almost all White. I value fairness, and was raised that way. But I'm not used to thinking about race, or talking about it. I don't know as much about it as you do. I want to learn more and not be judged for what I don't know already. That's not my fault. And yet you're blaming me.

Shakira: I can do that—not blame you, as long as I know you aren't just giving me some bullshit. The inequalities that exist today are so painful and so unfair. I need to know that you really care about them, too.

Kelsey: I do.

The conversation continued like that for a while. I had the feeling they'd reached a new level of openness and honesty with each other. I'm not saying there won't be conflicts in the future, but I really do think that Nonviolent Communication was helpful in this case. It certainly contributed to them talking together. And now, at least, they're willing to continue as roommates.

Making Mediation Work

As you can see in the example above, the skills involved in effective mediation are the same skills you'd use in any Nonviolent Communication interaction. You translate statements of judgment, criticism, or blame into expressions of feelings and needs and you check regularly to see how these expressions are being heard and responded to by the other party. It is crucial to go slowly—the more intense the feelings and needs being expressed, the slower. It is usually extremely helpful for each party to verbalize out loud what they understand of the other party's needs. This supports both parties feeling heard and understood. As always, self-empathy, in this case practiced by the mediator, is crucial. Meredith focused on her own needs stimulated by the roommates' conflict so that she could respond with presence and clarity as to what was going on for them.

In this situation, Meredith took a somewhat formal role of mediator. More often, you may have the opportunity to use NVC skills with people who are in conflict but who have not explicitly asked you to mediate. The process is essentially the same whether you have been formally designated as the mediator or not.

CONCLUSION:
Creating a Nonviolent World

In this book, we have focused on communication. But what is the link between the words we use and physical acts of violence? Where does violence begin, and end?

Violence, from an NVC perspective, is a tragic expression of unmet needs. The more human needs are experienced as unmet, the greater the chance that violence will occur. When we express unmet needs in the form of violence, we often imagine urgency and consider such actions "necessary" and even unavoidable. The use of violence is for the person's "own good," or for a "greater" good, such as ensuring justice or peace. Such thinking occurs in the paradigm of right and wrong and good and evil. It assumes that people need to be reformed and, to have care and consideration for others, must be punished and rewarded.

In this book we have considered the possibility of a very different world. This world, based on compassion, recognizes that human beings act out of wanting to meet positive needs. At every moment we have choices about how we will meet these needs. This awareness is crucial in choosing how we relate to others and ourselves; it is key in creating a world where the needs of all people can be met. A rock has no choice. We, as human beings, have arguably more choice than any living, breathing creature. As Viktor E. Frankl has observed, "The last of human freedoms [is] the ability to chose one's attitude in a given set of circumstances." I hope from reading this book that you feel a greater sense of choice in what you choose, what you think and feel, and how you respond to events in your life. The less choice we have—*the less choice we see or perceive ourselves as having*—the less we are fully alive.

Violence, in contrast, can be seen as leading to a kind of death—in the most extreme form, physical death and destruction; in more transmuted forms, a narrowing and diminishment of life and its expansiveness. When we don't fully connect with others, when we don't have full awareness and choice, when we confuse strategies for primary, life-expressing needs, we are, in effect, closing the aperture—even if slightly—on the fullness of life and all that we can experience and receive.

Is hitting a child necessary to serve life? Is killing another human being, bombing another nation, seeing that another suffer when we have suffered ourselves, necessary to meet needs for fairness, hope, safety, and justice? These are the questions I hope you will consider. Why? Because I believe the world depends on it. Given current circumstances, as pointed out in the interview at the end of this book, "We are getting to a point where our best protection is to communicate with the people we're most afraid of. Nothing else will work." As Carl Sandburg writes in his short poem, "Choose,"

> The single clenched fist lifted and ready,
> Or the open asking hand held out and waiting.
> Choose:
> For we meet by one or the other.

What would a nonviolent world look like? It would be a world where each person has the resources to feel compassion for another. It would be a world where the needs of all people are met—not just for themselves, their friends, family, town, state, country, or continent. Thinking in such a global and interconnected way may feel overwhelming, discouraging, and even impossible. How can you ensure the needs of people on the other side of the world are met, never mind on the next street over or in the next town? But think of the people you communicate with every day. Imagine if you and ten others started to communicate in a compassionate way. What if those ten people inspired ten others to do the same? Compassion, just like violence, can easily spread across the world. Like any great change, it begins with one person making a start and groups of people working together. You have the choice of contributing to that change. It is a choice you can make every day.

APPENDIX I

BEYOND GOOD & EVIL:
Marshall Rosenberg On Creating A Nonviolent World

An Interview by D. KILLIAN

I first met Marshall Rosenberg when I was assigned by a local paper to cover one of his "Nonviolent Communication" training seminars. Disturbed by the inequalities in the world and impatient for change, I couldn't imagine what use a communication technique could be in solving problems such as global warming or the debt of developing nations. But I was surprised by the visible effect Rosenberg's work had on individuals and families caught in conflict.

Nonviolent Communication, or NVC has four steps: observing what is happening in a given situation; identifying what one is feeling; identifying what one is needing; and then making a request for what one would like to see occur. It sounds simple, yet it's more than a technique for resolving conflict. It's a different way of understanding human motivation and behavior.

Rosenberg learned about violence at an early age. Growing up in Detroit in the thirties and forties, he was beaten up for being a Jew and witnessed some of the city's worst race riots, which resulted in more than forty deaths in a matter of days. These experiences drove him to study psychology in an attempt to understand, as he puts it, "what happens to disconnect us from our compassionate nature, and what allows some people to stay connected to their compassionate nature under even the most trying circumstances."

Rosenberg completed his PhD in clinical psychology at the University of Wisconsin in 1961 and afterward went to work with youths at reform schools. The experience led him to conclude that, rather than help people to be more compassionate, clinical psychology actually contributed to the conditions that cause violence, because it categorized people and thus distanced them from each other; doctors were trained to see the diagnosis, not the person. He decided that violence did not arise from pathology, as psychology taught, but from the ways in which we communicate.

Humanist psychotherapist Carl Rogers, creator of "client-centered therapy," was an early influence on Rosenberg's theories, and Rosenberg worked with Rogers for several years before setting out on his own to teach others how to interact in non-aggressive ways. His method became known as Nonviolent Communication.

No longer a practicing psychologist, Rosenberg admits that he has struggled at times with his own method, resorting to familiar behavior or fearing the risks involved in a nonviolent approach. Yet each time he has followed through with Nonviolent Communication, he has been surprised by the results. At times, it has literally saved his life.

On one occasion in the late 1980s, he was asked to teach his method to Palestinian refugees in Bethlehem. He met with about 170 Muslim men at a mosque in the Deheisha Camp. On the way into the camp, he saw several empty tear-gas canisters along the road, each clearly marked "Made in U.S.A." When the men realized their would-be instructor was from the United States, they became angry. Some jumped to their feet and began shouting, "Assassin! Murderer!" One man confronted Rosenberg, screaming in his face, "Child killer!"

Although tempted to make a quick exit, Rosenberg instead focused his questions on what the man was feeling, and a dialogue ensued. By the end of the day, the man who had called Rosenberg a murderer had invited him home to Ramadan dinner.

Rosenberg is founder and director of the nonprofit Center for Nonviolent Communication (www.cnvc.org). He is the author of Nonviolent Communication: A Language of Compassion *(PuddleDancer Press) and has just completed a new book, to be released by PuddleDancer in fall 2003, on the application of NVC in education:* When Students Love to Learn and Teachers Love to Teach. *He is currently working on a third book addressing the social implications of Nonviolent Communication.*

A tall, gaunt man, Rosenberg is soft-spoken but becomes animated when describing how Nonviolent Communication has worked for him and others. He has three children and currently lives in Wasserfallenof, Switzerland. Rosenberg is in great demand as a speaker and educator and maintains a relentless schedule. The day we spoke was his first free day in months. Afterward, he would be traveling to Israel, Brazil, Slovenia, Argentina, Poland, and Rwanda.

Killian: Your method aims to teach compassion, but compassion seems more a way of being than a skill or technique. Can it really be taught?

Rosenberg: I would say it's a natural human trait. Our survival as a species depends on our ability to recognize that our well being and the well being of others are, in fact, one and the same. The problem is that we are taught behaviors that disconnect us from this natural awareness. It's not that we have to learn how to be compassionate; we have to unlearn what we've been taught and get back to compassion.

Killian: If violence is learned, when did it start? It seems to have always been a part of human existence.

Rosenberg: Theologian Walter Wink estimates that violence has been the social norm for about eight thousand years. That's when a myth evolved that the world was created by a heroic, virtuous male god who defeated an evil female goddess. From that point on, we've had the image of the good guys killing the bad guys. And that has evolved into "retributive justice," which says that there are those who deserve to be punished and those who deserve to be rewarded. That belief has penetrated deep into our societies. Not every culture has been exposed to it, but, unfortunately, most have.

Killian: You've said that *deserve* is the most dangerous word in the language. Why?

Rosenberg: It's at the basis of retributive justice. For thousands of years, we've been operating under this system that says that people who do bad deeds are evil; indeed, that human beings are basically evil. According to this way of thinking, a few good people have evolved, and it's up to them to be the authorities and control the others. And the way you control people, given that our nature is evil and selfish, is through a system of justice in which people who behave in a good manner get rewarded, while those who are evil are made to suffer. In order to see such a system as fair, one has to believe that both sides deserve what they get.

I used to live in Texas, and when they would execute somebody there, the good Baptist students from the local college would gather outside the prison and have a party. When it came over the loudspeaker that the convict had been killed there was loud cheering and so forth— the same kind cheering that went on in some parts of Palestine when they found out about the September 11 terrorist attacks. When your concept of justice is based on good and evil, in which people deserve to suffer for what they've done, it makes violence enjoyable.

Killian: But you're not opposed to judgments.

Rosenberg: I'm all for judgments. I don't think we could survive very long without them. We judge which foods will give what our bodies need. We judge which actions are going to meet our needs. But I differentiate between life-serving judgments, which are about our needs, and moralistic judgments that imply rightness or wrongness.

Killian: You've called instead for "restorative justice." How is that different?

Rosenberg: Restorative justice is based on the question: how do we restore peace? In other words, how do we restore a state in which people care about one another's well being? Research indicates that perpetrators who go through restorative justice are less likely to repeat the behaviors that led to their incarceration. And it's far more healing for the victim, to have peace restored than simply to see the other person punished.

The idea is spreading. I was in England about a year ago to present a keynote speech at the international conference on restorative justice. I expected thirty people might show up. I was delighted to see more than six hundred people at this conference.

Killian: How does restorative justice work?

Rosenberg: I have seen it work, for example, with women who have been raped and the men who raped them. The first step is for the woman to express whatever it is that she wants her attacker to understand. Now, this woman has suffered almost every day for years since the attack, so what comes out is pretty brutal: "You monster! I'd like to kill you!" and so forth.

What I do then is help the prisoner to connect with the pain that is alive in this woman as a result of his actions. Usually what he wants to do is apologize. But I tell him apology is too cheap, too easy. I want him to repeat back what he hears her saying. How has her life been affected? When he can't repeat it, I play his role. I tell her I hear the pain behind all of the screams and shouting. I get him to see that the rage is on the surface, but beneath that lies the despair about whether her life will ever be the same again. And then I get the man to repeat what I've said. It may take three, or four, or five tries, but finally he hears the other person. Already at this point you can see the healing starting to take place—when the victim gets empathy.

Then I ask the man to tell me what's going on inside of him. How does he feel? Usually, again, he wants to apologize. He wants to say, "I'm a rat. I'm dirt." And again I get him to dig deeper. And it's very scary for these men. They're not used to dealing with feelings, let alone experiencing the horror of what it feels like to have stimulated in another human being such pain.

When we've gotten past these first two steps, very often the victim screams, "How *could* you?" She's hungry to understand what would cause another person to do such a thing. Unfortunately, most of the victims I've worked with have been encouraged from the very beginning by well-meaning people to forgive their attackers. These people explain that the rapist must have been suffering and probably had a bad childhood. And the victim does try to forgive, but this doesn't help much. Forgiveness reached without first taking these other steps is just superficial. It suppresses the pain.

Once the woman has received some empathy, however, she wants to know what was going on in this man when he committed this act. I help the perpetrator go back to the moment of the act and identify what he was feeling, what needs were contributing to his actions.

The last step is to ask whether there is something more the victim would like the perpetrator to do, to bring things back to a state of peace. For example, she may want medical bills to be paid, or she may want some emotional restitution. But once there's empathy on both sides, it's amazing how quickly they start to care about one another's well being.

Killian: What kinds of "needs" would cause a person to rape another human being?

Rosenberg: It has nothing to do with sex, of course. It has to do with the tenderness that people don't know how to get and often confuse with sex. In almost every case, the rapists themselves have been victims of some sort of sexual aggression or physical abuse, and they want someone else to understand how horrible it feels to be in this passive, weak role. They need empathy, and they've employed a distorted means of getting it: by inflicting similar pain on someone else. But the need is universal. All human beings have the same needs. Thankfully, most of us meet them in ways that are not destructive to other people and ourselves.

Killian: We've long believed in the West that needs must be regulated and denied, but you're suggesting the opposite: that needs must be recognized and fulfilled.

Rosenberg: I'd say we teach people to misrepresent their needs. Rather than educating people to be conscious of their needs, we teach them to become addicted to ineffective strategies for meeting them. Consumerism makes people think that their needs will be met by owning a certain item. We teach people that revenge is a need, when in fact it's a flawed strategy. Retributive justice itself is a poor strategy. Mixed in with all that is a belief in competition, that we can get our needs met only at other people's expense. Not only that, but that it's heroic and joyful to win, to defeat someone else.

So it's very important to differentiate needs from strategies and to get people to see that any strategy that meets your needs at someone else's expense is not meeting *all* your needs. Because anytime you behave in a way that's harmful to others, you end up

ALL HUMAN BEINGS HAVE THE SAME NEEDS. WHEN OUR CONSCIOUS-NESS IS FOCUSED ON WHAT'S ALIVE IN US, WE NEVER SEE AN ALIEN BEING IN FRONT OF US. OTHER PEOPLE MAY HAVE DIFFERENT STRATEGIES FOR MEETING THEIR NEEDS, BUT THEY ARE NOT ALIENS.

hurting yourself. As philosopher Elbert Hubbard once said, "We're not punished for our sins, but *by* them."

Whether I'm working with drug addicts in Bogota, Colombia, or with alcoholics in the United States, or with sex offenders in prisons, I always start by making it clear to them that I'm not there to make them stop what they're doing. "Others have tried," I say. "You've probably tried yourself, and it hasn't worked." I tell them I'm there to help them get clear about what needs are being met by this behavior. And once we have gotten clear on what their needs are, I teach them to find more effective and less costly ways of meeting those needs.

Killian: Nonviolent Communication seems to focus a lot on feelings. What about the logical, analytic side of things? Does it have a place here?

Rosenberg: Nonviolent Communication focuses on what's alive in us and what would make life more wonderful. What's alive in us are our needs, and I'm talking about the universal needs, the ones all living creatures have. Our feelings are simply a manifestation of what is happening with our needs. If our needs are being fulfilled, we feel pleasure. If our needs are not being fulfilled, we feel pain.

Now, this does not exclude the analytic. We simply differentiate between life-serving analysis and life-alienated analysis. If I say to you, "I'm in a lot of pain over my relationship to my child. I really want him to be healthy, and I see him not eating well and smoking," then you might ask, "Why do you think he's doing this?" You'd be encouraging me to analyze the situation and uncover his needs.

Analysis is a problem only when it gets disconnected from serving life. For example, if I said to you, "I think George Bush is a monster," we could have a long discussion, and we might think it was an interesting discussion, but it wouldn't be connected to life. We wouldn't realize this, though, because maybe neither of us has

I F I SAID TO YOU, "I THINK GEORGE BUSH IS A MONSTER, WE COULD HAVE A LONG DISCUSSION, AND WE MIGHT THINK IT WAS AN INTERESTING DISCUSSION, BUT IT WOULDN'T BE CONNECTED TO LIFE....MAYBE NEITHER OF US HAS EVER HAD A CONVERSATION THAT WAS LIFE-CONNECTING.

ever had a conversation that was life-connecting. We get so used to speaking at the analytic level that we can go through life with our needs unmet and not even know it. The comedian Buddy Hackett used to say that it wasn't until he joined the army that he found out you could get up from a meal without having heartburn; he had gotten so used to his mother's cooking, heartburn had become a way of life. And in middle-class, educated culture in the United States, I think that disconnection is a way of life. When people have needs that they don't know how to deal with directly, they approach them indirectly through intellectual discussions. As a result, the conversation is lifeless.

Killian: If we do agree that Bush is a monster, though, at least we'll connect on the level of values.

Rosenberg: And that's going to meet some needs—certainly more than if I disagree with you or if I ignore what you're saying. But imagine what the conversation could be like if we learned to hear what's alive behind the words and ideas, and to connect at that level. Central to NVC training is that all moralistic judgments, whether positive or negative, are tragic expressions of needs. Criticism, analysis, and insults are tragic expressions of unmet needs. Compliments and praise, for their part, are tragic expressions of fulfilled needs.

So why do we get caught up in this dead, violence-provoking language? Why not learn how to live at the level where life is really going on? NVC is not looking at the world through rose-colored glasses. We come closer to the truth when we connect with what's alive in people than when we just listen to what they think.

Killian: How do you discuss world affairs in the language of feelings?

Rosenberg: Somebody reasonably proficient in NVC might say, "I am scared to death when I see what Bush is doing in an attempt to protect us. I don't feel any safer." And then somebody who disagrees might say, "Well, I share your desire for safety, but

I'm scared of doing nothing." Already we're not just talking about George Bush, but about the feelings that are alive in both of us.

Killian: And coming closer to thinking about solutions?

Rosenberg: Yes, because we've acknowledged that we both have the same needs. It's only at the level of strategy that we disagree. Remember, all human beings have the same needs. When our consciousness is focused on what's alive in us, we never see an alien being in front of us. Other people may have different strategies for meeting their needs, but they are not aliens.

Killian: In the U.S. right now, there are some people who would have a lot of trouble hearing this. During a memorial for September 11, I heard a policeman say all he wanted was "payback."

Rosenberg: One rule of our training is: empathy before education. I wouldn't expect someone who's been injured to hear what I'm saying until they felt that I had fully understood the depth of their pain. Once they felt empathy from me, then I would introduce my fear that our plan to exact retribution isn't going to make us safer.

Killian: Have you always been a nonviolent revolutionary?

Rosenberg: For many years I wasn't, and I was scaring more people than I was helping. When I was working against racism in the United States, I must confess, I confronted more than a few people with accusations like "That was a racist thing to say!" I said this with deep anger, because I was dehumanizing the other person in my mind. And I was not seeing any of the changes I wanted.

An Iowa feminist group called HERA helped me with that. They asked, "Doesn't it bother you that your work is against violence rather than *for* life?" And I realized that I was trying to get people to see the mess around them by telling them how they were contributing to it. In doing so, I was just creating more resistance and more hostility. HERA helped me to get past just talking about not judging others, and to move on to what can enrich life and make it more wonderful.

Killian: You have criticized clinical psychology for its focus on pathology. Have you trained any psychotherapists or other mental-health practitioners in NVC?

Rosenberg: Lots of them, but most of the people I train are not doctors or therapists. I agree with theologian Martin Buber, who said that you cannot do psychotherapy as a psychotherapist. People heal from their pain when they have an authentic connection with another human being, and I don't think you can have an authentic connection when one person thinks of him- or herself as the therapist, diagnosing the other. And if patients come in thinking of themselves as sick people who are there to get treatment, then it starts with the assumption that there's something wrong with them, which gets in the way of the healing. So, yes, I teach this to psychotherapists, but I teach it mostly to regular human beings, because we can all engage in an authentic connection with others, and it's out of this authentic connection that healing takes place.

Killian: It seems all religious traditions have some basis in empathy and compassion — the bleeding heart of Christ and the life of Saint Francis are two examples from Christianity. Yet horrible acts of violence have been committed in the name of religion.

Rosenberg: Social psychologist Milton Rokeach did some research on religious practitioners in the seven major religions. He looked at people who very seriously followed their religion and compared them to people in the same population who had no religious orientation at all. He wanted to find out which group was more compassionate. The results were the same in all the major religions: the nonreligious were more compassionate. Rokeach warned readers to be careful how they interpreted his research, however, because within each religious group, there were two radically different populations: a mainstream group, and a mystical minority. If you looked at just the mystical group you found that they were more compassionate than the general population.

In mainline religion, you have to sacrifice and go through many different procedures to demonstrate your holiness, but the mystical minority see compassion and empathy as part of human nature. We *are* this divine energy, they say. It's not something we have to attain. We just have to realize it, be present to it. Unfortunately, such believers are in the minority and often persecuted by fundamentalists within their own religions. Chris Rajendrum, a Jesuit priest in Sri Lanka, and Archbishop Simon in Burundi are two men who risk their lives daily in the service of bringing warring parties together. They see Christ's message not as an injunction to tame yourself or to be above this world, but as a confirmation that we *are* this energy of compassion. Nafez Assailez, a Muslim I work with, says it's painful for him to see anyone killing in the name of Islam. It's inconceivable to him.

Killian: The idea that we're evil and must become holy implies moralistic judgment.

Rosenberg: Oh, amazing judgment! Rokeach calls that judgmental group the salvationists. For them, the goal is to be rewarded by going to heaven. So you try to follow your religion's teachings not because you've internalized an awareness of your own divinity and relate to others in a compassionate way, but because these things are "right" and if you do them, you'll be rewarded, and if you don't, you'll be punished.

Killian: And those in the minority, they've had a taste of the divine presence and recognize it in themselves and others?

Rosenberg: Exactly. And they're often the ones who invite me to teach Nonviolent Communication, because they see that our training is helping to bring people back to that consciousness.

Killian: You've written about "domination culture." Is that the same as "salvationism"?

Rosenberg: I started using the term "domination culture" after reading Walter Wink's works, especially his book *Engaging the Powers*. His concept is that we are living under structures in which the few dominate the many. Look at how families are structured here in the United States: the parents claim always to know what's right and set the rules for everybody else's benefit. Look at our schools. Look at our workplaces. Look at our government, our religions. At all levels, you have authorities who impose their will on other people, claiming that it's for everybody's well being. They use punishment and reward as the basic strategy for getting what they want. That's what I mean by domination culture.

Killian: It seems movements and institutions often start out as transformative but end up as systems of domination.

Rosenberg: Yes, people come along with beautiful messages about how to return to life, but the people they're speaking to have been living with domination for so long that they interpret the message in a way that supports the domination structures. When I was in Israel, one of the men on our team was an Orthodox rabbi. One evening, I read him a couple of passages from the Bible, which I had been perusing in his house after the Sabbath dinner. I read him a passage that said something like "Dear God, give us the power to pluck out the eyes of our enemies," and I said, "David, really, how do you find beauty in a passage like this?" And he said, "Well, Marshall, if you hear just what's on the face of it, of course it's as ugly as can be. What you have to do is try to hear what is behind that message."

So I sat down with those passages to try to hear what the speaker might have said, had he known how to put it in terms of feelings and needs. It was fascinating, because what was ugly on the surface could be quite different if you sensed the feelings and needs of the speaker. I think the author of that passage was really saying, "Dear God, please protect us from people who might hurt us, and give us a way of making sure that this doesn't happen."

Killian: You've commented that, among the different forms of violence — physical, psychological, and institutional, physical violence is the least destructive. Why?

Rosenberg: Physical violence is always a secondary result. I've talked to people in prison who've committed violent crimes, and they say: "He deserved it. The guy was an asshole." It's their thinking that frightens me, how they dehumanize their victims, saying that they deserved to suffer. The fact that the man went out and shot another person scares me, too, but I'm more scared by the thinking that led to it, because it's so deeply ingrained in such a large portion of humanity.

When I worked with the Israeli police, for example, they would ask, "What do you do when someone is shooting at you already?" And I'd say, "Let's look at the last five times somebody shot at you. In these five situations, when you arrived on the scene, was the other person already shooting?" No. Not in one of the five. In each case, there were at least three verbal exchanges before any shooting started. The police re-created the dialogue for me, and I could have predicted there would be violence after the first couple of exchanges.

I'VE WORKED WITH SOME PRETTY SCARY FOLKS, EVEN SERIAL KILLERS. BUT WHEN I STAYED WITH IT AND FORGOT ABOUT THE PSYCHIATRIC POINT OF VIEW THAT SOME PEOPLE ARE TOO DAMAGED EVER TO CHANGE, I SAW IMPROVEMENT.

Killian: You have said, though, that physical force is sometimes necessary. Would you include capital punishment?

Rosenberg: No. When we do restorative justice, I want the perpetrators to stay in prison until we are finished. And I am for using whatever physical force is necessary to get them off the streets. But I don't see prison as a punitive place. I see it as a place to keep dangerous individuals until we can do the necessary restoration work. I've worked with some pretty scary folks, even serial killers. But when I stayed with it and forgot about the psychiatric point of view that some people are too damaged ever to change, I saw improvement.

Once, when I was working with prisoners in Sweden, the administrator told me about a man who'd killed five people, maybe more. "You'll know him right away," he said. "He's a monster." When I walked into the room, there he was a big man, tattoos all over his arms. The first day, he just stared at me, didn't say a word. The second day, He just stared at me. I was growing annoyed at this administrator: *Why the hell did he put this psychopath in my group?* Already, I'd started falling back on clinical diagnosis.

Then, on the third morning, one of my colleagues said, "Marshall, I notice you haven't talked to him." And I realized that I hadn't approached that frightening inmate, because just the thought of opening up to him scared me to death. So I went in and said to the killer, "I've heard some of the things that you did to get into this prison, and when you just sit there and stare at me each day and don't say anything, I feel scared. I would like to know what's going on for you."

And he said, "What do you want to hear?" And he started to talk.

If I just sit back and diagnose people, thinking that they can't be reached, I won't reach them. But when I put in the time and energy and take a risk, I always get somewhere. Depending on the damage that's been done to somebody, it may take three, four, five *years* of daily investment of energy to restore peace. And most systems are not set up to do that. If we're not in a position to give somebody what he or she needs to change, then my second choice would be for that person to be in prison. But I wouldn't kill anyone.

Killian: For horrendous acts, don't we need strong consequences? Just making restitution might seem a light sentence for some.

Rosenberg: Well, it depends on what we want, we know from our correctional system that if two people commit the same violent crime, and one goes to prison while the other, for whatever reason, does not, there is a much higher likelihood of continued violence on the part of the person who goes to prison. The last time I was in Twin Rivers Prison in Washington State, there was a young man who had been in three times for sexually molesting children. Clearly, attempts to change his behavior by punishing him hadn't worked. Our present system does not work. In contrast, research done in Minnesota and Canada shows that if you go through a process of restorative justice, a perpetrator is much less likely to act violently again.

As I've said, prisoners just want to apologize — which they know how to do all too well. But when I pull them by the ears and make them really look at the enormity of the suffering this other person has experienced as a result of their actions, and when I require the criminals to go inside themselves and tell me what *they* were feeling when they did it, it's a very frightening experience for them. Many say, "Please, beat me, kill me, but don't make me do this."

Killian: You speak about a protective use of force. Would you consider strikes or boycotts a protective use of force?

Rosenberg: They could be. The person who has really spent a lot of time on this is Gene Sharp. He's written books on the subject and has a wonderful article on the Internet called "168 Applications of Nonviolent Force." He shows how, throughout history, nonviolence has been used to prevent violence and to protect, not to punish.

I was working in San Francisco with a group of minority parents who were very concerned about the principal at their children's school. They said he was destroying the students' spirit. So I trained them in how to communicate with the principal. They tried to talk to him, but he said, "Get out of here. Nobody is going to tell me how to run my school." Next I explained to them the concept of protective use of force, and one of them came up with the idea of a strike: they would keep their kids out of school and picket with signs that let everyone know what kind of man this principal was. I told them they were getting protective use of force mixed up with punitive force: it sounded like they wanted to punish this man. The only way protective use of force could work, I said, was if they communicated clearly that their intent was to protect their children and not to bad-mouth or dehumanize the principal. I suggested signs that stated their needs: "We want to communicate. We want our children in school."

And the strike was very successful, but not in the way we'd imagined. When the school board heard about some of the things this principal was doing, they fired him.

Killian: But demonstrations, strikes, and rallies are often presented as aggressive by the media.

Rosenberg: Yes, we've seen protesters cross the line in some of the antiglobalization demonstrations. Some people, while trying to show how terrible corporations are, take some pretty violent actions under the guise of protective use of force.

There are two things that distinguish truly nonviolent actions from violent actions. First, there is no enemy in the nonviolent point of view. You don't see an enemy. Your thinking is clearly focused on protecting your needs. And second, your intention is not to make the other side suffer.

Killian: It seems the U.S. government has trouble differentiating between the two. It tries to make war sound acceptable by appealing to our need for safety, and then it acts aggressively.

Rosenberg: Well, we do need to protect ourselves. But you're right, there is so much else mixed up with that. When the population has been educated in retributive justice, there is nothing they want more than to see someone suffer. Most of the time, when we end up using force, it could have been prevented by using different ways of negotiating. I have no doubt this could have been the case if we'd been listening to the messages coming to us from the Arab world for so many years. This was not a new situation. This pain of theirs had been expressed over and over in many ways, and we hadn't responded with any empathy or understanding. And when we don't hear people's pain, it keeps coming out in ways that make empathy even harder.

Now, when I say this, people often think I'm justifying what the terrorists did on September 11. And of course I'm not. I'm saying that the real answer is to look at how we could have prevented it to begin with.

Killian: Some in the U.S. think that bombing Iraq is a protective use of force.

Rosenberg: I would ask them, What is your objective? Is it protection? Certain kinds of negotiations, which have never been attempted, would be more protective than any use of force. Our only option is communication of a radically different sort. We're getting to the point now where no army is able to prevent terrorists from poisoning our streams or fouling the air. We are getting to a point where our best protection is to communicate with the people we're most afraid of. Nothing else will work.

This article originally appeared in *The Sun* magazine (www.thesunmagazine.org).

RESOURCES FOR LEARNING NONVIOLENT COMMUNICATION

I hope that you have enjoyed this book, tried applying some of the principles to your own life, and obtained some benefit in your relationship with yourself and others. If so, you may be wondering—what next? If at all possible, I would urge you to find some trainers who have more experience than you have with the NVC process to support you in your learning. The principles of NVC are not intellectually difficult to understand, but the application and practice of these principles to everyday life is extremely challenging for most of us. The CNVC web-site (www.cnvc.org/train.htm) can assist you in finding both trainers and groups supporting the learning and practice of NVC.

If there are no trainers in your geographical area, you may wish to start a practice group with others with similar interests. The book by Leu (below), which is coordinated with Rosenberg's book (below), is invaluable for this purpose. Many of the centers also offer tele-classes and individual training sessions and empathy sessions by telephone which work surprisingly well. For tele-classes you are not restricted to one geographical area. A number of list-serves also provide information and support for learning (below).

Books

(Unless otherwise indicated, all of the following may be ordered at www.cnvc.org/matls.htm or 1-800-255-7696)

1. Bryson, Kelly. *Don't Be Nice, Be Real: Balancing Passion for Self with Compassion for Others.* n.p. 2002.

This book draws from the author's many years working as a therapist with individuals and couples. He applies NVC to many of the types of relationship problems adults encounter and his way with words makes the reading enjoyable. Order at www.languageofcompassion.com. Quite a few of the chapters are also available to read for free at the web-site.

2. Hart, Sura and Victoria Kindle Hodson. *The Compassionate Classroom: Relationship Based Teaching and Learning*. Del Mar, CA: PuddleDancer Press, 2003.

This book provides an organized overview of NVC and has a large number of delightful activities and exercises for teaching NVC to children in a group setting. Many of these could be readily adapted for use with older children (i.e. adults).

3. Kashtan, Inbal. *Parenting From Your Heart*. Del Mar, CA: PuddleDancer Press, 2003.

This 48-page pamphlet is written by the Coordinator of the Center for Nonviolent Communication's Parenting Project. She shows clearly what it means to be compassionate both to yourself and the children you may be caring for. It includes many examples of using NVC in this challenging terrain.

4. Leu, Lucy. *Nonviolent Communication Companion Workbook: A Practical Guide for Individual, Group or Classroom Study*. Del Mar, CA: PuddleDancer Press, 2003.

This book provides a structured series of exercises and activities that are coordinated with Rosenberg's book *Nonviolent Communication: A Language of Life*. The first part of the book describes how to set up and run a practice group and contains invaluable advice distilled from many years of experience.

5. Rosenberg, Marshall B. *Life-Enriching Education*. Del Mar, CA: PuddleDancer Press, 2003.

    This book shows the application of NVC to the classroom. It includes both theory and examples of NVC in practice.

6. Rosenberg, Marshall B. *Nonviolent Communication: A Language of Life*. 2nd ed. Del Mar, CA: PuddleDancer Press, 2003.

    This is the "Bible" of NVC written by its developer. Although most of the theory in this book can be found in other NVC resources, this book contains Rosenberg's own examples and his experiences of using NVC around the world, including in high conflict and war-torn areas. If you want to start a practice group using the Leu workbook (see above), it would be helpful to have this book with which it is coordinated.

7. Haskvitz, Sylvia. *Eat by Choice, Not by Habit*. Del Mar, CA: PuddleDancer Press, 2005.

    This book describes a compassionate approach to issues of eating, food, physical well being and choice.

Audio-Tapes/CDs

1. Rosenberg, Marshall B. *Speaking Peace*. Louisville, CO: Sounds True, 2003.

    This is my favorite of the audiotapes or CDs of Rosenberg explaining NVC at an introductory level. I especially appreciate his captivating anecdotes, clear explanations and inspiring songs. I also value his showing how applying the NVC model can lead to change at both the individual and the institutional level. Other introductory tapes are also available.

2. Rosenberg, Marshall B. NVC: Create Your Life, Your Relationships, and Your World Harmony With Your Values. Louisville, CO: Sounds True, 2005.

   This set of 4 CDs covers the same material as does Rosenberg's book *Nonviolent Communication: A Language of Life*.

3. Rosenberg, Marshall B. A series of intermediate-level CDs from an International Intensive Training. I really enjoy listening to these CDs which raise many provocative issues and alternatives for how we relate to others and ourselves:

   Giraffe Fuel for Life. Gratitude exercises, reward & punishment, hearing feelings and needs rather than thoughts, what stops us from celebrating.

   Needs and Empathy. How to give empathy; distinguishing needs from strategies to meet them, other questions.

   Intimate Relationships. Making requests that meet our need for love, hearing the need behind the "No," the cost of hearing rejection, giraffe love, role plays.

   Creating a Life Serving System Within Oneself. Empathy for the Chooser and Educator, mourning in giraffe, restorative justice.

   Experiencing Needs as a Gift. Hearing the need behind the "No," the cost of giving from non-giraffe energy.

Video Testimonials

If you want to get a sense of how different people have felt the impact of learning NVC in their lives, check out the video testimonials at http://www.cnvc.org/video.htm. Ordinarily testimonials are considered a very low level of "proof" for the effectiveness of any intervention. What impressed me about these, which I read before going to my first intensive training in NVC, was the qualitative nature of the shift in people's experience of themselves and others as a result of incorporating NVC in their lives.

Articles

Articles about applications of NVC to prisons, education, conflict in the Middle East and other situations can be found at http://cnvc.org/bookchap.htm

Discussions/List-serves

The Synergy Communication group provides practice in using the NVC model interactively, including observations, feelings, needs and requests. It is free. http://groups.yahoo.com/group/synergycommunication/

The Pondering NVC group is a place to discuss your thoughts about NVC. Whereas the Synergy Communication group is where you should go to practice talking and listening using NVC, the Pondering NVC group is more for talking about general principles and ideas. http://groups.yahoo.com/group/PonderingNVC/

Resources for parents, including a list-serve where parents share challenges, ideas and experiences with parenting using NVC are available at http://www.cnvc.org/parents.htm

Web-sites

1.   Center for Nonviolent Communication: www.cnvc.org

This web-site contains a wonderful set of articles about applications of NVC, information about trainers and trainings offered around the world (including Marshall Rosenberg's schedule of trainings), and an online store selling books, audio and video materials.

2.   PuddleDancer Press: www.nonviolentcommunication.com

Major publisher of NVC materials, site contains good overview of NVC

3.   Regional groups in U.S. and Canada (for groups in other parts of U.S. and all over the world see http://cnvc.org/world.htm):

www.bcncc.org   British Colombia

www.BrooklynNVC.org   Brooklyn & lower Manhattan

www.nycnvc.org   New York City

www.nvctoronto.org/nearbyevents.html   Calendar of trainings in Northeastern United States and Eastern Canada

www.baynvc.org   San Francisco Area

www.stccc.us   Southern Tier of New York

www.nvctoronto.org Toronto - a good site for learning by phone

4.   Growing Compassion: www.growingcompassion.org

A place to practice nonviolent communication in tele-classes. Also a section on resources for NVC trainers and learners, including games, activities, etc.

GRATITUDE

We would like to express our appreciation to Dr. Marshall B. Rosenberg for creating the tool of Nonviolent Communication, his lifetime commitment to finding ways to meet the needs of all people, and his continuous sharing of this material all over the globe.

We would also like to thank the many trainers who have contributed so much to our growth and learning, including Walter Armstrong, Duke Duchscherer, Robert Gonzales, Dow Gordon, Sylvia Haskvitz, Rita Herzog, Nancy Kahn, Christine King, Gina Lawrie, Lucy Leu, Kit Miller, Ruby Phillips, Susan Skye, Wes Taylor, and Towe Widstrand.

We would like to especially thank NVC trainers Miki Kashtan, Inbal Kashtan and the late Julie Greene, the founders of the Bay NVC North America NVC Leadership Program, for their vision, clarity, and passion in sharing NVC and for their tremendous contribution to our learning and development. We would also like to thank Meganwind Eoyang and Nancy Kahn, current Bay NVC and Leadership Program trainers, for their open-hearted courage and support in living and modeling NVC consciousness, as well as the 2004 and 2005 LP support teams and all the participants. All of you have contributed profoundly to our integration of NVC and learning to balance compassion for ourselves and others.

The book would not be as fun or effective without the enthusiastic work of Andrew Jung, Sam Zavieh and Meredith Woitach who illustrated and contributed to our cartoons. We value the contributions of Michelle Russo, who helped create some of the exercises, Jonathan Crimes and Peter Przeradzki, who gave us feedback on an early draft, Inbal Kashtan who provided support on the revisions of the first edition, Jet and Martha, who helped with proof reading, and the Media Resource Center at Binghamton University for the scanning of the advertisements and the interview in the Appendix. We are also very grateful to Jill Connor, for her efforts and support in designing the cover, Charlotte Morse, who did the page lay-out juggling numerous pieces and pages, www.bigfoto.com for the photographs in Chapters One and Four, and Westcan Printing Group for producing the book. We are grateful to each for your patience and commitment, working on schedule with equanimity and a generosity of spirit.

Jane would like to express her thanks to Bill Connor, for supporting and encouraging her to create this "fourth baby." She is appreciative of the love and support of all of her family—Paul, Justin, Jolien, Jill, Jessicca and Jordan—without whom the meaning of compassion and caring would be so much less rich for her. She regrets that her parents, Sam and Rhoda Marantz, are not here to see this book, since they modeled caring for the needs of all people on this planet their entire lives. And now Jane has a much better idea of what went into the creation of Sam's physics book. She is grateful that dear Aunt Sara, who lives compassion every day, is here.

Jane is also appreciative of the support and contributions of Roxanne Manning, who has always been available to listen and assisted with editing and the development of the graphic model of Compassionate Communication, and Kanya Likanasudh for her continuous empathy and support for this project. She is also grateful to the many students who were enthusiastic and eager to contribute their experiences for this book. She would like to thank Leo Wilton, Sean Massey and the faculty and staff of the Division of Human Development for caring about her and her passion for NVC. She thanks Felicia Birnel, Arnie and Mera Eisen and Leo Wilton for hosting her while she was writing the preliminary edition of this book and doing Sloan-Kettering. She gives special thanks to her "buddies," Sue Ellen Cheairs, Kanya Likanasudh, Ava Gips, Harbert Rice, and Martha Lasley. She is grateful to all of the people at Binghamton University who have provided an environment where she could continue to grow and do what she loves for so many years. Finally, she wishes to thank her co-author, Dian Killian, who has shared and supported the vision of this book so ably with her talents, and provided an *in vivo* laboratory for working out our differences with grace and compassion.

Dian Killian is grateful to her partner, Martha Grevatt, for all her companionship, tenderness, laughter, and support; she is in awe to see that after almost ten years, love can continue to unfold with such surprising delight. Dian would also like to thank her NVC buddies, Jude Lardner, Lynda Smith, Kanya Likanasudh, Gail Epstein, Curtis Watkins, and Nancy Kahn, for such delicious friendship, connection, caring, intimacy, and support, as well as fellow assistants in the 2005 LP program who have become like family, especially Stuart Watson, Sue Holper, and Katy Dawson. Gratitude also to current students and all those who have been supportive of Brooklyn Nonviolent Communication, especially Sarah Jude, Nellie Todd Bright, Paul Merrill, Kit Miller, and "Big Dog" Judith, and friends on two continents who have been truer than blood, especially Grainne, Michael, Maria, Katharina, Baumy, Hugh, and Dor.

Warm appreciation also goes to her co-author, Jane Connor, who has been so delightful to work with, offering companionship, learning, fun, and, not least importantly, compelling deadlines.

Finally, Dian would like to thank her grandmother, Lillian Sophia Endress Seelen, who brought compassion and beauty into the world each day both with the quality of her presence and the strength of her voice.

BIBLIOGRAPHY

Bryson, Kelly B. *Don't Be Nice, Be Real: Balancing Passion for Self with Compassion for Others.* n.p. 2002.

Carkhuff, Robert R. *The Art of Helping.* 7th ed. Amherst, MA: Human Resource Development Press, 1993.

Eisler, Riane. *The Chalice and the Blade: Our History, Our Future.* San Francisco: HarperSanFrancisco, 1988.

Foucault, Michel. *Discipline and Punish: The Birth of the Prison.* New York: Random House, 1975.

Frankl, Viktor. *Man's Search for Meaning: An Introduction to Logotherapy.* New York:.Washington Square Press, 1969.

Gendlin, Eugene. *Focusing.* New York: Bantam Books, 1981.

Kohn, Alfie. *Punished by Rewards: The Trouble with Gold Stars, Incentive Plans, As, Praise and Other Bribes.* New York: Houghton Mifflin Company, 1995.

Lerner, Michael. *Spirit Matters.* Charlottesville: Hampton Roads Publishing Company, 2002

Leu, Lucy. *Nonviolent Communication Companion Workbook: A Practical Guide for Individual, Group or Classroom Study.* Del Mar, CA: PuddleDancer Press, 2003.

Maslow, Abraham. *Toward a Psychology of Being. New York:* John Wiley & Sons, 1998.

Miller, Alice. *Breaking Down the Wall of Silence to Join the Waiting Child.* London: Virago, 1992.

Myers, Wayland. *Nonviolent Communication: The Basics as I Know and Use Them.* Del Mar, CA: PuddleDancer Press, 2002.

Nagler, Michael N. *Is There No Other Way? The Search for a Nonviolent Future.* Berkeley: Berkeley Hills Books, 2001

Powell, John. *The Secret of Staying in Love. Allen, TX:* Thomas More Press, 1995.

Rogers, Carl. *On Personal Power.* New York: Delacorte, 1977.

Rosenberg, Marshall B. *Nonviolent Communication: A Language of Life.* 2nd ed. Del Mar, CA: PuddleDancer Press, 2003.

Said, Edward. *Orientalism: Western Conceptions of the Orient.* New York: Pantheon, 1995.

Wink, Walter. *The Powers That Be: Theology for a New Millennium.* New York: Doubleday Books, 1999.

INDEX

ABOUT THE AUTHORS

Jane Marantz Connor, Ph.D. is Director of the Division of Human Development at Binghamton University where she is also an Associate Professor of Human Development and a recipient of the Chancellor's Award for Excellence in Teaching. Aside from teaching Nonviolent Communication, her vocational passion is teaching her undergraduate course in Multicultural Psychology, which has evolved from a seminar of 25 students to a lecture hall class enrolling over 400 students a semester. She has a life-long commitment to issues of social justice and equality and is second vice-president of the Broome-Tioga National Association for the Advancement of Colored People, which gave her their award for Individual Accomplishment in Advancing Human Rights. Her doctorate is in psychology and she is a New York State licensed psychologist. She is the founder of the Southern Tier Center for Compassionate Communication in Binghamton, New York where she lives with her husband; they are the proud parents of three children and grandparents of two. She can be reached at jconnor@binghamton.edu.

Dian Killian, Ph.D., has a background in cultural studies and classical rhetoric. As a scholar and journalist, she has written frequently about social justice issues, including racism, immigration, and queer rights in publications such as *The Sun* magazine, *The Harvard Gay and Lesbian Review*, the *Lambda Book Report*, and the feminist monthly *Sojourner*, among others. She has also published poetry and fiction. As a political activist, she has worked as a union organizer and in the gay rights and anti-war movements. She and her partner were one of the first couples to receive a civil union in the state of Vermont and she recently testified on behalf of the labor movement in favor of civil marriage in the state on New York. In recognition of her activism, New York City Council granted her a "Hero Award" in 2002. In addition to her background in Nonviolent Communication, Killian has completed training in the Alternatives to Violence program and is a member of the Religious Society of Friends (Quakers). She lives in Brooklyn, New York where she directs Brooklyn Nonviolent Communication (www.BrooklynNVC.org).

FEEDBACK PLEASE!

We wrote this book to support the learning, understanding, and use of NVC, especially among younger persons and those in college or graduate school. Have we been effective? Did we meet your needs?

We are planning a later edition of this book in one or two years and would be grateful for input as to how we could make the current edition more meaningful and useful. We would love feedback (preferably in the form of observations, feelings, needs, requests), including page numbers if appropriate. If you like, this and the following pages can be removed and your feedback sent to the address below; you can also email us and we will send you an electronic version of this form. If you include your email address, we would be delighted to let you know about the release of further editions, workshops that may interest you, and any special discounts available.

Feedback:

1. What needs did reading this book meet for you? Please specify:

    Book as a whole: _____

    Exercises: _____

    Dialogues: _____

    Cartoons: _____

    Illustrations: _____

    Other: _____

2. What needs were *not* met? Please specify:

   Book as a whole: _____

   Exercises: _____

   Dialogues: _____

   Cartoons: _____

   Illustrations: _____

   Other: _____

3. What were your favorite parts of this book? Why?

   _____

   _____

   _____

4. What parts or aspects did you find most valuable? Why?

   _____

   _____

   _____

5. What were your least favorite parts?

   _____

   _____

   _____

6. What, if anything, would you like to add to this book, such as topics, further explanation, exercises, etc.?

   _____

   _____

   _____